THE ORTHO[

THE ACTS
OF THE APOSTLES

Spreading the Word

by Fr. Lawrence R. Farley

Ancient Faith Publishing
Chesterton, Indiana

THE ACTS OF THE APOSTLES
Spreading the Word
© Copyright 2012 by Lawrence Farley

One volume of *The Orthodox Bible Study Companion Series*

All rights reserved. No part of this publication may be reproduced by any means, electronic, mechanical, photocopying, recording, scanning, or otherwise, without the prior written permission of the publisher.

Published by   Ancient Faith Publishing
                A Division of Ancient Faith Ministries
                P.O. Box 748
                Chesterton, IN 46304

ISBN: 978-1-936270-62-0

Printed in the United States of America

Dedicated to David Thiessen:
after all these years,
still the Best Man

Table of Contents and Outline

Introduction to the Series 9
    A Word about Scholarship and Translation ❧ 9
    Key to the Format of This Work ❧ 11

Introduction to the Acts of the Apostles 13

I. Opening: The Ascension and the Promise of the Spirit (1:1–11) 17

II. The Church in Jerusalem (1:12—8:1a) 25
    1. The Gathering of the Disciples (1:12–26) ❧ 25
    2. Pentecost (2:1–47) ❧ 30
    3. Healing in the Temple and the First Arrest of the Apostles (3:1—4:31) ❧ 44
    4. Great Grace upon the Church: All Share Their Goods (4:32—5:16) ❧ 59
    5. Second Arrest of the Apostles (5:17–42) ❧ 65
    6. Jerusalem Ministry of Stephen (6:1—8:1a) ❧ 72

III. The Church Spreads to Judea and Samaria (8:1b–40) 93
    1. Persecution Spreads the Church to Judea and Samaria (8:1b–3) ❧ 93
    2. Samaritan Ministry of Philip (8:4–8) ❧ 94
    3. Philip and Simon the Magus (8:9–24) ❧ 95
    4. Philip and the Ethiopian Eunuch (8:25–40) ❧ 100

IV. The Church Spreads to the Gentiles (9:1—11:18) 105
    1. The Conversion of Saul (9:1–31) ❧ 105
    2. Peter Preaches to the Gentiles (9:32—10:48) ❧ 114

      a. Peter at Lydda (9:32–35) ❧ 114
      b. Peter at Joppa (9:36–45) ❧ 115
      c. Peter Comes to the Gentiles at Caesarea (10:1–23a) ❧ 117
      d. The Holy Spirit Poured Out upon the Gentiles (10:23b–48) ❧ 122
   3. Jerusalem Blesses the Gentile Mission (11:1–18) ❧ 129

V. The Church Founded at Gentile Antioch (11:19—15:35) 133

   1. Jerusalem Blesses the Church at Antioch (11:19–26) ❧ 133
   2. Antioch Sends Aid to Judean Poor (11:27—12:25) ❧ 136
   3. First Missionary Journey of Paul (13:1—14:28) ❧ 145
      a. Departure ❧ 145
      b. Cyprus ❧ 147
      c. Pisidian Antioch ❧ 150
      d. Iconium ❧ 160
      e. Lystra ❧ 162
      f. Return to Antioch ❧ 166
   4. Jerusalem Council Vindicates Gentile Mission (15:1–35) ❧ 168

VI. Paul's Further Journeys (15:36—21:16) 179

   1. Second Missionary Journey of Paul (15:36—18:22) ❧ 179
      a. Departure ❧ 179
      b. Philippi ❧ 185
      c. Thessalonica ❧ 195
      d. Athens ❧ 200
      e. Corinth ❧ 209
      f. Return to Antioch ❧ 216

2. Third Missionary Journey (18:23—21:16) ༷ 217
      a. Apollos at Ephesus ༷ 217
      b. Paul at Ephesus ༷ 219
      c. To Greece ༷ 233
      d. Return to Jerusalem ༷ 237

VII. Paul in Jerusalem
(21:17—26:32) 255
   1. Arrival (21:17–26) ༷ 255
   2. Arrest (21:27–36) ༷ 261
   3. Paul's Address to Jerusalem Jews
      (21:37—22:30) ༷ 265
   4. Paul's Address to the Sanhedrin
      (23:1–30) ༷ 275
   5. Paul's Address to Felix at Caesarea
      (23:31—24:27) ༷ 283
   6. Paul Appeals to Caesar (25:1–12) ༷ 293
   7. Paul's Address to Agrippa (25:13—26:32) ༷ 297

VIII. Paul and the Gospel in Rome
(27:1—28:31) 313
   1. Voyage to Rome and Shipwreck on Malta
      (27:1–44) ༷ 313
   2. Malta (28:1–10) ༷ 324
   3. Voyage to Rome (28:11–15) ༷ 328
   4. Paul at Rome (28:16–31) ༷ 329

A Postscript 335
   Luke's Narrative and Paul's Subsequent Fate ༷ 335
   "Acts 29": The Ongoing History of the Orthodox
      Church ༷ 336

Appendix
   A Chronolgy of Acts 339

Excurses:
- On the Ascension of Christ 21
- On the Feast of Pentecost 34
- On the Accuracy of Stephen's History 81
- On the Journey to Arabia 111
- On the Confrontation with Peter in Antioch 178
- Lessons from Paul's Speech Before the Areopagus 207
- On the Epistles to the Thessalonians 211
- On Writing the First Epistle to the Corinthians 226
- On Writing the Second Epistle to the Corinthians
  and the Epistles to the Galatians and the Romans 234
- On the Pastoral Office 247
- On St. Paul's Judaism 259
- On the Chronology of Paul's Time in Jerusalem 290
- On the Resurrection of Christ 306
- On the Church's Interaction with the Romans 310

About the Author 341
Also in the Series 343
Other Books by the Author 344

ॐ Introduction to the Series ॐ

A Word about Scholarship and Translation
This commentary was written for your grandmother. And for your plumber, your banker, your next-door neighbor, and the girl who serves you French fries at the nearby McDonald's. That is, it was written for the average layman, for the nonprofessional who feels a bit intimidated by the presence of copious footnotes, long bibliographies, and all those other things which so enrich the lives of academics. It is written for the pious Orthodox layman who is mystified by such things as Source Criticism, but who nonetheless wants to know what the Scriptures mean.

Therefore, it is unlike many other commentaries, which are written as contributions to the ongoing endeavor of scholarship and as parts of a continuous dialogue among scholars. That endeavor and dialogue is indeed worthwhile, but the present commentary forms no part of it. For it assumes, without argument, a certain point of view, and asserts it without defense, believing it to be consistent with the presuppositions of the Fathers and therefore consistent with Orthodox Tradition. It has but one aim: to be the sort of book a busy parish priest might put in the hands of an interested parishioner who says to him over coffee hour after Liturgy, "Father, I'm not sure I really get what St. Paul is saying in the Epistles. What does it all mean?" This commentary tries to tell the perplexed parishioner what the writers of the New Testament mean.

Regarding the translation used herein, an Italian proverb says, "All translators are traitors." (The proverb proves its own point, for it sounds better in Italian!) The point of the proverb, of course, is that no translation, however careful, can bring out all the nuances and meanings of the original, since no language can be the mathematical equivalent of another. The English translator is faced, it would seem, with a choice: either he can make the translation something of a rough paraphrase of the original and render it into flowing sonorous English; or he can attempt to make a fairly literal, word-for-word translation from the original with the resultant English being stilted, wooden, and clumsy.

These two basic and different approaches to translation correspond to two basic and different activities in the Church. The Church needs a translation of the Scriptures for use in worship. This should be in good, grammatical, and flowing English, as elegant as possible and suited to its function in the majestic worship of the Liturgy. The Church also needs a translation of the Scriptures for private study and for group Bible study. Here the elegance of its English is of lesser concern. What is of greater concern here is the bringing out of all the nuances found in the original. Thus this approach will tend to sacrifice elegance for literality and, wherever possible, seek a word-for-word correspondence with the Greek. Also, because the student will want to see how the biblical authors use a particular word (especially St. Paul, who has many works included in the canon), a consistency of translation will be sought and the same Greek word will be translated, wherever possible, by the same English word or by its cognate.

The present work does not pretend to be anything other than a translation for private Bible study. It seeks to achieve, as much as possible, a literal, word-for-word correspondence with the Greek. The aim has been to present a translation from which one could jump back into the Greek original with the aid of an interlinear New Testament. Where a single Greek word has been used in the original, I have tried to find (or invent!) a single English word.

The result, of course, is a translation so literally rendered from the Greek that it represents an English spoken nowhere on the planet! That is, it represents a kind of "study Bible English" and not an actual vernacular. It was never intended for use outside the present commentaries, much less in the worship of the Church. The task of producing a flowing, elegant translation that nonetheless preserves the integrity and nuances of the original I cheerfully leave to hands more competent than mine.

Key to the Format of This Work:
- The translated text is first presented in boldface type. Italics within these biblical text sections represent words required by English syntax that are not actually present in the Greek. Each translated text section is set within a shaded grey box.

> ༃ ༃ ༃ ༃ ༃
> **9 And having said these *things*, He was lifted up while they were looking, and a cloud took Him up from their eyes.**

- In the commentary sections, citations from the portion of text being commented upon are given in boldface type.

    After Jesus had finished His last discourse with His disciples, **He was lifted up while they were looking** on, and **a cloud took Him up from their eyes**. By the **cloud**, we are probably to understand the same

- In the commentary sections, citations from other locations in Scripture are given in quotation marks with a reference; any reference not including a book name refers to the book under discussion.

    They made first for **Cyprus**, where Barnabas was born (4:36).... It is possible that he asked to go with them, especially since Barnabas was his cousin (Col. 4:10).

- In the commentary sections, italics are used in the ordinary way—for emphasis, foreign words, etc.

    In those days of waiting for the Holy Spirit to come, they **all with the same-impulse were devoting themselves to the prayer**. The word rendered *same-impulse* is the Greek *omothumadon*, a favorite word of Luke's (used ten times in Acts).

❧ Introduction ☙

THE CHARACTERISTICS AND WRITING OF THE ACTS OF THE APOSTLES

The book commonly called the Acts of the Apostles is a door and a bridge. It is a door into the Church of the first century, telling us what that Church was like and how the Christian movement spread from Palestine into all the world. It is, in fact, the only door we have into that time, for it is the only document dating from the first century which describes church life then. (We may add perhaps the door is not so much wide open as it is ajar, for although it tells us what church life was like then, it does not tell us very much!) It is thus very precious, for without it we would have no firsthand description of how the Church lived, functioned, worshipped, and evangelized.

It is also a bridge, connecting the ministry of Jesus and His apostles in the four Gospels to the epistles that were written to the churches. When the Gospels end, Jesus' disciples are in Palestine, awaiting the Holy Spirit, existing as a Jewish messianic movement. The epistles were written mostly to Gentile churches spread across the Mediterranean world. How does one go from one to the other? The Acts of the Apostles (or Acts, as it will be called in this commentary) tells that tale.

The work was originally written as the second half of a two-volume work, the first half being the Gospel of St. Luke. Luke was a Gentile physician, born in Antioch and a later companion of St. Paul. He wrote this two-volume set to his Gentile friend Theophilus to further acquaint him with the controversial Christian movement, about which he had doubtless heard many slanders. In Luke 1:1–4, Luke tells Theophilus that he consulted many eyewitnesses and used previous sources when he wrote his Gospel, which told the story of Jesus. Luke further tells Theophilus in Acts 1:1–5 that he dealt in his first book with "all that Jesus began to do and teach," clearly intending by this to continue the story of what He later did through His disciples.

Like Luke's Gospel, the Acts do not record history simply for archival purposes. Luke writes history, but he makes a selection of events. (For example, he does not record what *all* the apostles did, the later title "Acts of the Apostles" notwithstanding, but focuses especially on the work of Peter and Paul.) He writes to make certain apologetic points, in order to commend this new Faith to his friend Theophilus—and through him, to the world at large.

1. Firstly, Luke intends to show that the Church and the Christian movement (the two were the same) were **not seditious and politically suspect** as many thought. The Church's Founder had been executed under Pontius Pilate for sedition, as the King of the Jews, a rival to the power of Caesar (Luke 23:2). Wherever this movement spread, there seemed to be riots (Acts 16:20–21; 17:6–8). Everywhere the sect was spoken against (28:22). Luke narrates some of its history to show that the Christians were no danger to the security of the Empire, and that their bad reputation was due solely to Jewish slander and envy. In this matter, Paul is a test case, for he was brought before Caesar precisely on charges of inciting riot.

2. Secondly, Luke writes to show that **the Church is the true Israel** and the inheritor of God's promises to His people (28:20). Judaism was a *religio licita*, a legal religion, and as such was entitled to protection under Roman law. Though the Jews denied that the Christian movement was a legitimate part of Judaism, stigmatizing it as a heresy, Luke strove to show that the Christians were entitled to the same legal privileges as the Jews, even though the movement now contained many Gentiles.

3. Thirdly, Luke intends to show how **God guides the Church by His Holy Spirit**, controlling every facet of its expansion. Thus the Spirit is with the Church as He was with Christ. Accordingly, the role of the Holy Spirit is prominent, as highlighted by the

phenomenon of speaking in tongues. (Indeed, some have said the book should be called "The Acts of the Holy Spirit.") Thus the Spirit's Presence is seen on the Day of Pentecost (2:1–4, 33), through the miracles of the apostles (e.g. 3:1f), and through divine judgment on those who lie to the apostles (5:1f). God's guiding hand is seen through the confirming outpouring of the Spirit when the Church moves into Samaritan territory (8:4f) and among the Gentiles (chs. 10–11). The apostles are led in the very routes they choose by the Spirit's miraculous guidance (16:6–10). The subtext of all this is clear: Since God guides the Church, to fight against the Christians is to fight against God (5:38–39). The Romans therefore would be well advised not to persecute the Church.

4. Finally, Luke writes to show his Jewish readers that **the inclusion of the Gentiles is the will of God**. Jews had no trouble in believing Gentiles had a place in the Kingdom, but they saw this place as a subordinate one, as servants of the Jews. By narrating the outpouring of the Spirit upon the Gentiles (chs. 10–11) and the Church's subsequent acceptance of them at its first council (ch. 15), Luke shows his Jewish readership that the Gentiles, *while remaining Gentiles*, have a place of equality with Jews in the Kingdom. Jews saw the Church's inclusion of the Gentiles as further evidence that the Christian movement was heretical and that it overthrew the foundational truths of Judaism. Luke shows that this inclusion is not heretical and does not threaten the truth of the Jewish Scriptures; rather, it is the will of God.

Where and when was the Acts of the Apostles written? Luke was a native and resident of Antioch, so it is possible he wrote from there. It is also possible he wrote Acts from Rome, if he remained there after being with Paul during his second imprisonment.

The time of the book's writing is also uncertain. Paul was imprisoned in Rome about AD 60 and spent at least two years there (28:30–31), so that Acts could not have been written before 62. It would seem it was written before the destruction of Jerusalem in 70, for had it been written after this, Luke surely would have alluded to this event. His concern was to show how Jewish envy and slander were behind much of the Christians' unpopularity, and the unpopularity of the Jews themselves after 70 would have been too useful to Luke's purpose not to mention. Also, after 70, the Jewish-Gentile tension ceased to be such a factor in church life, as the Christians and Jews increasingly went their own separate ways; but in Acts this dynamic is still prominent.

Paul was imprisoned a second time in about the autumn of 65 and martyred about the summer of 66. It was during this imprisonment that both Mark and Luke came to visit him in Rome (2 Tim. 4:11). It would seem Luke had access at that time to the notes Mark would use for his Gospel, and that Luke began writing his work then. That would mean that his Gospel was produced perhaps about the middle of 67 or later, and his Acts after that, perhaps 68 or 69. Since Nero died in the summer of 68, this would mean Acts was written after the first wave of persecution had passed, and Luke felt he had a fresh chance to commend his Faith to Roman society.

❧ I ☙

OPENING:
THE ASCENSION AND THE PROMISE OF THE SPIRIT
(1:1–11)

☙ ☙ ☙ ☙ ☙

1 1 The first word I made, Theophilus, about all that Jesus began to do and teach
2 until the day when He was taken up, after He had by the Holy Spirit commanded the apostles whom He had chosen
3 (to whom He also presented Himself living, after His suffering, by many proofs, appearing to them during forty days, and telling of the things about the Kingdom of God).
4 And eating with *them*, He ordered them not to depart from Jerusalem, but to wait for the promise of the Father, "Which you heard of from Me;
5 "for John baptized with water, but you *yourselves* will be baptized in the Holy Spirit after not many days."
6 And therefore when they had come together, they were asking Him, saying, "Lord, is it at this time You are restoring the Kingdom to Israel?"
7 He said to them, "It is not for you to know the times or the *appointed* times which the Father has set by His own authority,

> 8 "but you will receive power when the Holy Spirit has come upon you, and you will be My witnesses both in Jerusalem, and in all Judea and Samaria, and unto the end of the earth."

St. Luke dedicated his **first word** (or account, referring to his Gospel) to **Theophilus**. In Luke 1:3 Theophilus is given the title "most-excellent" (Gr. *kratiste*), a title used by Roman provincial governors, and it seems as if he held some state position. He was, I suggest, a highly placed friend of Luke who had heard reports of the new Christian Faith (not all of them favorable). Luke writes his two-volume work to commend the Faith to him, and as an outreach to Roman society at large.

That first account is characterized as **all that Jesus began to do and teach until the day when He was taken up** (Luke 24:50–51). The implication is that the present work contains an account of all that Jesus *continued* to do and teach through His disciples. There is thus a continuity between Jesus and His Body, the Church. (Thus Christ counts Saul's persecution of His Church as persecution of *Him*; 9:5.) What the Church does, Jesus does, in the sense that the Church is His instrument in the world. (This does not mean, of course, that Christ is responsible for all the misdeeds of men that are done in His Name.)

Luke then refers to the time that Jesus was with the apostles prior to His Ascension. **During** this **forty days**, He was not with them continuously, but **presented Himself** as **living by many proofs, appearing** to them at intervals and demonstrating that He was truly risen. (Luke 24:41–43 mentions that He ate a piece of broiled fish to prove that He was no phantom or hallucination; John 20:27 mentions that He invited Thomas to feel His wounds.) While with them, He was also teaching **the things about the Kingdom of God**. The content of this teaching is not given, but it seems to have included teaching about how the Hebrew Scriptures were fulfilled in His life and in the future work of the Church (see Luke 24:45–49, which forms the background to this entire passage).

Luke also speaks of Christ **by the Holy Spirit commanding the**

I. Opening　　　　　　　　　　　　　　　　　　　　　　　　　　Acts 1:1–8

apostles. This reference to the Holy Spirit refers to Christ's prophetic words to them. During one of the times that He was **eating with them** (Gr. *sunalizo*, literally "to eat salt with"; i.e., to share a meal), Christ did not just teach, but also spoke predicting their future life. In particular, **He ordered them not to depart from Jerusalem, but to wait for the promise** given by **the Father**. That is, Christ predicted that if they would wait in the city, they would be filled with the Holy Spirit **after not many days**. This was the reality they **heard of from** Him at their Last Supper (see John 14:16–17, 26; 15:26; 16:13–15). This was what made them greater than the disciples of John (compare Luke 7:28), for **John baptized with water** only, but they would **be baptized in the Holy Spirit** and fire (Luke 3:16). As they had been soaked with water during John's baptism, so they would be soaked with power in the next few days.

In narrating Christ's words about giving His directions to His apostles **by the Holy Spirit** (i.e., prophetically), Luke invites us to see later parallels in the prophetic ministry of the Church (e.g. Acts 11:28; 16:6, 7; 21:11). Just as Jesus once spoke to His disciples "by the Holy Spirit" while with them, so after His Ascension He continued to speak to them by the Holy Spirit through the prophets of the Church. The mode of speaking may have changed, but the Lord continued to guide His people.

As Christ spoke about the Kingdom of God during one of these times, **they were asking Him** if it was **at this time** that He was **restoring the Kingdom to Israel**. Throughout Christ's ministry, the apostles shared the expectations of their fellow Jews that the Kingdom would take a political form, and that Jesus would exalt Israel to a place of political freedom and prominence in the world. Now that the hidden will of God regarding His death and resurrection had been fulfilled (Luke 24:46), surely this was the time to fulfill their national hopes? Would the tyranny of Rome over Judea now be overthrown?

Jesus does not answer yes or no, but rather diverts them entirely from such national questions. The matter of **the times or the *appointed* times** (Gr. *chronos* and *kairos*, meaning the stretch of years and the times of opportunity and crisis) was not theirs to consider.

The Father had **set by His own authority** the rise and fall of nations. They were not called to such political considerations but to **be** His **witnesses** throughout the world, testifying to the Gospel facts they had seen and heard. (The nonpolitical nature of the apostles' work was surely of interest to loyal Romans such as Theophilus. The Church was no threat to the security of the Empire.)

To this end they would **receive power when the Holy Spirit** had **come upon** them in the days to come, and it was with this **power** (Gr. *dunamis*; compare our English word "dynamo") that they were to fulfill their appointed tasks. Their focus was on their own nation of Israel, but Christ was calling them to lift up their eyes to refocus upon a wider field. They were to be His **witnesses** and work **in Jerusalem** where they were, and in **all Judea** (that is, the Roman province of Judea, including Galilee). Even beyond their own nation, they were to witness in foreign **Samaria**, and even **unto the end of the earth**. Once again, Luke's Roman readers are invited to notice that the Church's task is witness, not revolution.

This geographical widening of focus not only forms the Church's apostolic mandate. It also forms the contents for the rest of Acts, for Luke goes on to narrate the spread of the Word to Jerusalem (chs. 2–7), then to Judea and Samaria (chs. 8–11), then to Gentile cities (chs. 11–21), and finally to Rome (chs. 22–28). When the Gospel reached Rome, the dark heart of the pagan world, it had in principle reached everywhere, for Rome was further from Israel than merely geography would allow. Spiritually speaking, Rome was as far away as you could get. (It is interesting that Psalm 8 of the so-called *Psalms of Solomon*, written shortly before this, celebrates Pompey coming to Israel from Rome as coming "from the end of the earth.") Paul's preaching the Gospel in Rome was a promise that missionaries would traverse all the globe with that saving message.

ॐ ॐ ॐ ॐ ॐ

9 And having said these *things*, He was lifted up while they were looking, and a cloud took Him up from their eyes.
10 And as they were staring into heaven while

> **He was going, behold! two men in white garb stood beside them,**
> **11 and they also said, "Men of Galilee, why do you stand looking into heaven? This Jesus, who has been taken up from you into heaven, will come in the same way as you beheld Him go into heaven."**

After Jesus had finished His last discourse with His disciples, **He was lifted up while they were looking** on, and **a cloud took Him up from their eyes**. By the **cloud**, we are probably to understand the same cloud that obscured Him from view once before, on the Mount of Transfiguration (Luke 9:34), so that Jesus was received into the immediate Presence of the Father. Since Jesus emerged from that cloud on the previous occasion, the disciples now **stood looking into heaven**, wondering if He would reappear.

Suddenly (the suddenness signaled by **behold!**), **two men in white garb** were standing beside them, obviously angelic messengers like those who attended Christ's Resurrection. They asked the **men of Galilee why** they still remained there. Jesus would not reappear beside them, as He had after the cloud vanished on the night of His Transfiguration (Luke 9:36). Instead, He would **come in the same way as** they **beheld Him go into heaven**—that is, descending from heaven, from the Presence of the Father. There would be no more post-Resurrection appearances. The next time they saw Him would be when He returned to judge the world.

> ### ❦ EXCURSUS
> #### On the Ascension of Christ
>
> The Ascension of Christ is related by St. Luke without any theological commentary. Reading the Epistle to the Hebrews about the high priesthood of Christ (e.g. Heb. 7:26—8:2) and the Epistle to the Ephesians (e.g. Eph. 4:8f), we may add the following:

Christ's Ascension was not simply His relocation from earth to heaven, with the accompanying end of His resurrection appearances. It was the culmination of His exaltation, the first step of which was His Resurrection and the glorification of His body. Through His Ascension, Christ assumed His place at the right hand of the Father in heaven, sharing all the power and rule of the universe, having fully overcome the limitations of time and space that accompanied His earthly ministry. Part of this heavenly rule involves His high-priestly ministry to His disciples. As the glorified Head of His Body, He is present before God as the sacrificed Lamb, the eternal and effective Offering present in the eucharistic worship of His Church.

The question is sometimes asked, "What do this final glorious liberation from the limitations of time and space and His sharing in the Father's authority have to do with His physical ascent from the earth's surface?" Bluntly put, since heaven is not located several miles above the clouds, why did Christ vertically ascend? And where did His Body go?

It is helpful at the outset to realize how little we know of these spiritual and heavenly realities. The departed saints are with God and before His throne (Rev. 4—5), but we can have no accurate idea of the spatial dimensions of this. The question, "Where?" is one that rapidly gets lost in the labyrinth of the transcendence of heavenly realities and the power of God. How the spirits of just men made perfect (Heb. 12:23) gather around the Heavenly Presence we cannot know, much less how the glorified Body of Christ relates to that Presence. All we can say is that somewhere those spirits and that Body remain—with the full recognition that the spatial word "somewhere" must not lead us to project onto that statement our earthly understandings of location and space.

That means, if we take our almost complete ignorance seriously, we cannot say that Christ's vertical ascent from the earth can have nothing to do with His escape from earthly limitations. It is possible this is an example of what C. S. Lewis (in a collection of essays entitled *They Asked for a Paper*) called "transposition." In Lewis's thought, transposition is the process whereby a richer and more complex reality relates to a poorer and simpler one.

Thus, when the richer reality of (for example) the music of a full symphony orchestra is transposed into the poorer reality of a piano piece, certain things in that poorer reality have to have two functions. The notes of the piano will have to represent not just the notes the piano would play in the orchestra, but the sounds of the stringed and wind instruments as well.

Perhaps in the same way, in our poorer physical world, vertical ascent serves two purposes—being involved both in simple physical ascent (as in mountain-climbing) and in the process of Christ's glorification.

Those who know only the poorer medium will never be able fully to understand the richer one. One who knows only the music of the piano and who has never heard an orchestra will not be able to see how the piano notes can represent other sounds as well. Similarly, one who knows only physical realities will not be able to see how a physical ascent can also serve the process of what we may call Christ's escalating transcendence. It is only by experiencing the richer world that one can truly see how the phenomenon of ascent can serve this higher purpose.

❧ II ☙

THE CHURCH IN JERUSALEM
(1:12—8:1a)

§II.1. The Gathering of the Disciples

> ☙ ☙ ☙ ☙ ☙
> 12 Then they returned to Jerusalem from the mountain called *the Mountain* of Olives, which is near Jerusalem, a Sabbath day's journey.
> 13 And when they had entered, they went up into the upper-room, where they were staying; that is, Peter and John and James and Andrew, Philip and Thomas, Bartholomew and Matthew, James *the son* of Alphaeus, and Simon the Zealot, and Judas *the son* of James.
> 14 These all with the same-impulse were devoting themselves to the prayer, with the women, and Mary the Mother of Jesus and His brothers.

After the Ascension **they returned to Jerusalem** from the *Mountain* **of Olives**, on the eastern slopes of the city. They were **near Jerusalem**, only **a Sabbath day's journey** away, which is little over half a mile. (Luke stresses this to show they were obeying Christ's order not to leave Jerusalem.) After they returned, they **went up into the upper-room**, probably the same room where they had met for the Last Supper. This was now the central place for meetings of the disciples in Jerusalem.

Luke then lists the Eleven. **Peter** comes first as the head of the apostles. He is followed here by **John**, who seemed to be his best friend (they are often paired: Luke 22:8; Acts 3:1; 8:14). **James** and **Andrew** come next as the brothers of John and Peter. The order of the rest of the list is different from the order in Luke 6:14f, in that **Philip** is here paired with **Thomas** and **Bartholomew** with **Matthew**, whereas in the former list, Philip and Bartholomew are paired, and Matthew is paired with Thomas. The rearranged order may be haphazard, or it may represent new close relationships among the Twelve. Luke's main point in listing the apostles is to show that all remained steadfast except Judas the traitor.

In those days of waiting for the Holy Spirit to come, they **all with the same-impulse were devoting themselves to the prayer**. The word rendered *same-impulse* is the Greek *omothumadon*, a favorite word of Luke's (used ten times in Acts). It indicates the united purpose of the Church, a harmony of heart and will that testifies to the grace and presence of God. During those days, the apostles were not simply loitering about the city. They were seeking God in fervent prayer and adoration. The use of the article (Gr. *te proseuche*; *the* prayer) perhaps indicates formal Jewish liturgical prayer.

The Eleven were joined by **the women** of the group, including not only the wives of the apostles (for Peter was married: see Luke 4:38; 1 Cor. 9:5), but also Mary Magdalene, Joanna the wife of Chuza, and Susanna (see Luke 8:2–3). Singled out in this group were **Mary the Mother of Jesus and His brothers**. The family of Jesus, who knew Him most intimately, were convinced that He was the risen Messiah and joined with His apostles. The presence of His earthly family thus attests to the authenticity of Christ's mission.

ॐ ॐ ॐ ॐ ॐ

15 And in these days Peter arose in the middle of the brothers (a crowd of about one hundred and twenty names was in the same *place*), and said,

16 "Men, *my* brothers, it was necessary that the Scripture be fulfilled, which the Holy Spirit foretold through the mouth of David about

Judas, who became a guide to those who took Jesus.

17 "For he was numbered out among us and received his portion in this service."

18 (Now this *man* acquired a field with the reward of his unrighteousness; and becoming prone, he burst in the middle and all his bowels spilled *out*.

19 And it became known to all who were dwelling in Jerusalem; so that in their own language that field was called Hakeldama, that is, "Field of Blood.")

20 "For it is written in the Book of Psalms, 'Let his residence be made a wilderness, and let no one dwell in it'; and 'His episcopate let another take.'

21 "It is therefore necessary *that* of those men who have gone with us all the time that the Lord Jesus went in and out among us—

22 "beginning with the baptism of John, until the day that He was taken up from us—one of these become a witness with us of His resurrection."

23 And they stood *apart* two *men*, Joseph called Barsabbas (who was also called Justus), and Matthias.

24 And they prayed and said, "You, O Lord, knower of the hearts of all, reveal which one of these two You have chosen

25 "to take the place of this service and apostleship from which Judas turned aside to go to his own place."

26 And they gave lots for them, and the lot fell upon Matthias; and he was added *to be* with the eleven apostles.

It was during one of those gatherings that **Peter arose in the middle of the brothers**. (The location is not specified; it could have been the house containing the same upper room as in v. 13, or it could have been the Temple; compare Luke 24:53.) Peter was the spokesman of the Twelve and the one appointed by Christ to strengthen the others by his leadership (Luke 22:32). He therefore assumes that lead now in order to rectify a deficiency. The **crowd** which had gathered for the regular prayer was **about one hundred and twenty names**. (Luke uses the word **names** instead of "persons" because each one was well known to all the others, as one big intimate family.)

He addresses them as **men, *my* brothers** (a term that would include the women, being simply an affectionate term for one's kin; compare its use in Acts 23:6). Though Jesus appointed twelve original witnesses as the nucleus of the restored Israel (Luke 22:30), since the defection of Judas they were reduced to eleven. Judas was once **numbered out among** them, being as fully apostolic as the others, and he **received his portion in** the apostolic **service** just as the others did. He also received authority to heal and exorcise when sent out (Luke 9:1–2). Nonetheless, he fell away from his calling and **became a guide** and support **to those who took Jesus** in the Garden of Gethsemane. This had to be, for **it was necessary that the Scripture be fulfilled**. **David** had **foretold about Judas** through his prophecy in **the Book of Psalms**. In Psalm 69:25, David wrote, **"Let his residence be made a wilderness,"** and in Psalm 109:8 (LXX), **"His episcopate let another take."**

In the original context of these psalms, David said his enemy would die early in life, falling by the judgment of God. His foe's residence would therefore be uninhabited, desolate as the wilderness. His job (Gr. *episcope*, "office") would be taken over by another after he died prematurely. These psalms referred to the enemies of David and his dynasty. Since that dynasty culminated in Jesus, the curses invoked upon the foes of the House of David fall upon Judas also.

Peter applies these curses to Judas not out of spite, but because they were so completely fulfilled in him, for Judas did die prematurely as under the judgment of God. Peter did not have to tell his

II. The Church in Jerusalem   Acts 1:15–26

hearers the fate of Judas since they all knew it, but Luke relates the tale in a parenthesis.

Luke says that Judas **acquired a field** with the money given to him for betraying Christ (or more accurately, the priests bought it later in his name; Matt. 27:6–8). This was the Potter's Field, across the Kidron Valley. There Judas hanged himself (Matt. 27:5). It appears that what he used to hang himself tore or gave way so that he fell onto the sharp rocks below, and **becoming prone** as he landed on them, **he burst in the middle and all his bowels spilled** *out*. Luke relates this grisly end to show how Judas died as the judgment of God. This horrible end **became known to all who were dwelling in Jerusalem, so that** the field where he died came to be known as **Hakeldama, "Field of Blood"**—the name change being an abiding testimony to his guilt.

Since Judas had died, it was **necessary** that he be replaced so that the Church could begin with its original complement of twelve apostles as the foundation of the renewed Israel. One must be chosen to **become a witness with** them of Christ's **resurrection**, and therefore he must have been with them all the time of Christ's ministry, from **the baptism of John** months before until Christ **was taken up** a few days before.

Two of that group fulfilled those conditions, and they **stood** them apart from the others: **Joseph called Barsabbas** (literally, "son of the Sabbath," probably because he was born on a Sabbath day) **who was also called Justus** when among the Gentiles, **and Matthias**. Both equally met the qualifications, so it was for the Lord Jesus to choose His twelfth apostle, not them. This would be done by casting lots, the time-honored method for invoking the divine choice (Prov. 16:33).

They prayed before casting lots that the lot might reveal Christ's choice. Their prayer was to the **Lord** as the **knower of the hearts of all**, and thus as the only fit judge for such a choice. He could see what the others could not. Let the lot reflect His choice of the two for this task. **Judas** had held **the place of** that **service** (Gr. *diakonia*) **and apostleship**, but he had **turned aside** from that place **to go to his own place**—that is, to go where he belonged, to Gehenna.

The contrast is between his **place** (Gr. *topos*) with the apostles and his own **place** apart from them. Judas had disastrously decided to go his own way, **turning aside** from the straight path before his feet. The word rendered *turn aside* is the Greek *parabaino*, rendered "transgress" in Matt. 15:3; Judas did not merely veer off the main road, but transgressed the holy office given to him. Let his replacement now be revealed!

The parallel between the two men, Judas and his successor, is perhaps more apparent in the Greek than in the English. The word rendered *portion* in verse 17 is the Greek *kleros*, the same word rendered *lot* in verse 26, for portions were often determined by casting lots. Thus Judas turned away from that which the lot of destiny had given him, and his successor was chosen by the same divine lot.

The usual method for casting lots was to write the names of the candidates on small pebbles and place them in an urn. One would be drawn, and this was the chosen lot. When the lot was drawn, it **fell upon Matthias, and he was added** *to be* **with the eleven apostles**. The full number of the apostles had been restored, and the Church was thus ready to fulfill its appointed task of witness to the world.

§II.2. Pentecost

> **2** 1 And when the day of Pentecost had fully come, they were all together in the same place.
> 2 And suddenly from heaven there was a noise like a violent, driving wind, and it filled the whole house where they were sitting.
> 3 And there appeared to them tongues as of fire, dividing up and sitting on each one of them.
> 4 And they were all filled with the Holy Spirit and began to speak with other tongues, as the Spirit was giving them to declare.

II. The Church in Jerusalem   Acts 2:1–4

St. Luke now relates the birthday of the Church. This took place **when the day of Pentecost had fully come**—that is, when the fifty days after Passover had been fulfilled. (The word *Pentecost* comes from the Greek word for "fifty.") In the Jewish calendar, it originally marked the firstfruits of the wheat harvest (Ex. 34:22). It was ten days since the Lord had ascended, and His disciples had spent this time blessing God in the Temple and worshipping privately as Christians in the upper room.

It was early in the day, about 9:00 A.M. **They were all together in the same place**—probably the upper room that was the gathering place for their Christian worship. It was the custom for pious Jews to attend the Temple offering of the firstfruits and the sacrifices soon after dawn; no doubt they had been there earlier and returned to the upper room for their own Christian worship. This detail of them being **all together in the same place** is significant, for the Spirit would come to unite them as one Body.

Suddenly there was a noise like a violent, driving wind, and the noise **filled the whole house where they were sitting**. It was like listening to a hurricane as the Divine Spirit filled the house.

In Luke's statement that the wind came **from heaven**, we detect echoes of the prophecy of Ezekiel 37:9. In that prophecy of the resurrection of the nation, Ezekiel first prophesied to a valley of dry bones, which came together and were covered with sinews and skins. Then he prophesied to the breath and the Spirit (the Hebrew *ruach* means both breath and Spirit), and from the four winds the Divine *Ruach* came into the former corpses so that they lived. Thus God promised He would put His Spirit within them (Ezek. 37:14). The coming of the Pentecostal Spirit "from heaven" thus fulfilled this word of the Divine *Ruach* coming "from the four winds." This was no earthbound wind, but one that came straight from the throne of God in heaven.

John the Baptizer had promised that the Messiah would baptize in the Holy Spirit and fire (Luke 3:16), and it is significant that the Spirit also came as the Fire of God. This fire began **dividing up and sitting on each one of them**, so that each one received his personal share of the Spirit. The Spirit not only unites Christian with Christian, but He also preserves the uniqueness of each one. The fire assumed the form of **tongues**, for the Spirit came to enable them to declare with their tongues the mighty saving acts of God in Christ. As if in pledge of this new boldness to witness they were receiving, when **they were all filled with the Holy Spirit**, they also **began to speak with other tongues, as the Spirit was giving them to declare**. (The word rendered *declare* is the Greek *apophtheggomai*, used for the loud declarations of the prophet or holy man.)

This speaking in tongues was unique in salvation—men had prophesied before, but none had spoken in tongues like this. It came as something brand new, as evidence that God was doing a new thing in the earth through His Church. There is no reason to think the apostles knew what they were saying (in 1 Cor. 14:14, St. Paul says when he prays in a tongue, his mind remains unfruitful). But they were speaking true languages of the world nonetheless—languages recognized by those international pilgrims then in Jerusalem.

---

5 Now there were Jews dwelling in Jerusalem, reverent men from all nations under heaven.
6 And when this sound happened, the multitude came together and were confounded, because each one was hearing them speak in his own language.
7 And they were beside *themselves* and marveled, saying, "Behold, are not all these who are speaking Galileans?
8 "And how is it that we *ourselves* each hear them in our own language to which we were born?
9 "Parthians and Medes and Elamites and those dwelling in Mesopotamia, Judea and Cappadocia, Pontus and Asia,
10 "Phrygia and Pamphylia, Egypt and the parts of Libya toward Cyrene, and those sojourning from Rome, both Jews and proselytes,

II. The Church in Jerusalem   Acts 2:5–13

> 11 "Cretans and Arabs—we hear them in our tongues speaking of the great *deeds* of God."
> 12 And all were beside *themselves* and perplexed, saying to one another, "What does this mean?"
> 13 But others were deriding and saying, "They have been filled with sweet-wine."

Luke then explains that **there were Jews dwelling in Jerusalem** at that time, **reverent men** who came as pilgrims from **all nations under heaven** for the Feast of Pentecost. At the sound of a roomful of people all speaking loudly in various languages at the same time, this international **multitude** that heard this commotion not unnaturally **came together** (probably at the house). They **were confounded because each one was hearing them speak in his own language**—even though **all** of those who were doing the **speaking** were **Galileans**. How did such men learn all these languages?

Those who gathered about the door were indeed a mixed crowd. There were Jews who were **Parthians, Medes, and Elamites** (all from outside the Roman Empire, descendants of those Jews who remained in the Babylonian captivity). There were Jews who were **dwelling in Mesopotamia**, between the Parthian and Roman Empires. Within the Roman Empire, there were Jews from nearby, in other parts of **Judea** (or Palestine), as well as from northward in **Cappadocia, Pontus,** and the province of **Asia** further west. There were Jewish pilgrims from **Phrygia** (between Cappadocia and Asia) and **Pamphylia** (south of Phrygia). Jews were there from the sizable Jewish population in **Egypt** and from further west, **the parts of Libya** (that is, Africa) **towards** the city of **Cyrene** (a city on the north coast of the African continent). There were many Jews **sojourning** in Jerusalem **from Rome, both** those born **Jews** and also **proselytes**, Gentiles who had converted to Judaism. There were even **Cretans** (who came from the far-off island) and **Arabs** (from distant Arabia). Each one in this crowd heard the Christians **speaking of the great *deeds* of God**, declaring loudly in those foreign languages the mighty things God had done through His Son.

The question was, what did this inexplicable hubbub mean? Those locals who had joined the crowd (who could not understand the languages and who heard only a commotion) wrote the whole thing off. For them it could only mean **they have been filled with sweet-wine** (Gr. *gleukos*, a highly intoxicating wine).

❧ EXCURSUS
ON THE FEAST OF PENTECOST

The Holy Spirit was sent from heaven on the Day of Pentecost, ten days after Christ's Ascension. It seems this day was chosen by God, not only because there were many pilgrims present in Jerusalem at that time for the feast (for they were present a day or so before Pentecost also), but also because of the typological significance of the day. In the Judaism of that day, Pentecost not only was the feast of the firstfruits of the wheat harvest, it also commemorated the giving of the Law, since it was considered that the Law was given on Mount Sinai fifty days after the Passover in Egypt.

This was therefore a fitting day for the bestowal of the Spirit and the beginning of the Church's work of evangelism. For just as Pentecost was the celebration of the firstfruits (Ex. 34:22), so on this day the firstfruits of Israel were gathered into the Kingdom, as many Jews came to believe in Jesus as the glorified Messiah (Acts 2:41). Furthermore, just as Pentecost commemorated the giving of the Law, so through the giving of the Spirit was the Law of God written in the hearts of the people (Heb. 8:10; 2 Cor. 3:3).

The crowd of pilgrims added to the Church that day was also significant, for the international nature of the crowd testified to the international nature of the Church. Just as these Jews came from all over the world, so the Church was destined by God to spread throughout the world.

The different tongues spoken by the apostles at that time also witnessed to the Church's international calling—and to its unity. For just as the Christians all miraculously spoke different languages and yet were one, so in the Church is the fractured disunity of men overcome. As the kontakion for Pentecost says, "when God distributed the tongues of fire, He called all to unity." Thus Pentecost reverses the curse of the tower of Babel, for there diverse tongues separated one man from another, whereas here the diverse tongues bring all together in Christ.

༄ ༄ ༄ ༄ ༄

14 But Peter, having stood with the Eleven, lifted up his voice and declared to them, "Men of Judea, and all you dwelling in Jerusalem, let this be known to you, and give ear to my words.

15 "For these *men* are not drunk, as you *yourselves* take *them to be*, for it is the third hour of the day.

16 "But this is what was spoken of through the prophet Joel:

17 "'And it will be in the last days,' God says, 'that I will pour out My Spirit upon all flesh; and your sons and your daughters will prophesy, and your young *men* will see visions, and your elder *men* will dream dreams.

18 "'Even upon My slaves and upon My *female-*slaves I will in those days pour out My Spirit, and they will prophesy.

19 "'And I will give wonders in the heaven above, and signs upon the earth beneath, blood and fire and vapor of smoke.

20 "'The sun will be changed into darkness and the moon into blood before the great and manifest Day of the Lord will come.

> **21** "'And it will be *that* everyone, whoever calls upon the Name of the Lord, will be saved.'

St. Luke does not say much about location or logistics for this speech but concentrates on the message itself. If the disciples were in the house they used in 1:13, it would appear that **Peter** went outside to address the crowd, along **with the Eleven** others, so that they **stood** together as a united witness for the truth of Peter's message. Peter **lifted up his voice and declared to them** (the word for *declare* is the Gr. *apophtheggomai*, the same word used in v. 4 for the loud proclamations of inspired men). Peter was declaring loudly to his audience of pilgrims and locals, with the prophetic authority to speak for God.

He began by dismissing (perhaps with a smile?) their interpretation that the noise was caused by **these *men*** being **drunk**. Not likely, he says, for it was just **the third hour of the day**, 9:00 A.M. The time for getting drunk, he jokingly says, is later! Instead, the noise was the fulfillment of **what was spoken of through the prophet Joel**.

Joel had predicted (in Joel 2:28–32) that **in the last days**, Messiah would come and God would **pour out** His **Spirit** abundantly **upon all flesh**. In the days of old, the Spirit was given only to prophets, princes, and sages. But in the days of the Messiah, things would be different. **All flesh**, all persons, would receive the Spirit, not just the prophets. **Young *men*** would **see visions**, and **elder *men*** would **dream dreams**, as God revealed Himself to all (visions and dreams were ways that God revealed Himself to His prophets). Even the humblest, the **slaves and *female*-slaves**, would receive the Spirit, so that they would **prophesy**. In those days, all God's people would enjoy the closeness to God formerly known only to the few prophets.

Those days would be days of wonder. God would **give wonders** everywhere—**in the heaven above** and **upon the earth beneath**. Chaos would reign (**blood and fire and vapor of smoke** are cited, the signs of the desolation of war and smoking cities), and even nature would begin to turn unnatural. The **sun would be changed into darkness and the moon into blood**. These were the classic apocalyptic signs, signs that the great and manifest Day of the Lord was at hand. Peter mentions them here because just over a month before, these signs had begun to be fulfilled. In the middle of the day, at the crucifixion of Jesus, the sun was changed into darkness (Luke 24:44)—a sign that the Day of the Lord was drawing near and the days prophesied by Joel had indeed come.

That was good news, for Joel said that in those days, **everyone, whoever calls upon the Name of the Lord, will be saved**. It was this invocation of the Name of the Lord Jesus that Peter was about to urge upon his audience (2:39; compare 22:16). (We note in passing that in Joel 2:32 LXX, the "Lord" refers to Yahweh, whereas Peter here applies the title to the divine Christ.)

> ৯ ৯ ৯ ৯ ৯
> 22 "Men of Israel, hear these words: Jesus the Nazarene, a man attested to you by God with *works* of power and wonders and signs which God did through Him in your midst, just as you yourselves know—
> 23 "this *Man*, delivered up by the appointed intention and foreknowledge of God, you nailed up by the hands of lawless *men* and destroyed,
> 24 "whom God raised up, having loosed the birth pangs of death, since it was not possible for Him to be held fast by it.
> 25 "For David says of Him, 'I was always foreseeing the Lord before me; for He is at my right *hand* that I may not be shaken.
> 26 "'Therefore my heart was glad and my tongue exulted; moreover even my flesh will dwell in hope;
> 27 "'because You will not leave my soul behind to Hades, nor give *over* Your holy one to see decay.
> 28 "'You have made known to me the ways of

life; You will fill me with the gladness of Your Presence.'
29 "Men, *my* brothers, it is permitted to speak with boldness to you about the patriarch David that he both died and was buried, and his tomb is with us to this day.
30 "And therefore, being a prophet, and knowing that God had sworn to him with an oath to seat the fruit of his loins upon his throne,
31 "he foresaw and spoke of the resurrection of the Christ, that He was neither left behind to Hades, nor did His flesh see decay.
32 "This Jesus God raised up, to which we *ourselves* are all witnesses.
33 "Therefore having been exalted to the right *hand* of God, and having received from the Father the promise of the Holy Spirit, He has poured out this which you *yourselves* both see and hear.
34 "For it was not David who ascended into the heavens, but he himself says, 'The Lord said to my Lord, "Sit at My right hand,
35 "'"until I put Your enemies as a footstool for Your feet."'"
36 "Therefore let all the House of Israel know certainly that God has made Him both Lord and Christ—this Jesus whom you *yourselves* crucified."

After Peter's opening citation of the Scriptures, he launched into his main message—that **Jesus the Nazarene** had risen from the dead. He appealed to what his listeners already **knew**: that He was **a man attested by God** by all sorts of miracles. Jesus' reputation as a wonder-worker was well known to all. And so was His execution. He was **delivered up** to death and **destroyed**. Peter is emphatic about who was responsible for this atrocity—**you nailed** Him **up**, and even

II. The Church in Jerusalem   Acts 2:22–36

used **the hands of lawless *men***, the hated Gentiles, to do this. Yet this all occurred **by the appointed intention and foreknowledge of God**, who works all things to fulfill His will, even the wickedness and failings of men. The execution of Jesus thus was not proof that He was not the Christ. His death also served the divine purposes.

Though they condemned Jesus, **God** overturned their sentence and **raised** Him **up** again—only fitting, since it **was not possible** for the Prince of Life **to be held fast** by death. (The agonies of death are described as **birth pangs** since in this case, like a woman's birth pangs, they led finally to new life.)

Did it seem strange that Messiah should die and be raised? It should not seem strange, since this also was predicted by their Law. In Psalm 16:8–11, **David** sees God as always before his face (the meaning here of **foreseeing the Lord**), always near, **at his right hand** to help him through any disaster. That was why he need not fear even death, as **even** his flesh **will dwell in hope**. God would **not leave** his **soul behind to** languish in **Hades**, the land of the dead, nor would He **give over** his **holy one**, His pious servant, **to see decay**. Instead, David would know **the ways** of endless **life** in God's **Presence**.

All Peter's hearers knew of this psalm. Peter drives his point home. **It was permitted** for him to **speak with boldness**, without any fear of contradiction—**the patriarch David,** who wrote about triumphing over death, **both died and was buried, and his tomb** was **with** them all so that all could verify that fact. What then of his words? In merely secular literature, David's words would be taken simply as a reference to being healed of a life-threatening illness, and that would be that. But David's words were not merely secular literature. David was **a prophet**, and as a prophet, his words were a deep well of meaning, with significance beyond that of mere secular poetry. Moreover, David **knew that God had sworn to him with an oath to seat the fruit of his loins upon his throne** (2 Sam. 7:12–16), and that his House had a glorious future.

David's glowing words about not being abandoned to Hades or seeing corruption therefore had their final fulfillment not in David himself, but in his future descendant. The prophetic significance of this psalm ultimately concerned the resurrection of the Christ, for Jesus indeed was **neither left behind to Hades, nor did His flesh see decay**. On the contrary, **this Jesus God raised up**—to which the apostles standing there (the **we** is emphatic in the Greek) **were all witnesses**.

That was what all the commotion meant. Jesus was **exalted to the right *hand* of God** and **received from the Father the promise of the Holy Spirit** of which Joel spoke. Having become the source for the Spirit in this age, **He has poured out this** phenomenon which they did **both see and hear**.

This exaltation of Jesus to the right hand of God so that He shared all the rule of the Father was also prophesied in the Scriptures. **It was not David who ascended into the heavens**, even though he wrote of such an ascension. (Indeed, the tomb containing his body could be visited by any, proof that David did not ascend.) Rather, David **himself** says it was his **Lord** the Messiah who was invited by **the Lord** God to **sit at** God's **right hand** in the heavenlies (Ps. 110:1).

There could therefore be no doubt. **All the House of Israel** should **know certainly** and with the assurance of fulfilled Scripture that **God has made** Jesus **both Lord and Christ**—**this** same **Jesus whom** they not long ago **crucified**. The Sanhedrin debased Him as a deceiver, but God had in turn exalted Him as Lord over all.

꙳ ꙳ ꙳ ꙳ ꙳

37 Now when they heard *it*, they were stabbed in the heart and said to Peter and the rest of the apostles, "Men, *our* brothers, what shall we do?"

38 And Peter *said* to them, "Repent, and let each one of you be baptized in the Name of Jesus Christ for the forgiveness of your sins; and you will receive the gift of the Holy Spirit.

39 "For the promise is for you and for your children, and for all those afar, as many as the Lord our God will call to *Himself*."

II. The Church in Jerusalem   Acts 2:37–41

> 40 And with many other words he testified and was exhorting them, saying, "Be saved from this crooked generation!"
> 41 So therefore, those who had welcomed his word were baptized; and there were added in that day about three thousand souls.

Convinced by Peter's argument that Jesus was the Christ, the hearers **were stabbed in the heart** at the enormity of what they had done. They had done the unthinkable—they had disowned God's Messiah and handed Him over to be crucified. Given this catastrophe, they thought there was no hope for them, and they cried out, **"What shall we do?"** How could they escape the (as they thought) inevitable wrath of God?

Peter assured them God was not implacable, and divine retribution for their act was not inevitable. Let them become Jesus' disciples and they would be pardoned. That is, they must **repent** of their rejection of Jesus and of all their sins. If they would turn from all known sin and strive to live in holiness, they would avoid the judgment of God (see Luke 13:2–3).

They must also **each one** of them **be baptized in the Name of Jesus Christ for the forgiveness of** their **sins**. The reference to the **Name of Jesus Christ** is to the Name invoked as they received baptism, for it was upon Jesus as the Messiah that they called as they received baptism (22:16). This immersion brought them **the forgiveness of sins**, for Jesus promised that His disciples would know God's pardon, and baptism was how one became His disciple.

If they became the disciples of Jesus through repentance and baptism, they would **receive the gift of the Holy Spirit** just as the apostles had moments before. The promise of the Holy Spirit (1:4) was not just for those who had already aligned themselves with Jesus during His ministry. God willed to pardon and empower all, even those who before now had opposed Jesus. **The promise** was **for you and for your children** (or descendants) **and for all those afar**, living in the distant lands of the Diaspora. All Israel might come and freely partake of God's grace. Through the apostles' word, God was **calling to *Himself*** His people, and He would receive all those He summoned.

Peter did not end his appeal here, but **with many other words** urged them to accept baptism and become Jesus' disciples. Only so could they **be saved from** the **crooked** and perversely rebellious **generation** they were in. His appeal did not go unheeded. **About three thousand souls** who heard him **welcomed his word**, and these **were baptized** (possibly in the Jordan River). On the Feast of the Firstfruits, the spiritual firstfruits of the Church were harvested.

What did this baptism entail? The liturgical components are not mentioned, but it would appear from 8:14–17 and 19:5–6 that it involved baptism proper (that is, immersion in water) and the laying on of hands, and that it was through this entire rite that they **received the gift of the Holy Spirit**. St. Luke does not mention such liturgical details, since this was not necessary—the baptized Christians knew what their baptism entailed. He only mentions those details in 8:14–17 and 19:1–7 because those situations were unusual; it was necessary to stress that in those cases, the Samaritans and disciples of John received the same Christian baptism as everyone else.

༃ ༃ ༃ ༃ ༃

42 And they were devoting *themselves* to the apostles' teaching and to the sharing, to the breaking of bread and to the prayers.
43 And fear was happening in every soul, and many wonders and signs were happening through the apostles.
44 And all those who had believed were in the same *place*, and were having everything in common;
45 and they were selling their properties and possessions, and were dividing them up with all, as anyone might have need.
46 And day by day devoting *themselves* with the same-impulse in the Temple and breaking bread from house to house, they were partaking

II. The Church in Jerusalem   Acts 2:42–47

> of their food together with exultation and simplicity of heart,
> 47 praising God and having favor with all the people. And the Lord was adding day by day those who were being saved in the same *place*.

Those who were baptized **were devoting *themselves*** to their new way of life. The verb rendered *devote* is the Greek *proskartereo*, the same verb used in 1:14 to describe the determined focus of the disciples upon prayer, and in 8:13 to describe the almost bodily attachment of Simon the Sorcerer to Philip. The new converts made their new way of life their constant occupation.

This new life involved four components: **the apostles' teaching, the sharing, the breaking of bread,** and **the prayers. The apostles' teaching** refers to the authoritative transmission from the apostles of Jesus' life and teaching. **The sharing** (Gr. *koinonia*) refers to the entire communal life of new disciples. This included the sharing of goods for those in need (v. 45). **The breaking of bread** is a formula indicating the eating of meals (see its use in 27:35)—which meals culminated in the eucharistic memorial. **The prayers** refers to the formal prayers of the Christian community (note the article—"*the* prayers"—Gr. *tais proseuchais*). The disciples functioned as a kind of Christian synagogue, offering the same prayers as their Jewish brothers, though doubtless with a more Christian expression.

During this time, **fear was happening in every soul** (that is, every person), and this corresponded to the **many wonders and signs** which **were happening through the apostles** (such as related in 3:1f and 5:15–16). (The same verb, *egineto*, "were happening," is used in both parts of the sentence, inviting one to see the parallelism.) Christ's miracles through the apostles brought awe to all who saw them.

All those who had believed were in the same *place* (Gr. *epi to auto*; compare its use in 1:15)—that is, they gathered together as a single community, and such was their unity that they **had everything in common**. The rich among them felt such concern for their comrades that they voluntarily began **selling their properties and**

possessions that the apostles might give some of the liquidated price to help those among them who **had need**. There is no suggestion that this was to be a blueprint for Christian communities everywhere, for it does not appear to have been the case in the other churches mentioned by Luke later in his account. Rather, this extraordinary generosity at Jerusalem was occasioned by the great poverty of the Christian poor there (see Rom. 15:26), and is mentioned here as evidence of the unity that prevailed in those early golden days (compare Acts 4:32–35).

They continued **with the same-impulse** (Gr. *omothumadon*), preserving the unity of spirit that prevailed in the upper room (1:14). They worshipped **in the Temple** (since they were the true Israel) and also **from house to house** in smaller groups, **breaking bread** and sharing meals **with exultation and simplicity of heart**. That these communal meals (culminating in the Eucharist, as we suggested) were taken in joy reflects the grace of God, for joy is the hallmark of His Kingdom. In all their worship, whether publicly in the Temple or privately in homes, they continued **praising God and having favor with all the people**. This favor also was a sign of God's grace, for as Solomon says, when a man's ways please the Lord, He makes even his enemies to be at peace with him (Prov. 16:7). The Church therefore went from strength to strength, as **the Lord** Jesus **added** more **day by day in the same** *place* (Gr. *epi to auto*). His new converts (**those who were being saved**) were added onto the already existing community of the faithful in Jerusalem.

§II.3. Healing in the Temple and the First Arrest of the Apostles

3 1 Now Peter and John were going up into the Temple at the hour of prayer, the ninth *hour*.
2 And a certain man, being lame from his mother's womb, was being carried, whom they were putting day by day at the gate of

II. The Church in Jerusalem — Acts 3:1–10

> the Temple (the *gate* called Beautiful), to ask alms of those who were going into the Temple.
>
> 3 And seeing Peter and John about to go into the Temple, he was asking to receive alms.
>
> 4 And Peter, with John, stared at him and said, "Look at us!"
>
> 5 And he *fixed his* attention on them, expecting to receive something from them.
>
> 6 But Peter said, "Silver and gold I do not possess, but what I do have, this I give to you: In the Name of Jesus Christ the Nazarene—walk!"
>
> 7 And taking hold of him by the right hand, he raised him up. And immediately his feet and his ankles were strengthened.
>
> 8 And leaping up, he stood and was walking; and he entered with them the Temple, walking and leaping and praising God.
>
> 9 And all the people saw him walking and praising God,
>
> 10 and they were recognizing him that he was the one sitting for alms at the Beautiful Gate of the Temple, and they were filled with astonishment and amazement at the thing that had happened to him.

Luke begins his story of the Church in Jerusalem by relating one of the wonders done by the apostles and its aftermath. As loyal Jews, the Christians would regularly meet in the Temple for prayer. One day, **Peter and John were going up into the Temple** area **at the hour of prayer**—in particular, **the ninth *hour***, 3:00 P.M., the time of the evening sacrifice. (Other hours of prayer were at the morning sacrifice at dawn and at sunset.) They were headed into the inner courts to pray during the evening sacrifice along with their fellow Jews. In order to get there, they had to pass through **the *gate* called Beautiful**.

There were many gates or doors in the Temple, but this one was called "the Beautiful Gate" because it was so richly adorned with Corinthian bronze. So exquisite was it that Josephus (a Jewish historian of the time) said it far exceeded in value the gates plated with silver and set in gold (*Wars*, 5, 5, 3).

At this gate was a beggar who was **lame from his mother's womb**. His friends **carried** him and **put** him at this prominent spot **day by day** so that he could sit begging in a place through which many pious Jews would pass. As **Peter and John** were **about** to pass by him **to go into the Temple** (that is, into the inner courts), the beggar was **asking to receive alms** from them. He was not speaking to them directly, but to all within the sound of his voice, perhaps staring at the ground as he chanted his plaintive cry hour after hour.

It would seem that the Lord silently spoke to Peter and John and stirred their hearts to take action, so that it was Jesus Christ who healed the man (compare 9:34). Certainly there is no record of Peter and John conferring together about what they would do. **Peter, with John, stared at** the man, seeing him not just as another faceless beggar, but as the man whom Jesus was about to heal. They caught his attention by commanding, **"Look at us!"** In response, the beggar *fixed his* **attention on them** with a hopeful smile, naturally **expecting to receive something from them**. Since the apostles made a point of saying, "Look at us!" he no doubt expected a suitably generous gift.

The gift was more generous than he dared hope. When the beggar extended his hand to receive their coins, Peter responded by saying that his gift was not of that type. **Silver and gold** Peter did **not possess** and could not give him. But what he had, this he would give him: **In the Name of Jesus Christ the Nazarene—walk!**

Having said this, Peter **took hold of him by the right hand** (perhaps still held out in expectation of a gift) and **raised him up**, pulling him to his feet. St. Luke records the result with a physician's eye for detail—**immediately his feet and ankles were strengthened, and leaping up, he stood** upright **and was walking** (for the cause of his lameness was located in his feet and ankles).

The man was shocked—and elated. When Peter and John

II. The Church in Jerusalem   Acts 3:11–16

continued their progress through the gate into the courts of **the Temple, he entered with them**. He was so overcome with joy that **walking** with the apostles was not enough. He could not contain himself, but was **leaping** up and down, trying out limbs he had never used before, and **praising God** with loud shouts for his new vitality. God had prophesied that the lame man would **leap** like this, and so it was (see Is. 35:6 LXX, where the same word, *allomai*, is used).

Naturally **all the people saw** this spectacle and **were recognizing him** as the former beggar. They were **filled with astonishment and amazement**, and as they shared news of this miracle, a crowd began to gather.

> ༃ ༃ ༃ ༃ ༃
>
> 11 And while he was holding onto Peter and John, all the people ran together to them at the portico (the one called "Solomon's"), full of astonishment.
>
> 12 But when Peter saw *this*, he answered to the people, "Men of Israel, why do you marvel at this, or why do you stare at us, as if by our own power or piety we had made him walk?
>
> 13 "The God of Abraham, Isaac, and Jacob, the God of our fathers, has glorified His Servant Jesus, whom you *yourselves* delivered up and denied before the presence of Pilate, when he had judged to release that One.
>
> 14 "But you *yourselves* denied the Holy and Righteous One, and asked for a man *who was* a murderer to be granted to you,
>
> 15 "but killed the Leader of Life, whom God raised from the dead, to which we *ourselves* are witnesses.
>
> 16 "And through the faith in His Name—His Name has made this *man* solid whom you observe and know; and the faith which is

> **through Him has given him this wholeness before you all.**

Peter and John returned with their new friend still **holding onto** them with joy as they left the Temple through the Beautiful Gate and entered the adjacent **portico**, and **all the people ran together** to find them there. This portico was **the one called Solomon's**. It was located east of the Temple structure and was often used by the pious for meetings or discussions. Members of the Sanhedrin would teach in those terraces in the week after Passover, and the Child Jesus attended such a session there (Luke 2:46). This portico or porch was also the scene of Christ's confrontation with His foes during the Feast of Dedication (John 10:22f). It was to become a favorite meeting place for the Christians.

As the crowd stood gaping at the man, **Peter saw *this***, and also an opportunity to proclaim the Gospel. He asked them **why** they **marveled** at this miracle, and **why** they **stared at** Peter and John, **as if by** their **own power or piety** they **had made** the lame man **walk**. This was not their work, but the work of Jesus, who did many such miracles.

This was proof that **the God of** their **fathers had glorified His Servant Jesus**, exalting Him to His right hand so that He could pour out such miracles (compare 2:33). This same Jesus is the one they **delivered up and denied** (that is, disowned) a few weeks previously **before the presence of Pilate when he had** already **judged to release that One**. Pilate had already given his judgment that Jesus was innocent and should be released (Luke 23:13–16). But they would have none of this. It was they (the **you** is emphatic in vv. 13, 14) who **denied** their own Messiah, **the Holy and Righteous One** (these were titles of the Messiah), and when Pilate offered to grant them Jesus as part of the customary Passover amnesty, they **asked for a man *who was* a murderer to be granted** instead (Luke 23:18–19).

Here was crushing irony: They spared from execution the man of death, but handed over to death the Leader of Life. The word here translated *Leader* is the Greek *archegos*. It is used in Numbers 13:2f LXX for the tribal leaders; the word also has the meaning "source," since

II. The Church in Jerusalem　　　　　　　　　　　　Acts 3:17–26

those leaders were fathers of dynasties. In describing Jesus as **the Leader of Life**, Peter affirms Him to be the Prince of Israel, the source of their life and salvation. This was the One they disowned and killed—the very One **whom God raised from the dead**, annulling their false judgment of His Messiah. To this fact they, Peter and John and the rest of apostles (the **we** is emphatic), were **witnesses**.

Peter stresses that it is the Name of Jesus that has wrought this miracle. The apostles have no power of their own to do such works. It is only their **faith in** Jesus' **Name** and power that **has made this man solid** in his feet and ankles, and the **wholeness** they can all see in the man proves Jesus is the Messiah.

> ꕥ ꕥ ꕥ ꕥ ꕥ
>
> 17 "And now, brothers, I know that you acted in ignorance, just as your rulers did also.
> 18 "But the things which God preproclaimed by the mouth of all the prophets that His Christ should suffer, He has thus fulfilled.
> 19 "Repent therefore and return, that your sins may be wiped away, that *appointed* times of reviving may come from the presence of the Lord;
> 20 "and that He may send Jesus, the Christ preappointed for you,
> 21 "whom it is necessary for heaven to welcome until the times of restoration of all things about which God spoke by the mouth of His holy prophets from ages *past*.
> 22 "Moses indeed said, 'The Lord your God will raise up for you a prophet like me from your brothers; Him you shall hear in everything, whatever He may speak to you.
> 23 "'And it shall be that every soul, whoever does not hear that prophet, shall be destroyed from the people.'
> 24 "And all the prophets who have spoken, from

> Samuel and *his* successors onward, also proclaimed this day.
> 25 "You *yourselves* are the sons of the prophets and of the covenant which God decreed to your fathers, saying to Abraham, 'And in your seed all the families of the earth will be blessed.'
> 26 "For you first, God raised up His Servant, and sent Him to bless you by turning each one *of you* from your evil *acts*."

After such an indictment of the people of Jerusalem, doubtless many in the crowd were cut to the heart at the thought that they had killed God's Christ. Some perhaps began weeping. Peter softens his tone somewhat, calling them **brothers** and acknowledging that they **acted in ignorance**, along with their **rulers** in the Sanhedrin. They did not mean to kill their Messiah, and this ignorance meant that their hearts were not hardened. Repentance and mercy were still possible. Christ died not only through their hostility, but also because of God's providential will for the salvation of the world. (We see a parallel in the sufferings of Joseph; his brothers sold him into Egyptian slavery out of hostility, but God meant all along to use this to give life; Gen. 45:5.) **God** had **preproclaimed by the mouth of all the prophets that His Christ should suffer** (e.g. Is. 53), and He had in this way **fulfilled** it through them.

Their case, therefore, was not hopeless. Let them now **repent and return** to God and their **sins** would be **wiped away**—not just the sin of rejecting the Christ, but all their offenses. And then *appointed times of reviving* would **come** directly **from the presence of the Lord**. The word rendered *reviving* is the Greek *anapsuxis*, a word meaning "respite, relief, refreshment." The word is used in Exodus 8:15 LXX for relief from divine judgment, and the thought here is of the long-prophesied times when Israel could know God's forgiveness. After years of languishing in the shadow of death (Luke 1:79), here were times when they could relax and be refreshed by the waters of rest.

II. The Church in Jerusalem — Acts 3:17–26

If all Israel would repent and be saved, God would also **send Jesus, the Christ preappointed** for them. The word *preappointed* points to the fact that Jesus' works were all part of God's eternal plan. Christ had ascended into **heaven** to be **welcomed** by all the angels there as He sat at God's right hand. **It was necessary** for Him to reign from there **until the times of restoration of all things about which God had spoken by the mouth of His holy prophets**. God had promised that His Kingdom would finally be consummated in a new heaven and a new earth (compare Is. 65:17), and that all that was broken would finally be mended. Christ would return from heaven and bring the fullness of this Kingdom. Let Israel repent, rejoicing that one day they would find such life from the dead (Rom. 11:15).

As an example of what **God had spoken by the mouth of His prophets**, Peter offers what **Moses** said in Deuteronomy 18:15f: **The Lord** their **God** would **raise up a prophet like** Moses; **Him** they must **hear in everything**, for **whoever** would **not hear that prophet** would **be destroyed from the people**.

In the original context, Moses was telling the people they should not rely upon mediums and diviners to learn God's will (Deut. 18:9–14). Instead, they should heed the prophets, for God would raise up prophets who would declare His will even as Moses had. Just as Christ embodied in Himself the line of Davidic kings, so He also embodied this line of prophets. Moses' words about Israel relying on a prophet to learn God's will found their ultimate fulfillment in Jesus.

That all Israel's prophets culminate in Him finds expression in the singular noun "prophet," for Moses does not say that God will raise up "prophets" (in the plural) like him, but **a prophet** like him. Jesus is that prophet like Moses, for, like Moses, He declares God's Word so authoritatively that to reject Him is to reject God and His covenant. In this way, Jesus is a second Moses, for He brings a second covenant.

It was not just Moses who prophesied of Jesus, but **all the prophets, from Samuel and *his* successors onward, also proclaimed this day** of salvation. They all spoke of a time when God's Kingdom would come, and Peter's hearers were **the sons of** these **prophets**, the inheritors of their words. They should therefore believe what their fathers had said.

God had **decreed** a **covenant** with **Abraham**, promising him that **in** his **seed all the families of the earth would be blessed** (Gen. 12:1–3). Peter's hearers were **sons** and inheritors **of** that **covenant** also, and so could expect to be blessed as the **first** among the families and nations of the earth. For **God raised up His Servant** Jesus, bringing Him to the People through the baptism of John, and **sent Him to bless** them with the blessing promised them in the covenant with Abraham. This blessing could be enjoyed by **each** of them if they would only **turn from** their **evil *acts*** in repentance and baptism. (The blessing is said to come to **each one** because each one was baptized individually.)

ॐ ॐ ॐ ॐ ॐ

4 1 And as they were speaking to the people, the priests and the captain of the Temple, and the Sadducees, came up to them,

2 being annoyed because they were teaching the people and proclaiming in Jesus the resurrection from the dead.

3 And they laid hands on them and put them in jail until the next day, for it was already evening.

4 But many of those who had heard the Word believed; and the number of the men came to be about five thousand.

5 And it happened on the next day that there were gathered together in Jerusalem their rulers and elders and scribes,

6 and Annas the high-priest, and Caiaphas and John and Alexander, and as many who were of high-priestly descent.

7 And when they had stood them in the middle, they were inquiring, "In what power or in

> what name have you *yourselves* done this?"
> 8 Then Peter, having been filled with the Holy Spirit, said to them, "Rulers and elders of the people,
> 9 "if we *ourselves* are being investigated today for a benefit done to an ailing man, as to how this *man* has been saved,
> 10 "let it be known to all of you, and to all the people of Israel, that by the Name of Jesus Christ the Nazarene, whom you *yourselves* crucified, whom God raised from the dead—by this *Name* this *man* stands here before you healthy.
> 11 "This One is the stone which was disdained by you, the builders, which became the head of the corner.
> 12 "And there is not in any other the salvation; for there is no other name under heaven that has been given among men, by which it is necessary for you to be saved."

The message Peter and John were delivering to the crowds in the portico of Solomon was interrupted by the arrival of **the priests, the captain of the Temple, and the Sadducees**. This captain was the *sagan*, the chief of the Temple police, the officers responsible for maintaining order in the sacred courts. The delegation represented all those responsible for the Temple. They were **annoyed because** the apostles **were teaching the people** as if *they* were God's authoritative teachers. The word rendered *annoyed* is the Greek *diaponeomai*, indicating that they were not just irked, but indignant and angry (compare its use in 16:18).

In particular, they objected to the apostles **proclaiming in** the case of **Jesus the resurrection of the dead**. (The Sadducees did not believe the dead would be raised.) They therefore **laid hands on them** (presumably with the help of the Temple police) **and put them in jail until the next day. It was already evening**, and the Sanhedrin court met only in the day. The damage (as they would have thought it) was already done, however, for **many of those who had heard the Word** just preached **believed** it, and **the number of the men alone came to be about five thousand**—an increase of about two thousand since the Day of Pentecost.

Court convened the next day. It was an impressive gathering, consisting of the **rulers** (members of the Sanhedrin), **elders and scribes, Annas** the high-priest (officially retired), **Caiaphas** (the officially appointed high-priest), **John** (possibly Annas's son), **Alexander** (possibly another member of Annas's family), and **as many who were of high-priestly descent**. They **stood** the apostles **in the middle** as the accused. Expecting to cow them by such an assembly, they began **inquiring, "In what power or in what name have you yourselves done this?"** The *you* is emphatic, and the thought is, "What right do the likes of you have to be acting like this? Who gave you the authority to do this?" Peter and John were among those who fled the night their Nazarene leader was arrested, and perhaps the authorities expected they could be intimidated and bullied into submission now.

If so, they were mistaken. Christ had promised that when His disciples stood before rulers and authorities, the Holy Spirit would teach them what to say (Luke 12:11–12). It was so now. **Peter** was then **filled with the Holy Spirit** (the aorist tense of the verb indicates a fresh infilling that moment) and went on the offensive. He begins with a withering irony: **"If we are being investigated today for a benefit done to an ailing man, as to how this *man* has been saved** or healed," he will tell them plainly. That is, are they really trying them for the terrible crime of helping a sick man? Is this a crime now? Be that as it may, he continues, it is by Jesus' Name that the man has been healed.

In his response, Peter is very clever. He was asked, in general terms, by whose authority they were teaching and spreading the heresy of one who had been condemned by their court as a deceiver. In response, Peter focuses not upon the *teaching* (which could be disputed), but upon the *healing* (which could not). And he replies in a very aggressive manner. He does not just say, "My authority

II. The Church in Jerusalem — Acts 4:13–22

comes from Jesus the Nazarene," but "My authority comes from Jesus the Messiah, the Nazarene—the One you crucified, the One God raised from the dead." He is not so much answering the question as accusing them of opposing God.

Peter goes on, proving his point by quoting the Scripture. Alluding to Psalm 118:22, he says that Jesus is **the stone which was disdained** as worthless by them, God's appointed leaders and **builders**, but which God nonetheless made **the head of the corner**. They had cast away the stone as unusable for building purposes, but it turned out to be the cornerstone, the most valuable stone in the structure. Jesus is no deceiver, and they reject Him in vain, for God has enthroned Him as His Messiah.

They hope to find **the salvation** of Israel (Gr. *he soteria*, "*the salvation*") in someone else, thinking the Messiah is still to come. They are wrong. **There is not in any other** man **the salvation** they are seeking, for **there is no other name under heaven given among men** by which Israel can find its appointed redemption. Jesus is the Messiah, and through Him alone can Israel (and the world) **be saved**. The lame man was saved by Jesus (v. 9), and it is Jesus alone who can save His people.

---

13 Now as they observed the boldness of Peter and John, and grasping that they were unlettered and unlearned men, they were marveling, and were recognizing them that they were with Jesus.

14 And seeing the man who had been healed standing with them, they had nothing to contradict *them with*.

15 But when they had ordered them to depart out of the council, they were taking counsel with one another,

16 saying, "What will we do with these men? For that a known sign has happened through them is manifest to all those dwelling in

Jerusalem, and we are not able to deny *it*.
17 "But that it may not spread any further among the people, let us threaten them to speak no longer to any men in this name."
18 And when they had called them, they ordered them not to expound or teach at all in the Name of Jesus.
19 But Peter and John answered and said to them, "Whether it is righteous before God to hear you rather than God, you judge,
20 "for we *ourselves* are not able not to speak *about* what we have seen and heard."
21 And when they had threatened them further, they dismissed them (finding nothing for which they might punish them) because of the people, for they were all glorifying God for what had happened;
22 for the man was more than forty years old upon whom this sign of curing had happened.

The Sanhedrin **observed the boldness of Peter and John** and were amazed at this unexpected change in them. When last they dealt with them, the apostles fled in fear (Mark 14:50), yet here they stood in utter defiance. (The righteous indeed are bold as a lion; Prov. 28:1.) Knowing too that **they were unlettered and unlearned men** (that is, not rabbinically trained), **they were marveling** at their skill in disputing using the Scriptures. Such bold use of the Scriptures reminded them only too clearly of Another, and they began **recognizing** that **they were with Jesus**. Who else could have taught these fishermen this way, making them most wise? (Compare the troparion for Pentecost). The members of the Sanhedrin would have loved to **contradict** them and ram their words back down their throats, denying that any miracle had been done, just as Jesus' foes attempted to do when He healed the blind man (John 9:24f). But **seeing the man who had been healed standing with them** (perhaps after he entered as a witness for the apostles), there was nothing they could say.

II. The Church in Jerusalem   Acts 4:23–31

They therefore **ordered them to depart out of the council** while they planned their next move. (We may think that the Church learned of these deliberations as sympathetic friends of Joseph of Arimathea and Nicodemus, themselves members of the council, reported this to them.)

The council members were **not able to deny** that **a known sign had happened through them**, for all the city knew it by now. All they could do was pretend to offer clemency for this first "offense" and **threaten them to speak no longer to any men in this name** of Jesus. Let them cease their loud **expounding** (Gr. *phtheggomai*; to speak loudly, bombastically); let them not spread Jesus' **teaching** any further.

Once again, Peter and John do not waver nor cease their attack. Since the Sanhedrin are the judges of Israel, they ask them to **judge** and pronounce upon this: **whether it is righteous before God to hear** them **rather than God**. Whom do *they* think God wants them to heed, given the choice? As for them (the **we** is emphatic), they already know the answer to that question, so that they are **not able not to speak** *about* **what** they **have seen and heard**.

After the obligatory **threatening**, the Sanhedrin **dismissed them**. Luke mentions the main motive for their release. Though it was true that they could **find nothing for which they might punish them**, the main motive was **because of the people**; the Sanhedrin feared a riot. The people knew the healing was a miracle, for the lame man was **more than forty years old**—well past the age when any non-miraculous healing could be expected.

               ꙮ ꙮ ꙮ ꙮ ꙮ

23 And when they had been dismissed, they went to their own and declared all that the chief-priests and the elders had said to them.
24 And when they heard *this*, they lifted their voices to God with the same-impulse and said, "O Master, it is You who made the heaven and the earth and the sea, and all things in them,
25 "who said through Your servant our father

> David, the mouth of the Holy Spirit, 'Why did the nations snort, and the peoples devise empty *things*?
> 26 "'The kings of the earth stood by and the rulers were gathered in the same *place* against the Lord and against His Christ.'
> 27 "For in truth in this city there were gathered against Your holy Servant Jesus whom You anointed, both Herod and Pontius Pilate, with the nations and the peoples of Israel,
> 28 "to do whatever Your hand and Your intention predestined to happen.
> 29 "And now, Lord, look upon their threats, and give that Your slaves may speak Your Word with all boldness,
> 30 "while You stretch out Your hand to cure and signs and wonders happen through the Name of Your holy Servant Jesus."
> 31 And when they had besought, the place where they had gathered was shaken, and they were all filled with the Holy Spirit, and were speaking the Word of God with boldness.

After they had been **dismissed** by the Sanhedrin, Peter and John **went to their own** people, who were anxiously awaiting word from them as they feared for their safety. When they learned of the threats from their rulers, they turned to God, the true Ruler of Israel, praying that He might help them. God was the One who **made the heaven and the earth and the sea, and all things in them**, and who ruled them as a **Master** ruled his slaves. He used all to fulfill His plans for the salvation of the world—even the sinful rebellion of men. He could also use the opposition of the Sanhedrin to further His plans.

God's sovereignty over all was proven by what their **father David** had spoken in Psalm 2:1–2 as the instrument and **mouth of the** prophetic **Holy Spirit**. In that psalm, David spoke of **the kings of the earth and the rulers** being **gathered in the same *place* against**

II. The Church in Jerusalem   Acts 4:32–37

the Lord and against His Christ as they laid siege to Jerusalem. This poetry was prophetic of the alliance of the Gentile **Pontius Pilate** (representative of the **kings of the earth**) and **Herod** (representative of Israel's **rulers**) as they conspired in this city of Jerusalem against Jesus at the time of His trial (Luke 23:1–12). These plans proved to be **empty** *things*, as God used them to **do whatever** His **hand and intention predestined to happen**. Their opposition only served to further God's plan.

God was equally capable of using the **threats** of the Sanhedrin to further His purposes now, and so the Church prayed that God would **give** them grace that they **may speak** His **Word with all boldness**, and not be intimidated by their bullying. In response, God was asked to **stretch out** His **hand to cure** and give **signs and wonders through the Name of** His **holy Servant Jesus** as the proof of their preaching.

God heard their prayer. Even as Mount Sinai shook at God's Presence and the foundations of the Temple's thresholds once shook before Him (Ex. 19:18; Is. 6:4), so **the place where they had gathered** (probably the upper room) **was shaken**. This shaking was the sign of God's Presence, for they **were all filled with the Holy Spirit** and in the days to come **were speaking the Word of God with boldness**, even as they prayed.

This fresh infilling with the Holy Spirit was not a repetition of the events of Pentecost, just as Peter's infilling with the Spirit at his trial was not another baptism in the Spirit. Rather, both these infillings were the fruit of that first Pentecostal initiation. That initial Pentecostal experience made the Christians into God's prophets (2:17–18), and these subsequent experiences were part of that prophetic life.

§II.4. Great Grace upon the Church: All Share Their Goods

> 32 And the multitude of those who believed were of one heart and soul, and not one said that any of their possessions was his own; but everything was in common to them.

> 33 And with great power the apostles were rendering witness to the resurrection of the Lord Jesus, and great grace was upon them all.
> 34 For there was not anyone impoverished among them, for as many as were owners of fields or houses were selling *them* and bringing the prices of the *things* sold,
> 35 and laying them at the feet of the apostles, and they were giving away to each, as any had need.
> 36 And Joseph, the one surnamed Barnabas by the apostles (which translated is "Son of Exhortation"), a Levite of Cypriot descent,
> 37 and who possessed a field, sold *it* and brought the money and laid *it* at the feet of the apostles.

Luke then relates a story illustrating how God was with the fledgling Christian community as they began their mission, even as He was with Israel at the beginning of their history when they began their conquest of Canaan. In Israel's early days, they also did supernatural wonders through the power of God in their midst, such as the crossing of the Jordan (Josh. 3–4) and the conquest of Jericho (Josh. 6). Then came the disobedience of Achan, as he "misappropriated" (*nosphizomai*, Josh. 7:1 LXX, the same word used in Acts 5:2, 3) some of the dedicated things from Jericho. That is, he took some of the spoils, which had been dedicated to Yahweh and were not to be taken as booty by the Israelites. Achan kept quiet about this act, trying to deceive Joshua and the leaders, but God brought the sin to light, and Achan paid the ultimate price. This judgment on Achan showed God was truly with His People, and they could expect to be victorious if only they obeyed Him.

Luke records the Christian counterpart of that story, the judgment upon the sin of Ananias and Sapphira (5:1–11), to show that God is again with His People in power, just as He was in those early days. As the background to that story, Luke first shows how

II. The Church in Jerusalem   Acts 5:1–11

the Christian people lived in the unity of love and generosity, being **of one heart and soul**, even to the point of wealth among them being **common to them** all. Just as it was God's intention for His people that there be no poor among them (Deut. 15:4), so **there was not anyone impoverished among** the Christians, for those with wealth sold their **fields or houses** and brought the sales to **the feet of the apostles,** who **were giving away** the money **to each, as any had need**.

Prominent among such benefactors was **Joseph, the one surnamed Barnabas by the apostles.** (His feast day in the Church is June 11.) The name **Barnabas** is **translated** by Luke as **Son of Exhortation** (Gr. *paraklesis*). It perhaps represents the Hebrew *bar-nebbiya*, "son of prophecy" (i.e. a prophet), for prophecy could be characterized as spiritual exhortation (1 Cor. 14:3). Certainly Barnabas's role was that of a prophet and teacher (Acts 13:1). He was also **a Levite of Cypriot descent**, and he owned some property in the area, which he sold and gave the proceeds of to the apostles.

Luke mentions him at this place in his narrative to prepare his readers for Barnabas's role in the story of the conversion of Saul (9:26–27). It is also possible that Barnabas's example (and the admiration it won him from the apostles) inspired Ananias and Sapphira to sell their property, since they wanted to be similarly esteemed.

---

5 1   But a certain man named Ananias, with his wife Sapphira, sold a property
    2   and misappropriated some of the price for himself, his wife also co-knowing, and bringing a certain part *of it*, he laid *it* at the feet of the apostles.
    3   But Peter said, "Ananias, why has Satan filled your heart to lie to the Holy Spirit and to misappropriate some of the price of the field?
    4   "While it remained *unsold*, did it not remain

> with you? And having been sold, was it not under your authority? Why is it that this practice was put in your heart? You have not lied to men, but to God."
>
> 5 And as he heard these words, Ananias fell down and expired; and great fear came upon all who heard *of it*.
> 6 And the young men arose and picked him up, and after carrying him out, they buried him.
> 7 Now an interval of about three hours happened, and his wife came in, not knowing what had happened.
> 8 And Peter answered her, "Tell me if you rendered the field for so much?" And she said, "Yes, for so much."
> 9 Then Peter said to her, "Why is it that it was agreed by you to test the Spirit of the Lord? Behold, the feet of those who have buried your husband are at the door, and they will carry you out *too*."
> 10 And she fell immediately at his feet and expired; and the young men came in and found her dead, and carrying *her* out, they buried *her* beside her husband.
> 11 And great fear came upon the whole Church, and upon all those hearing these things.

After giving this background, St. Luke relates the sin of **Ananias** and **his wife Sapphira**. Like the others in the Jerusalem Church, they **sold a property** and **laid** money from the sale **at the feet of the apostles**. But unlike the others, Ananias **misappropriated some of the price for himself, his wife also co-knowing** about it. (The verb rendered *co-knowing* is the Gr. *sunoida*, here having the sense of being implicated in a crime, of collusion.) The sale of the property was completely voluntary, and even after the sale, what he did with the money was under his authority. He was free to give

II. The Church in Jerusalem   Acts 5:1–11

only part of the money. His sin consisted not of keeping back some of the money, but of lying about it and claiming that the gift to the apostles represented the full price of the land.

Just as the prophet Elisha knew of the secret sin of Gehazi (2 Kin. 5:26), so Peter knew of the sin of Ananias and his wife. He confronted him, asking him **why Satan** had **filled** his **heart to lie to the Holy Spirit** (for to lie to the Church was to **lie not to men but to God**). No sooner had Peter spoken these words than the judgment of God fell upon the deceiver, and he **fell down and expired**. **The young men** of the community **arose and picked him up** in his clothes **and after carrying him out, they buried him**. In that climate, burial was immediate—and all the more since the one who died did so under divine judgment.

After **about three hours**, Sapphira **came in** to where Peter still was (perhaps in the house whose upper room they were using), **not knowing what had happened**. No doubt Peter and others were there, waiting for her return. She was perhaps told that they were waiting to see her, and to her inquisitive look **Peter answered her, "Tell me if you rendered the field for so much?"** Here was the mercy of God and a chance for her to save herself. She must have known from the question she was caught, but she continued to brazen it out, saying, **"Yes, for so much."** As Peter asked her husband why he allowed Satan to fill his heart with evil, so he asked the same of Sapphira: **Why** was it that she **agreed to test the Spirit of the Lord?** To **test** the Lord (Gr. *peirazo*, here and in Ex. 17:2) was a great sin, tantamount to repudiating His covenant. For this rebellion, God's judgment would surely befall her as it had befallen her husband. **The feet of those who buried** him were **at the door**, waiting to carry her dead body out as well.

At this sentence, she also instantly **expired** where she stood, and when **the young men** checked her, they **found her dead** as well, and **buried *her* beside her husband**. As the two were united in their sin, so they were united in death under the judgment of God. Because of this, **great fear came upon the whole Church, and upon all those hearing these things** in Jerusalem who were not Christians. Surely God was with the disciples of Jesus!

Many have wondered if such a judgment was not somewhat severe. A sentence of death for a simple deception about money and prestige? But one may make the same objection about the sin of Achan—why judge a simple matter of theft and its cover-up so severely?

In fact, the issue was not one of lying about money, but of cherishing darkness in one's heart while standing so close to the light. The light of God shone with great radiance in those days, as "great grace was upon them all" (4:33). It took great hardness of heart to stand so close to that cleansing light and still abide in darkness. It was this rebelliousness of heart that was judged, for rebellion is as the sin of witchcraft (1 Sam. 15:23). The sin of Ananias and Sapphira was no trivial one, but their joint determination to trifle with God by sinning against the unity of the Church.

> 12 And through the hands of the apostles many signs and wonders were happening among the people, and everyone was with the same-impulse in Solomon's portico.
> 13 But none of the rest dared to join them; but the people magnified them.
> 14 And more of those believing in the Lord were added, multitudes of men and women,
> 15 so that they even carried out the ailing into the streets, and laid them on cots and pallets, so that when Peter came, at least his shadow might overshadow some of them.
> 16 And also the multitude from the cities around Jerusalem were coming together, bringing the ailing or troubled by unclean spirits; and everyone was being healed.

Luke concludes this story by showing how God, who was with His people to judge the rebels, continued to be with the apostles in power. **Through the hands of the apostles many signs and**

wonders continued. The unity of the Church continued also, as **everyone** was meeting **with the same-impulse** (Gr. *omothumadon*; compare its use in 1:14; 2:46; 4:24) **in Solomon's portico** to listen to the apostolic teaching.

However, the apostles enjoyed such esteem that **none of the rest** of the Christians **dared to join them** in easy familiarity. They knew that God was with the apostles in a powerful way, and they did not presume to question their authority or to trifle with them. All **the people** of the city **magnified** the apostles as men of power and did not harass them as they met in the Temple courts.

As a result of all this, the Church grew even more, with **multitudes of men and women** converting to the Faith. So great was the apostles' reputation in the city that people **even carried out the ailing into the streets** where **Peter** routinely walked so that **at least his shadow might overshadow some of them** and heal them.

§II.5. Second Arrest of the Apostles

> ॐ ॐ ॐ ॐ ॐ
>
> 17 And the chief-priest arose, with all those with him (being the faction of the Sadducees), and they were filled with jealousy;
> 18 and they laid hands upon the apostles and put them in a public jail.
> 19 But an angel of the Lord during the night opened the doors of the prison, and bringing them out, he said,
> 20 "Go and having stood, speak to the people in the Temple all the words of this Life."
> 21 And hearing *this*, they entered into the Temple about dawn and were teaching. Now when the chief-priest and those with him had arrived, they called together the council, even all the senate of the sons of Israel, and sent to the prison-house for them to be brought.
> 22 But the attendants who arrived did not find

> them in the prison; and they returned and declared *this*,
> 23 saying, "We found the prison-house closed in all security and the guards standing at the doors; but when we had opened *it*, we found no one inside."
> 24 Now when the captain of the Temple and the chief-priests heard these words, they were perplexed about them as to what would happen *about* this.
> 25 But someone arrived and declared to them, "Behold, the men whom you put in the prison are standing in the Temple and teaching the people!"
> 26 Then the captain departed with the attendants and brought them without violence (for they were afraid of the people, lest they be stoned).

Luke then tells of a second arrest (this time of all the apostles), focusing not only upon their fearless proclamation of the Gospel, but also upon their supernatural release from prison and the advice of the respected Gamaliel (vv. 34–39). The message is clear: God is with the apostles, and so to oppose them is to oppose God. St. Luke expects his Roman audience to get the message and give support to the new Christian movement.

In narrating the arrest, Luke is emphatic about what motivated **the chief-priest** and **the faction of the Sadducees** (those who ran the Temple): **jealousy**. It was jealousy of the Christians' popularity with the people that was behind Jewish opposition to the new Faith (compare 17:4–5), and it was this Jewish jealousy that should be blamed for the tumult that accompanied the Christian message, not the Christian message itself.

Driven by this jealousy, the Temple authorities **laid hands upon the apostles** (probably as they taught in Solomon's portico) and **put them in a public jail**. They were to be held there until their trial the next morning. But then came the unexpected—and proof that

God was with the apostles. **An angel of the Lord during the night opened the doors of the prison** and brought them out, directing them once they were outside to **go**, and having taken their stand as before, to **speak to the people in the Temple all the words of this Life** and salvation. (The jailbreak seems to have been accompanied by a divine blinding of the eyes of the guards.) When the Temple gates opened at **about dawn**, the apostles **entered into the Temple** and continued **teaching** the people as before.

St. Luke relates the aftermath of the jailbreak for maximum comic effect—and to show how God confounds those who resist Him, making fools of those who fancy themselves to be wise. **The chief-priest and those with him arrived** for the scheduled trial and **called together the council, even all the senate of the sons of Israel**. The whole august assembly sat in solemn state, preparing to judge their prey, whom they imagined to be languishing in prison and worrying about their fate. When all was ready, **they sent to the prison-house** for the apostles **to be brought**. We are left to picture their perplexity when **the attendants** arrived empty-handed with the message, **"We found the prison-house closed and locked in all security and the guards standing at the doors; but when we had opened *it*, we found no one inside."** This was impossible! What was going on? Had the apostles supporters among the jailers?

Their perplexity was increased when a second message reached them: **"Behold, the men whom you put in prison are standing in the Temple and teaching the people!"**—in direct defiance of their order (but in obedience to the angelic order). The solemn senate was humiliated. They had no choice but to go and have them **brought** again—but **without violence**. The reason they were gathered without being manhandled and given this police escort to the council was not any lack of fury on the part of the council. Rather, **they were afraid of the people, lest** the arresting attendants **be stoned**. This popular support is mentioned to show the apostles were guiltless of any crime. The apostles, for their part, though they could have resisted (relying on the people for support), voluntarily went with the arresting officers. The last time they stood before the Sanhedrin, they had been able to bear witness boldly to Jesus. Doubtless they were looking forward to another such opportunity.

> ꙳ ꙳ ꙳ ꙳ ꙳
> 27 And when they had brought them, they stood them in the council. And the chief-priest asked them,
> 28 saying, "We ordered you *strictly* not to teach in this name, and behold, you have filled Jerusalem with your teaching and intend to bring this man's blood upon us!"
> 29 But Peter and the apostles answered and said, "It is necessary to obey God rather than men.
> 30 "The God of our fathers raised up Jesus, whom you *yourselves* had laid *violent* hands on by hanging Him on a tree.
> 31 "This One God exalted to His right *hand as* a Leader and a Savior, to give repentance to Israel and forgiveness of sins.
> 32 "And we *ourselves* are witnesses of these words; and *so is* the Holy Spirit, whom God has given to those obeying Him."

The apostles then **stood in** the middle of **the Council** as the accused. The charge is then stated, and we can still feel the exasperation of the accusers: **"We ordered you *strictly* not to teach in this name, and behold, you have filled Jerusalem with your teaching!"** Not only had they continued teaching when they were forbidden to do so, but all the city was echoing with their words. More than that, **"you intend to bring this man's blood upon us"** and make it out that His death at their hands was unjust. We note that in their contempt for Jesus, they cannot even bring themselves to say His Name—He is **"this man."**

Peter (once again the mouthpiece for **the apostles**) is impenitent and does not deny the charge. Rather, He simply repeats that **it is necessary** for them **to obey God** and continue preaching **rather**

II. The Church in Jerusalem   Acts 5:33–40

than obey **men** like themselves and cease. With this one sentence, Peter sweeps away their accusation as unjust, asserting boldly that God is with the apostles, not with the Jewish Supreme Court.

Having answered the charge, Peter continues his defiance, saying again that the **God of** their **fathers** was the One who **raised up Jesus**, bringing Him to Israel through John's baptism. They were the ones who **laid *violent* hands** upon Him **by hanging Him on a tree** as one accursed (Deut. 21:23). God, however, reversed their verdict, for He **exalted** Him **to His right *hand***, raising Him up and investing Him with all the divine authority in heaven. Jesus was the appointed **Leader** who would lead Israel to victory, and who as **Savior** would save them from disaster. It was through Jesus, the One they crucified, that God would **give repentance to Israel**—that is, a chance to regain divine favor (compare Heb. 12:17), such as the **forgiveness of sins** with its attendant blessings.

Of **these words** (or things), the apostles were all **witnesses**—as was **the Holy Spirit, whom God had given** through Christian baptism **to those obeying Him** by becoming disciples of Jesus. That is, the works of the Holy Spirit (such as the miracles done by the apostles) were the Holy Spirit's witness that Jesus was the Messiah.

ॐ ॐ ॐ ॐ ॐ

33 But when they heard *this*, they were infuriated and were intending to destroy them.

34 But a certain Pharisee named Gamaliel, a teacher of the Law honored by all the people, stood in the council and ordered to put the men outside for a short *time*.

35 And he said to them, "Men of Israel, pay attention to what you are about to do with these men.

36 "For before these days Theudas arose, saying he was somebody, and a number of men joined with him, about four hundred. And he was destroyed; and all who were obeying him were dispersed and came to nothing.

> 37 "After this man, Judas of Galilee arose in the days of the census and turned away *some* people after him. That one perished too, and all those who were obeying him were scattered out.
> 38 "And now I say to you, withdraw from these men and let them *alone*, for if this intention or this work be from men, it will be torn down;
> 39 "but if it is from God, you will not be able to tear them down; perhaps you may even be found fighting against God."
> 40 And they were persuaded by him; and after calling the apostles to *them*, they beat them and ordered them to speak no more in the Name of Jesus, and dismissed them.

When the Council heard such defiant words, **they were infuriated** to the core (Gr. *diaprioo*; literally "sawn through") and **were intending to destroy them** as they destroyed Jesus. But in the midst of that murderous assembly, **a certain Pharisee named Gamaliel**, one who was **honored by all the people, stood in the Council** to speak, ordering first that the apostles be **put outside**. (As a Pharisee, he also had little sympathy for the Sadducees there; compare 23:6f.) He also had a greater and more far-sighted wisdom than many present.

He counseled that they must **pay attention to what** they were **about to do** with the apostles. Let them not be so hasty to persecute them! They could afford to wait. Let them remember the example of **Theudas**. He **arose** in Israel, **saying he was somebody** specially chosen by God, **and a number of men joined with him, about four hundred**. Despite those impressive numbers, when **he was destroyed, all who were obeying him were dispersed** and the whole thing **came to nothing**.

Which Theudas Luke refers to is unknown. The name Theudas was a common one, being short for Theodorus, Theodotus, and Theodosius. It could have been the Theudas mentioned by Josephus,

II. The Church in Jerusalem — Acts 5:41–42

who tried to cross the Jordan River miraculously and was killed by the Romans (though this would mean Josephus was mistaken in his dates). It could have been another Theudas, not mentioned by Josephus. Whichever man is referred to, Gamaliel calls the council to learn from the example that the work of such imposters eventually comes to naught.

Or they might learn from the example of **Judas of Galilee**, who protested against the Roman **census** in AD 6 and whose deluded followers also were **scattered out** after his death. Such false prophets were always arising. The council should **withdraw** from the apostles and **let them *alone***. Time would tell if their words were true. If their **intention** and counsel or **this work** of theirs was merely **from men, it would be torn down** and overthrown soon enough. But if it were **from God**, the Council would **not be able** to defeat them, however many of them they killed. Indeed, they would then be killing God's true prophets, and would thereby **even be found fighting against God**!

The council members **were persuaded by him** and decided not to destroy the apostles as they first intended. After calling the apostles back to the council, **they beat them** (flogging them with the traditional Jewish forty lashes less one) as a punishment for disobeying their previous order and as an incentive to **speak no more in the Name of Jesus** or spread His teaching. It was a minor punishment.

ॐ ॐ ॐ ॐ ॐ

41 They therefore went from the presence of the council, rejoicing that they had been *judged*-worthy to be dishonored for the Name.
42 And every day, in the Temple and from house to house, they did not cease teaching and preaching *the Good News* of the Christ *being* Jesus.

The apostles **went from the presence of the council** back to their brethren. They were not dispirited, but were **rejoicing that they had been *judged*-worthy to be dishonored** by a flogging **for**

the Name of Jesus. The Lord had promised them that their reward for such dishonor would be great (Luke 6:22–23). Far from obeying this last order from the Sanhedrin, **every day, in the Temple and from house to house, they did not cease teaching and preaching** as they had previously done. They continued to fill Jerusalem with their teaching (v. 28), contending that the One their rulers had killed was **the Christ**.

§II.6. Jerusalem Ministry of Stephen

> **6** 1 Now in these days while the disciples were being multiplied, a murmuring occurred on the part of the Hellenists against the Hebrews, because their widows were being overlooked in the daily service.
> 2 And the Twelve called to *them* the multitude of the disciples and said, "It is not pleasing for us to leave the Word of God to serve tables.
> 3 "Brothers, from among you, look over seven men witnessed to, full of the Spirit and of wisdom, whom we will appoint over this need.
> 4 "But we *ourselves* will pay attention to the prayer and to the service of the Word."
> 5 And the word pleased all the multitude, and they chose Stephen, a man full of faith and of the Holy Spirit, and Philip, Prochorus, Nicanor, Timon, Parmenas, and Nicolas, a proselyte from Antioch,
> 6 whom they stood before the apostles, and after praying, they laid their hands on them.

Luke's account of the Church's work in Jerusalem culminates in the story of Stephen, whose martyrdom was the catalyst for the Church's scattering and expansion. Stephen was chosen as one of

II. The Church in Jerusalem — Acts 6:1–6

seven almoners, whose work would evolve into the diaconate when the Church spread beyond Jerusalem (compare the references to deacons in Phil. 1:1; 1 Tim. 3:8f). Like many divine developments in the Church, the institution began with a crisis.

The Christians in Jerusalem **were being multiplied** by God, with the inevitable difficulty of caring for so many poor among them. Some of the Christians were **Hellenists** (that is, Greek-speaking Jews of the Diaspora), while others were **Hebrews** (that is, Aramaic-speaking Jews from Palestine). The **widows** of the Hellenistic group **were being overlooked in the daily service** (Gr. *diakonia*), the daily distribution of food or money to the needy. This neglect need not have been deliberate. It is possible that the Greek-speaking widows could not communicate well with some of the Hebrew-speaking people administering the distribution. Whatever the cause of the neglect, **a murmuring occurred** as the Hellenists began complaining bitterly about their Hebrew brethren. Something had to be done administratively to preserve unity.

The Twelve could have supervised the distribution themselves, but this would mean less time devoted to teaching—the task given them by Christ. It would **not** be **pleasing** or fitting for them to **leave** preaching **the Word of God**, the Gospel, **to serve tables**—a humble task others could do as effectively as they. They therefore **called to *them* the multitude of the disciples** to offer this solution: Let them **look over** and select from among themselves **seven men witnessed to** by others for their honesty, **full of the Spirit and of wisdom**. These men the Twelve would **appoint over this need**.

The Twelve, for their part (the **we** is emphatic), would **pay attention to the prayer, and to the service** (*diakonia*) **of the Word**. That is, they would restrict themselves to presiding at the liturgical prayers of the Church and to their work of preaching and teaching. This **word pleased all the multitude**, and they acted accordingly, choosing seven men. These they **stood before the apostles** to be commissioned by them, and **after praying, they laid their hands on them**, appointing and ordaining them to this work.

We note in this whole event the corporate and conciliar nature of the Church. The Twelve did not decide on a course of action by themselves and simply impose it on the Church like despots. They called the **multitude of the disciples** to offer their solution, and the acceptance of this by the multitude was a sign that this course of action had the divine approval. The apostles respected the dignity of the Church as a whole.

It is significant that all of the seven deacons had Greek names, for the Hellenists chose men from their own ranks to make sure their widows would be cared for. **Stephen** comes first in the list, described as **a man full of faith and of the Holy Spirit**, possibly a reference to his wonder-working (v. 8). **Philip** is mentioned next, doubtless because of his role as an evangelist in the chapters following (8:5f). **Prochorus** is traditionally held to be the amanuensis of St. John the Beloved Disciple. It is said that Prochorus later became bishop of Nicomedia and was martyred at Antioch. **Nicolas** was a Gentile from Syrian Antioch who was a proselyte, or convert to Judaism. Later tradition makes him responsible for the sect of the Nicolaitans, denounced in Revelation 2:6, 15.

---

7   And the Word of God was growing; and the number of the disciples was being multiplied extremely in Jerusalem, and a great crowd of the priests were obeying the Faith.

8   And Stephen, full of grace and power, was doing great wonders and signs among the people.

9   But some of those from what was called "the Synagogue of the Freedmen," both Cyrenians and Alexandrians, and from Cilicia and Asia, arose and debated with Stephen.

10 And they were not strong enough to withstand the wisdom and the Spirit with which he was speaking.

11 Then they suborned men to say, "We have heard him speak blasphemous words against Moses and God."

II. The Church in Jerusalem   Acts 6:7–12

> **12 And they set in motion the people, the elders, and the scribes, and they came upon him and carried him off, and brought *him* to the council.**

This crisis over, the Church continued to thrive. Indeed, **the Word of God**, or the Gospel, **was growing** and **the number of the disciples was being multiplied extremely** by God to such an extent that even **a great crowd of the** Jewish **priests were obeying the Faith** and receiving baptism. (At this point, there was no inconsistency felt in offering Jewish sacrifice and being a Christian. Indeed, even St. Paul would later offer such sacrifices as a part of his respect for the Temple and his Jewish heritage; 21:23–24.)

Stephen was not just administering the daily distribution. He was also **doing great wonders and signs among the people**, even as the apostles were. It seems that he worshipped in **"the Synagogue of the Freedmen,"** a Greek-speaking synagogue in Jerusalem founded by freed slaves or their sons from **Cyrene, Alexandria, Cilicia,** and **Asia**. Some Jews in this synagogue disagreed with Stephen and his Christian convictions, being alarmed by and jealous of the growth of the Christian movement. They therefore arranged a formal **debate** with Stephen at the synagogue. They were, however, **not strong enough to withstand the wisdom and the Spirit with which he was speaking** and were bested in the debate.

This public humiliation only made his opponents more determined to do away with Stephen, by fair methods or foul. If they could not destroy his credibility in public debate, they would eliminate him by other means. Thus they **suborned men to say, "We have heard him speak blasphemous words against Moses and God."** That is, they secretly arranged for men to bring this charge against him, for blasphemy was a capital offense. They also **set in motion** or stirred up **the people, the elders, and the scribes** to believe the charge. This mob turned against him, and **they came upon him** (possibly as he was walking in the streets?) and **carried him off, and brought *him* to the council** for trial.

> ꙮ ꙮ ꙮ ꙮ ꙮ
> 13 And they stood false witnesses *before them* who said, "This man does not cease speaking against this holy place, and the Law;
> 14 "for we have heard him say that this Jesus the Nazarene will tear down this place and change the customs which Moses delivered to us."
> 15 And staring at him, all those sitting in the council saw his face like the face of an angel.

At the trial, Stephen's foes **stood false witnesses** before the council. These witnesses, trying to prove the charges that Stephen had spoken blasphemous words against Moses and God (v. 11), testified, **"This man does not cease speaking against this holy place** (i.e. the Temple) **and the Law; for we have heard him say that this Jesus the Nazarene will tear down this place and change the customs which Moses delivered to us**, abolishing the Law." If such were true, this would indeed constitute blasphemy against Moses (by saying his Law would be abolished) and against God (saying His Temple would be torn down).

This was not the first time false witnesses had been used, nor the first time Jesus would be accused before the council of threatening to tear down the Temple. At Jesus' own trial, false witnesses were found who testified that Jesus said He would tear down the Temple and rebuild it in three days (Mark 14:57–58). It is tempting to think these were the same witnesses, recycled by the Sanhedrin to try their testimony again.

Though the false witness against Jesus was utterly baseless, the charges against Stephen were not so much utter lies as distortions. From Stephen's defense, it seems he did teach that the Temple and the Law were not God's ultimate goal or provision for Israel, but that they had a provisional nature. It was Jesus who was the final goal of Israel's sacred history. This did not mean, of course, that Jesus would tear down the Temple, or that pious Jews should forsake their cultural inheritance in the Law. But it did mean that these things were not final or constitutive in the Kingdom of God. The false witnesses ignored such nuances and presented Stephen's teaching in its worst possible light.

Stephen, however, was not cowed by these lies. All those in the council **staring at him** in their midst **saw** that **his face** was **like the face of an angel**. That is, his eyes were burning with an inner radiance and joy, a kind of ferocious serenity. The grace of martyrdom was upon him, and he already belonged to the Kingdom.

> ༄ ༄ ༄ ༄ ༄
>
> **7** 1 And the chief-priest said, "Are these things thus?"

After these accusations at the trial, **the chief-priest** (probably Caiaphas) invited Stephen to make his defense to these charges, saying, **"Are these things thus?"** By way of reply, Stephen does not deal with the individual charges directly. Most probably he despaired of receiving a fair trial. Instead, he uses his reply to make the Christian case, accusing his judges in turn of turning the Temple and the Law into idols and appealing to them to repent of this and of their rejection of Jesus.

To understand Stephen's reply, we first have to understand the mentality against which he was arguing. That mentality said that the Temple was the final phase of God's dealing with Israel, that the worship of God must always presuppose the Temple, and that communion without God was impossible without it. In his public teaching, Stephen had spoken against this view, and it was this teaching his adversaries were distorting (6:13). Stephen therefore presents this teaching and the Christian understanding of the Temple in its undistorted form.

In sum, he argues that Israel had been a pilgrim people, always led by God—though reluctantly—to new ways. Thus, the Temple is not the final phase of their spiritual pilgrimage, but merely one part of God's ongoing dealing with Israel. The goal of communion with God finds its fulfillment in Jesus, not in the Temple, and the

Temple cannot be indispensable for divine worship. This is apparent even from the history of the Temple itself, for the Temple was not built until long after Moses' time, even after the time of David, and even then it could not contain God. Because the Temple was but one phase in God's dealing with His pilgrim people, they must be prepared now to move on to the next phase—that of finding in Jesus the locus of God's saving Presence. This means they must also now repent of their long-entrenched habit of resisting those sent by God to lead them. They had not recognized God's purposes in Joseph, Moses, and all the prophets, even as they had not recognized His purpose in Jesus. They must now repent of their murder of God's Messiah and their perennial lawlessness.

> ॐ ॐ ॐ ॐ ॐ
>
> 2 And Stephen said, "Brothers and fathers, hear *me*! The God of glory appeared to our father Abraham while he was in Mesopotamia, before he dwelt in Haran,
>
> 3 "and said to him, 'Go out from your land and your relatives, and come into the land that I will show you.'
>
> 4 "Then he went out from the land of the Chaldeans and dwelt in Haran. And from there, after the death of his father, *He* resettled him into this land in which you *yourselves* are now dwelling.
>
> 5 "And He did not give him an inheritance in it, not a foot's length; and *even* when he had no child, He promised that He would give it to him and to his seed after him as a possession.
>
> 6 "But God spoke thus, that his seed would be a sojourner in another land, and that they would enslave and mistreat them for four hundred years.
>
> 7 "And 'whatever nation in which they will serve *as slaves* I *Myself* will judge,' said God,

II. The Church in Jerusalem — Acts 7:2–16

> 'and after these things they will come out and worship Me in this place.'
>
> 8 "And He gave him the covenant of circumcision; and thus he begot Isaac, and circumcised him on the eighth day; and Isaac *begot* Jacob, and Jacob the twelve patriarchs.
>
> 9 "And the patriarchs were jealous of Joseph and sold him into Egypt. And God was with him,
>
> 10 "and took him out from all his tribulations, and gave him grace and wisdom before Pharaoh, king of Egypt; and he appointed him governor over Egypt and his whole house.
>
> 11 "Now a famine came over all Egypt and Canaan, and great tribulation, and our fathers were not finding food.
>
> 12 "But when Jacob heard that there was wheat in Egypt, he sent our fathers first.
>
> 13 "And on the second *visit* Joseph was made known to his brothers, and Joseph's family was manifest to Pharaoh.
>
> 14 "And Joseph sent and called Jacob his father and all his relatives, seventy-five souls.
>
> 15 "And Jacob went down into Egypt and died, he and our fathers.
>
> 16 "And they were removed to Shechem, and laid in the tomb which Abraham had purchased for a sum of silver from the sons of Hamor in Shechem.

Stephen makes his case by reviewing Israel's sacred history and showing how his foes' Jewish view of the Temple is at odds with it. Far from the Temple being necessary to experience God, their **God appeared** in His **glory** to their **father Abraham while he was in Mesopotamia**, long before the Temple was ever built. God called him to **go out from** his **land** and his **relatives and** to **come into the**

land that He would later **show** him. That is, God called Abraham to be a pilgrim, not even telling him his final destination. In doing this, He set the pattern for his descendants, the people of Israel. They also were called to spiritual pilgrimage, not knowing their final destination, but trusting in the guiding hand of God.

Even after God **resettled** Abraham **into this land** of Canaan, **He did not give him an inheritance in it, not** even **a foot's length**, but Abraham continued to live as a nomad. Though God **promised that He would give** the land **to him and to his seed after him**, He also said that **his seed would be a sojourner in another land** (that is, in Egypt) and that it was only after **four hundred years** that He would return them to Canaan. The nature of Israel as a pilgrim people was thus written into their history for many, many years. God did not immediately give Abraham the Promised Land, but instead **gave him the covenant of circumcision.** This covenant was carried by **Isaac** and **Jacob** and **the twelve patriarchs**, and it testified to them that God was calling His people to walk by faith.

The patriarchal history of Israel also proved something else: that Israel did not always recognize those sent to them by God. Thus the **patriarchs were jealous of Joseph** and rejected him, despite his prophetic dreams (Gen. 37:5f), and **sold him into Egypt**. However, **God was with him**, even though his brethren rejected him. He exalted Joseph, for Pharaoh **appointed him governor over** all **Egypt**.

In the same way, Stephen implies, Israel had not recognized Jesus as Messiah and through jealousy delivered Him to death. God was with Jesus just as He was with Joseph, overturning Israel's rejection and exalting Jesus to His right hand. In Joseph's time, his brethren did not recognize their royal lord was Joseph when they met him in Egypt. It was only afterwards, **on the second *visit***, that **Joseph was made known to his brothers**. In the same way, Stephen implies, Israel did not recognize their Messiah was Jesus when they first knew Him. It is only now, at a later time, that they may come to recognize Him.

It was through Joseph that **Jacob** and the fathers **went down into Egypt**. From there, after their death and the Exodus from

Egypt, **they were removed to Shechem** (Josh. 24:32), now in hated Samaritan territory. Even in death, therefore, they were pilgrims in the land.

❦ EXCURSUS
On the Accuracy of Stephen's History

The accuracy of St. Stephen's recounting of his own sacred history is sometimes criticized. I would suggest that this criticism is unfair—not only because as a Jew, Stephen would be very familiar with the details of his own history and thus unlikely to make the elementary mistakes of which he is sometimes accused, but also because he was guided by the Holy Spirit in his arguments (6:3, 10; Luke 12:11–12). I would offer therefore the following.

1. In 7:2–3, Stephen says that God called Abraham while he was in Ur, before he moved to Haran, while Genesis 11:31—12:4 says that God called Abraham while he was in Haran. From God's words in Genesis 12:1, however, it is apparent that this call in Haran was a renewal of a previous call given in Ur, for Abram was told to "leave his birthplace" (Gen. 11:28)—a reference to leaving Ur, not Haran. Accordingly Genesis 15:7 and Nehemiah 9:7 speak of Abraham being called from Ur, and it is this first and definitive calling to which Stephen refers.
2. In 7:14, Stephen says that seventy-five souls came into Egypt, while Genesis 46:27 mentions only seventy. The Septuagint of this verse gives the number as seventy-five, as does the Hebrew fragment of Exodus 1:5 from the Dead Sea scrolls. It is this variant that seems to have been current in Palestine at that time, and this is the one Stephen quotes. (The extra persons are the sons and grandsons of Ephraim and Manasseh.)
3. In 7:16, Stephen says that Abraham was the one who

purchased the tomb from the sons of Hamor in Shechem, while Genesis 33:18–19 says it was Jacob who bought this tomb. In Stephen's rehearsal of this, however, he is concerned not just for burial of one of the patriarchs, but of all of them ("Jacob and our fathers," v. 15), and it seems that he is thinking of the burial arrangements made throughout the patriarchal period. Jacob's purchase of the tomb from the sons of Hamor was not the first time the patriarchs had dealings in Shechem—Abraham must have made alliances with the local Shechemites when he built his altar in Shechem (Gen. 12:6–7). Thus Abraham laid the groundwork for future purchases from the sons of Hamor through his alliances with them, and it was on this foundation that Jacob worked when he made the actual purchase (possibly in Abraham's name).

I would suggest it is on this basis that Stephen telescopes the entire history when he says that Abraham purchased the land from the sons of Hamor, for it was on the basis of his alliances that the final purchase was made. It is not necessary, however, to say that this reconstruction of patriarchal history is solely the work of Stephen. It seems likely that it was a local Samaritan tradition (which was happy to find as much patriarchal involvement in their territory as possible), and that it was to this tradition that Stephen refers.

17 "But as the time of the promise was drawing near which God had confessed to Abraham, the people grew and were multiplied in Egypt,
18 "until there arose another king over Egypt who did not know Joseph.
19 "This one dealt craftily with our race, and

mistreated our fathers to make them expose their infants so that they would not keep alive.

20 "And it was at this *appointed* time that Moses was born; and he was beautiful to God; and he was nurtured three months in the house of his father.

21 "And after he had been exposed, the daughter of Pharaoh took him away and nurtured him as her own son.

22 "And Moses was disciplined in all the wisdom of the Egyptians, and he was powerful in his words and works.

23 "But when forty *years'* time was fulfilled, there arose upon his heart *the desire* to look over his brothers, the sons of Israel.

24 "And when he saw one being hurt, he assisted him and did vengeance for the one being oppressed by striking the Egyptian.

25 "And he thought that his brothers had insight that God was giving them salvation by his hand; but they did not have insight.

26 "And on the following day he appeared to them as they were fighting, and he was reconciling them to peace, saying, 'Men, you are brothers—why do you hurt one another?'

27 "But the one who was hurting his neighbor pushed him aside, saying, 'Who appointed you a ruler and judge over us?

28 "'Are you wanting to destroy me in the same way as you destroyed the Egyptian yesterday?'

29 "And at this word, Moses fled and became a sojourner in the land of Midian, where he begot two sons.

30 "And after forty years had been fulfilled, an angel appeared to him in the wilderness of

Mount Sinai, in the flame of a burning bush.
31 "And when Moses saw it, he was marveling at the vision; and coming to it to look *closely*, there came the voice of the Lord:
32 "'I *Myself* am the God of your fathers, the God of Abraham and Isaac and Jacob.' And Moses trembled and was not daring to look *closely*.
33 "But the Lord said to him, 'Loose the sandals from your feet, for the place on which you are standing is holy ground.
34 "'I have certainly seen the oppression of My people in Egypt, and have heard their groans, and I have come down to take them out. And now come, I will send you to Egypt.'
35 "This Moses whom they denied, saying, 'Who made you a ruler and a judge?'—this one God sent to be both a ruler and redeemer with the hand of the angel who appeared to him in the bush.
36 "This one led them out, doing wonders and signs in the land of Egypt and in the Red Sea and in the wilderness for forty years.
37 "This one is the Moses who said to the sons of Israel, 'God will raise up for you a prophet like me from your brothers.'
38 "This one is he who was in the church in the wilderness with the angel who was speaking to him on Mount Sinai, and who was with your fathers, and he welcomed living oracles to give us,
39 "to whom our fathers did not want to become obedient, but pushed him aside and in their hearts turned back to Egypt,
40 "saying to Aaron, 'Make for us gods who will go before us; for this Moses who led us from

II. The Church in Jerusalem   Acts 7:17–43

> the land of Egypt—we do not know what happened to him.'
> 41 "And in those days they made a calf and brought a sacrifice to the idol and were being glad in the works of their hands.
> 42 "But God turned and delivered them up to worship the army of heaven; as it is written in the Book of the Prophets, 'Was it to Me that you offered *slaughtered* victims and sacrifices forty years in the wilderness, O House of Israel?
> 43 "'You also took up the tent of Moloch and the star of the god Rephan, the patterns you made to worship them. I also will resettle you beyond Babylon.'

Stephen next surveys the Mosaic period of Israel's history. Moses was born in a time of crisis, when **there arose another king over Egypt who did not know Joseph** and who felt no loyalty to him and his kin. This Pharaoh enacted a policy in which the Hebrews were required **to expose their** male **infants** by casting them into the Nile (Ex. 1:22). **It was at this *appointed* time that Moses was born.**

Because he was a very beautiful baby (literally, **beautiful to God**, a Hebrew superlative) his parents could not bear to cast him into the Nile but **nurtured** him secretly for **three months**. At length such a growing baby could not be kept secret, and he was **exposed** and set adrift in a basket on the Nile (Ex. 2:3f), delivered, as it were, into the hands of God. He was found by **the daughter of Pharaoh** (that is, one of the extended royal family), who **nurtured him as her own son**. The result was that he **was disciplined** and educated **in all the wisdom of the Egyptians**, doubtless having a career befitting one of his social position. Tradition makes him a military leader, one who was **powerful in his words and works**, one whose orders carried authority and who did military exploits.

At length (Stephen quotes a rabbinical tradition that makes

it after **forty *years***), **there arose upon** Moses' **heart *the desire* to look over** and champion the cause of **his brothers, the sons of Israel. When he saw one being hurt** and beaten by an Egyptian, **he assisted** his countryman, **striking** and unintentionally killing the Egyptian. Moses was hoping to begin his work of helping his fellow Hebrews, and **he thought that his brothers** would have **insight that God was giving them salvation** from their burdens **by his hand**. But he was wrong. For **on the following day, he appeared** as two of them **were fighting**, and when he tried to assert his authority over them to reconcile them, the aggressor in the fight **pushed him aside**, repudiating him and saying, **"Who appointed you a ruler and judge over us?"** Upon learning that his killing of the Egyptian was becoming widely known, **Moses fled and became a sojourner in the land of Midian**, in northwestern Arabia. Like the Patriarchs, Moses also lived as a pilgrim and a man of faith, sojourning in a land not his own.

While he was in this pagan land, **an angel appeared to him in the wilderness of Mount Sinai, in the flame of a burning bush**. Stephen stresses that the call of both Abraham and Moses occurred while far from Canaan, for God was not confined to one place. Indeed, wherever God revealed Himself was **holy ground**. The God who promised the Land of Canaan to the seed of Abraham now was fulfilling His word, for He would **send** Moses **to Egypt** to save his people. (The divine Presence is here called **an angel** because God reveals His Presence not in fullness but as a theophany, as "the Angel of the Lord"; Ex. 3:2.)

Stephen focuses on Moses, showing thereby how Moses prefigures Jesus. Indeed, **Moses** himself **said to the sons of Israel, "God will raise up for you a prophet like me from your brothers"** (Deut. 18:15f), and Jesus was this One.

Jesus was indeed like Moses. **Moses** was the very one **whom they denied, saying, "Who made you a ruler and judge?"** even though **God sent** him **to be both ruler and redeemer** for them. Jesus was denied by Israel too. Moses was **doing wonders and signs**, and Jesus also was known as a wonder-worker. Moses was **in the church**, God's assembly (Gr. *ekklesia*), while they were **in the wilderness**, and **on**

II. The Church in Jerusalem — Acts 7:44–50

Mount Sinai, he **welcomed living oracles to give** to Israel. In the same way, Jesus also was with His Church, and He also gave to Israel the true Word of the Father speaking in Him.

Just as Jesus paralleled Moses and fulfilled Moses' prophecy of Another coming like himself, so also the Israel of Jesus' day paralleled their rebellious ancestors. Israel in Moses' day **did not want to become obedient** to Moses, **but pushed him aside and in their hearts turned back** to the gods of **Egypt**. For scarcely had they been set free from Egyptian bondage when they were **saying to Aaron, "Make for us gods who will go before us."**

This was not an isolated act of rebellion, either. They also **worshipped the army of heaven**, all the stars and planets of heaven. That is, though they sacrificed to Yahweh, idolatry and rebellion were in their hearts even in that wilderness period, and God did not accept their worship. The idolatry Amos denounces **in the Book of the Prophets** (the Book of the Twelve Prophets in the Hebrew canon) had its root in those early days. Amos 5:25–27 (quoted in the Greek Septuagint form) says that Israel carried foreign gods with them even then, and it was for this entrenched habit of idolatry that God would **resettle** them **beyond Babylon**, casting them from His holy land.

Stephen's hearers could not miss the intended parallel. He was saying that because they had rejected Jesus as their fathers had rejected Moses, God would again cast them from the land. Israel of old had the Tent of Witness, but was judged for the idolatry hidden in their hearts. The Israel of Stephen's day, though possessing the Temple, also hid rebellion in their hearts and would also be judged.

꒰ ꒰ ꒰ ꒰ ꒰

44 "Our fathers had the Tent of Witness in the wilderness, just as He who spoke to Moses directed to make it according to the pattern he had seen.
45 "And having welcomed it in turn, our fathers brought it in with Joshua upon dispossessing the nations whom God drove out before the

> face of our fathers, until the days of David,
> 46 "who found grace before God, and asked that he might find a tabernacle for the God of Jacob.
> 47 "But Solomon built for Him a house.
> 48 "But the Most High does not dwell in a *place* made-with-hands, as the prophet says,
> 49 "'Heaven *is* My throne, and earth *is* the footstool of My feet; what kind of house will you build for Me,' says the Lord, 'or what place for My rest?
> 50 "'Did not My hand make all these things?'

Stephen concludes his speech before his accusers. He had been accused of speaking against the Holy Place (that is, the Temple), and here he clarifies his teaching about the Temple. The Temple had become for Israel the end and goal of all God's dealings with them, but in this they were misled. The static Temple structure was not God's original purpose for Israel, and its presence misled Israel into thinking that God could somehow be contained within it. That in turn led to the proud complacency with which they were even now afflicted.

Originally, their **fathers had the Tent of Witness**, a portable shrine to be carried from place to place as God led Israel **in the wilderness**. This was the provision **Moses** was **directed to make according to the** divine **pattern he had seen**, and it represented God's will for His pilgrim people. This Tent, not a static Temple, continued to be the way God dealt with Israel even in the days of **Joshua** when the wilderness wandering was over, and right up **until the days of David**. David was disturbed that he dwelt in a royal palace while God's Ark was housed behind simple tent curtains (2 Sam. 7:2). He therefore was determined to **find a tabernacle for the God of Jacob**.

The word rendered *tabernacle* is the Greek *skenoma*, the same word used in Psalm 132:5 LXX, which passage Stephen here cites. The word *skenoma* meant any lodging or dwelling place. Its original humble meaning of "tent" (compare *skene*, "tent," in v. 44) is here contrasted with the more munificent and static **house** which **Solomon** actually **built** later.

Even so, **the Most High does not dwell in a *place* made-with-hands, as the prophet** Isaiah **says** (Is. 66:1–2)—and as even Solomon acknowledged in his dedication prayer (1 Kin. 8:27). The word translated *made-with-hands* is the Greek *cheiropoietos*, connected with the classic Hebrew denunciation of the pagan idols that were made by human hands (Ps. 135:15). In using this word, Stephen is insinuating that Israel has made the Temple into an idol, thinking that with it they could somehow box God in. God's **hand made all these things**, even **heaven and earth**—did they think they could **build a place for** His **rest** where He would reside? Stephen was not guilty of speaking against the Temple—*they* were guilty of making the Temple into an idol!

> ৯ ৯ ৯ ৯ ৯
>
> 51 "Stiff-necked and uncircumcised in heart and ears, you *yourselves* always resist the Holy Spirit; as your fathers *did*, you *yourselves* also *do*.
>
> 52 "Which of the prophets did your fathers not persecute? And they killed those who had preproclaimed the coming of the Righteous One, whose betrayers and murderers you *yourselves* have now become—
>
> 53 "you who received the Law at the direction of angels, and did not keep *it*!"

Stephen now comes to the climax of his defense, rounding on his accusers with a counter-accusation. By refusing to be led by God into new ways through Christ, they were **stiff-necked and uncircumcised in heart and ears**, stubbornly refusing to let the truth into their hearts or hear it with their ears. They were the ones (the **you** is emphatic) who **always resist the Holy Spirit** and rebel against God's guidance—**as** their **fathers** *did* in the wilderness, they

Acts 7:54—8:1a THE BOOK OF ACTS

were **also** doing now. They were doing exactly what their **fathers** did, for they **persecuted** every single one of **the prophets** and **killed those** prophets **who had preproclaimed the coming of the Righteous One**, the Messiah. Like father, like son! Their fathers killed the prophets who predicted the Messiah, and they **betrayed and murdered** the Messiah Himself! They **received the Law** and claimed to be so loyal to it that they were incensed at the thought of its being changed (6:13–14), but they **did not keep it**.

༃ ༃ ༃ ༃ ༃

54 Now hearing these *things*, they were infuriated and were gnashing their teeth at him.

55 But being full of the Holy Spirit, he stared into heaven and saw the glory of God, and Jesus standing at the right *hand* of God,

56 and he said, "Behold, I observe the heavens opened up and the Son of Man standing at the right *hand* of God!"

57 But they cried out with a great voice, and shut their ears, and they rushed down upon him with the same-impulse.

58 And when they cast him outside of the city, they were stoning *him*, and the witnesses put off their garments at the feet of a young man called Saul.

59 And they were stoning Stephen as he called upon *the Lord* and said, "Lord Jesus, welcome my spirit!"

60 And falling on his knees, he cried out with a great voice, "Lord, do not stand this sin against them!" And having said this, he fell asleep.

8 1a And Saul consented to destroying him.

Those of the Sanhedrin listening to this **were infuriated and were gnashing their teeth** in murderous rage at him. But Stephen

II. The Church in Jerusalem Acts 7:54—8:1a

was **full of the Holy Spirit** as a true prophet (6:5), and as a prophet, **he stared into heaven and saw** in a vision **the glory of God and Jesus standing at the right *hand* of God**. It was as the Scripture said: young men were indeed seeing visions (Joel 2:28; Acts 2:17). In ecstasy he said to them, **"Behold, I observe the heavens opened up and the Son of Man standing at the right *hand* of God!"**—doubtless standing to deliver heaven's verdict on the innocence of Stephen (in antiquity judges normally delivered their verdicts standing).

This final confession of Jesus as the glorified Messiah was all the Sanhedrin could stand. **They cried out with a great voice and shut their ears**, unable to hear any more of his words (thus proving Stephen's accusation that they were uncircumcised in ears). **They rushed down upon him with the same-impulse** (Gr. *omothumadon*; compare its use in 1:14; 2:46; 4:24; Stephen's foes were as united in their rage as the Church was united in peace). They **cast him outside of the city** and began **stoning** *him* in an act of lynch-mob violence.

Luke adds that **the witnesses** of Stephen's words in the Sanhedrin **put off their garments**, leaving them **at the feet of a young man called Saul**. This is to show how Saul opposed the Church and to prepare us for mention of him later.

Stephen's death was like that of his Master, full of confidence and serenity. As Jesus committed His spirit into the hands of His Father (Luke 23:46), so Stephen **called upon** the **Lord Jesus** to **welcome** his **spirit** also. As the rocks flew and struck him, he sank to **his knees** in prayer and **cried out with a great voice, "Lord, do not stand this sin against them!"** Like his Lord, Stephen also prayed for his murderers (Luke 23:34). Luke intends us to see the contrast between the Sanhedrin and the protomartyr: They cried out with a great voice of murderous rage (v. 57), while Stephen **cried out with a great voice** of forgiveness for that rage. His prayer was that on the Last Day, this sin anyway might not stand up to witness against them. This grace-filled prayer was his last word. Having said this, **he fell asleep**, dying in the Lord. His flesh would awake again at the final resurrection. St. Stephen's Feast Day in the Church is December 27.

Thus the work of the Church in Jerusalem came to its climax. It was as the Lord said: He would give them a mouth and a wisdom none of their opponents could contradict, and some of them would be put to death (Luke 21:15–16).

∞ III ∂

THE CHURCH SPREADS TO JUDEA AND SAMARIA (8:1b–40)

§III.1. Persecution Spreads the Church to Judea and Samaria

> **8** **1b** And in that day a great persecution happened against the church in Jerusalem; and they were all dispersed throughout the regions of Judea and Samaria, except the apostles.
> **2** And reverent men buried Stephen and made great lamentation over him.
> **3** But Saul was ravaging the church, entering house after house; and dragging men and women, he was delivering *them* up to prison.

After Stephen's martyrdom, **a great persecution** began **against the church in Jerusalem**. It seems that the Jewish authorities, having eliminated Stephen, were determined to press their advantage and stop the expansion of the Church, if not wipe it out entirely. The rank and file were, for the time being at least, **all dispersed throughout the regions of Judea and Samaria**. Like seed, they were sown in the surrounding fields (the verb translated *disperse*, the Greek *diaspeiro*, cognate with "Diaspora," literally means "to sow out," as seeds are sown). The twelve **apostles**, however, were exempt from this persecution, doubtless because of the great esteem in which they were held by the people (compare 5:26).

Stephen also, because his piety was recognized by **reverent** and pious **men** in Jerusalem, was given proper burial with **great lamentation**, even though such ritual lamentations were usually denied those who had been executed as he was. Though all the Christians in Jerusalem suffered, it seems the Hellenists among them suffered especially, since they (and their champion Stephen) had been the most vocal in their outreach.

For his part, though, **Saul** began **ravaging the church** in Jerusalem, persecuting the heretics (as he regarded them) with great ferocity. The word rendered *ravage* is the Greek *lumainomai*, the usual word used for a wild beast tearing apart a body. Not content with arresting them if they confessed Jesus in public, he began **entering house after house, dragging** away **men and** even **women, delivering** *them* **up to prison**. Keeping quiet about one's faith provided no safety from persecution. Saul found out who the Christians were and pulled them out from the privacy of their own homes.

§III.2. Samaritan Ministry of Philip

> 4 Therefore, those who were dispersed went about preaching *the good news* of the Word.
> 5 And Philip went down to a city of Samaria and was heralding the Christ to them.
> 6 And the crowds with the same-impulse were paying attention to what was said by Philip, as they heard and saw the signs he was doing.
> 7 For many who had unclean spirits, they were coming out, shouting with a great voice; and many who had been paralyzed and lame were healed.
> 8 And there was much joy in that city.

Many of **those who were dispersed** were Hellenists, and they continued **preaching** *the good news* (*euaggelizo*) **of the Word** about Jesus with the same boldness they had in Jerusalem. Prominent among them was **Philip**, one of the seven deacons (feast day in

III. The Church Spreads to Judea and Samaria   Acts 8:9–13

the Church, October 11). He **went down to a city of Samaria** to continue his work of preaching.

Which Samaritan city is not indicated. It is unlikely that it was the capital Sebaste (the old city of Samaria of pre-exilic days), since this was a Hellenistic city, and the impression is given that most of Philip's converts were ethnic Samaritans, not Hellenists. The city of Gitto, eleven miles southeast of Caesarea, is a possibility, since it was the birthplace of Simon the Sorcerer (as reported by Justin Martyr, *Apology*, ch. 26). I would suggest, however, the major city of Shechem (then called Sychar) as the most likely candidate, especially since Christ had laid a foundation there during His ministry (John 4:4f).

Whatever the exact location of Philip's residence, he had great success in his preaching, since the crowds **heard and saw the signs he was doing**. In particular, **many who had unclean spirits** were spectacularly exorcised, since the demons were **coming out, shouting with a great voice**. Also, many who had been paralyzed and lame were healed, and this also provided spectacular witness to the truth of Philip's message. The great **joy in that city** witnessed to the coming of the Kingdom in their midst.

§III.3. Philip and Simon the Magus

> ༄ ༄ ༄ ༄ ༄
>
> 9 Now there was a certain man named Simon, who was previously in the city doing magic *arts*, astonishing the people of Samaria, saying he himself was someone great,
> 10 to whom all, from little to great, were paying attention to him, saying, "This *man* is the Power of God called Great."
> 11 And they were paying attention to him because for a considerable time he had astonished them with his magic *arts*.
> 12 But when they believed Philip preaching *the good news* about the Kingdom of God and

> the Name of Jesus Christ, they were being baptized, both men and women.
> 13 And even Simon himself believed; and after being baptized, he attached himself to Philip; and as he was observing signs and great works *of power* happening, he was being astonished.

Such success also attracted problems. One such problematic convert was Simon. He was a magus (from the Gr. *magos*; compare the plural "magi" in Matt. 2). The term *magos* originally meant a member of the Persian priestly class, skilled in ancient sciences such as astrology. By the time of the first century, the term often came to mean simply a fortuneteller, a cheap charlatan. It is here used to mean one who practices *mageia*, the magic arts (*mageuo* is the verb used in 8:9), a term including the casting of spells and the use of incantations for healing and other supernatural acts. Simon had become very adept in these supernatural occult practices, and had used them to make a career for himself as a local wonder-worker. He had concocted an entire gnostic worldview to go along with his work.

It seems he taught there were many divine emanations or **powers of God**, each with its own name and place in the celestial hierarchy, and that he himself was the incarnation of one of them, bearing the title "**the Great** Power." Tradition tells us he was accompanied by one Helen, a former prostitute, who he said was another emanation or divine power, emitted by himself, presumably before his incarnation in Samaria (Justin Martyr, *Apology*, ch. 26). All **the people of Samaria, from little to great, were paying attention to him**, accepting his claims, for they were **astonished** by the supernatural feats he could perform by **his magic *arts***.

Such demonic wonders, however, could not compete with the authentic divine power working through Philip. The populace therefore **believed** Philip's message that **the Kingdom of God** was being manifested on earth through **the Name of Jesus Christ**, and **they were being baptized, both men and women**. Indeed, **even Simon himself believed** and accepted Philip's message, and **after being**

III. The Church Spreads to Judea and Samaria   Acts 8:14–24

baptized, he attached himself to Philip and followed him around, continually **being astonished** at Philip's miracles. Luke mentions Simon's conversion and amazement here to show the superiority of the Gospel over the popular paganism of the day.

ಌ ಌ ಌ ಌ ಌ

14 Now when the apostles in Jerusalem heard that Samaria had welcomed the Word of God, they sent them Peter and John,

15 who came down and prayed for them, that they might receive the Holy Spirit.

16 For He had not yet fallen upon any of them; they had only been baptized in the Name of the Lord Jesus.

17 Then they were laying their hands on them, and they were receiving the Holy Spirit.

18 Now when Simon saw that the Spirit was given through the laying on of the hands of the apostles, he brought them money,

19 saying, "Give me also this authority, that on whomever I lay my hands he may receive the Holy Spirit."

20 But Peter said to him, "Your silver perish with you, because you supposed you *could* acquire the gift of God with money!

21 "You have no portion or inheritance in this word, for your heart is not straight before God.

22 "Repent therefore of this wickedness of yours, and beseech the Lord if perhaps the intention of your heart may be forgiven you.

23 "For I see that you are in the gall of bitterness and in the bond of unrighteousness."

24 But Simon answered and said, "Beseech the Lord for me yourselves, that nothing of what you have said may come upon me."

Philip (along with Stephen) was on the cutting edge of apostolic universalism and openness to other cultures, and as such, he boldly offered baptism even to the Samaritans. Jews had little use for Samaritans and considered them unclean. Philip's willingness to concede that Samaritans too could become true disciples of Jesus and receive the forgiveness of sins was revolutionary. But even Philip was not sure Samaritans were able to receive the Holy Spirit, the crown and culmination of baptism (2:38)—or at least he did not consider himself competent to make such a determination on his own. He therefore deferred to the judgment of the Twelve in Jerusalem, the mother church.

It was in response to Philip's work in Samaria that **the apostles in Jerusalem sent Peter and John.** (These two seem to have exercised a general supervision over such expansion; compare 11:22.) They **came down** from Jerusalem to the Samaritans **and prayed for them, that they might receive the Holy Spirit**, in completion and fulfillment of the usual baptismal initiation. This was not because only the apostles could lay hands upon them so that they would receive the Holy Spirit—presumably after the apostles left, the work continued in Samaria with others (such as Philip or his successors) administering the full baptismal initiation, including the laying on of hands (as Paul did with the Ephesians; compare 19:5–6). Rather, the apostles were called at this time to investigate Philip's work and set their seal upon it, giving the weight of apostolic authority to the decision that Samaritans too could receive the same full baptismal initiation as Jews—including the laying on of hands for the Holy Spirit. The Gospel in all its fullness was thus spilling over the boundaries of Judaism, with Samaritans now also receiving the same Pentecostal gift as the Jews.

This bestowal of the Holy Spirit must have been done with some outward manifestation, such as the Samaritans crying out with joy as the Spirit fell upon them. (There is no reason to think that speaking in tongues formed part of these manifestations, since Luke does not mention it here, and he seems careful to mention it when it occurs at other times.) This apostolic work greatly impressed **Simon**, and when he **saw the Spirit was given through the laying on of the**

hands of the apostles, he brought them money, requesting that in exchange for this, they **give** him **also this authority** to grant the Holy Spirit. Old habits die hard, and the old self-promoter saw in the authority to give such experiences a great moneymaker. What would the people give him if he could bestow such powerful experiences as this! He might even recover his old popularity!

It is impossible to know the depth or authenticity of Simon's conversion. It is possible that it was genuine, but superficial, and that his old ways reasserted themselves and overcame him, the seed of the Word not able to bear fruit in such shallow soil. His desire to buy spiritual authority with money would later give the Church a name for such a sin—"simony," named after Simon.

Peter reacts violently to Simon's offer to **acquire the gift of God with money**—"**Your silver perish with you**" (literally, "May your silver be with you to destruction!"—or as we would say, "To hell with your money, and you!"). Simon's error was not a well-intentioned one. It occurred because his **heart** was **not straight before God**, but crooked and perverted by greed. He was filled with **the gall of bitterness**, poisoned by envy of Philip, and held in **the bond of unrighteousness**, unable to walk in obedience to Christ. As such he had **no portion or inheritance in this word** or matter, nothing to do with the work of the Holy Spirit. Not only was Simon not to receive the authority to bestow the Spirit, he could not receive the Spirit at all, even for himself. Let him **repent** of his entire attitude of greed and **beseech the Lord** Jesus that he could be **forgiven** his wicked plans for self-promotion. Rather than prayer for the Holy Spirit, better Simon should pray for forgiveness, that he might escape the judgment of God! By refusing Simon's offer, Peter shows the apostles are motivated by sincerity alone, and not by any base desire. Luke expects his audience to note this.

Simon is stricken by this bold response, and he asks Peter and John to **beseech the Lord** for him themselves, that he might escape this impending judgment. In Simon's fear, Luke bids us see the power of the apostles. They spoke as prophets, discerning the intent of Simon's heart and uttering the judgment of God (as Peter had done against Ananias and Sapphira). Luke means his Roman hearers to learn from Simon's deference and to respect the apostles themselves.

We may add in passing that from the writings of St. Justin Martyr and others we learn that Simon's repentance also was superficial, and that after the apostles departed, Simon continued on his path of wickedness. He is regarded as the father of the gnostic heresy, ending up finally in Rome and propagating his errors until he died.

§III.4. Philip and the Ethiopian Eunuch

> ॐ ॐ ॐ ॐ ॐ
>
> 25 And therefore, when they had testified and spoken the Word of the Lord, they returned to Jerusalem and were preaching *the good news* to many villages of the Samaritans.
> 26 But an angel of the Lord spoke to Philip, saying, "Arise, and go toward the south on the road going down from Jerusalem to Gaza." (This is a wilderness.)
> 27 And he arose and went, and behold! an Ethiopian man, a eunuch, a court-official of Candace, queen of the Ethiopians, who was over all her treasury, who had come to Jerusalem to worship.
> 28 And he was returning and sitting in his *traveling*-chariot, and was reading the prophet Isaiah.
> 29 And the Spirit said to Philip, "Go up and join this *traveling*-chariot."
> 30 And when Philip had run up, he heard him reading Isaiah the prophet, and said, "Do you know what you are reading?"
> 31 And he said, "How might I be able to, unless someone guides me?" And he called Philip to come up to sit with him.
> 32 Now the passage of the scripture which he was reading was this: "He was led as a sheep to the

> slaughter, and as a lamb before its shearer *is* mute, thus he does not open his mouth.
> 33 "In his humiliation his judgment was taken away; who will describe his generation? For his life is taken from the earth."
> 34 And the eunuch answered Philip and said, "I beseech *you*—about whom does the prophet say this? About himself, or about some other?"
> 35 And Philip opened his mouth and, beginning from the Scripture, he preached the *good news of* Jesus to him.
> 36 And as they were going along the road they came upon some water; and the eunuch says, "Behold! Water! What hinders me from being baptized?"*
> 38 And he ordered the traveling-chariot to stand *still*, and they both went down into the water, Philip and the eunuch, and he baptized him.
> 39 And when they came up from the water, the Spirit of the Lord snatched Philip, and the eunuch did not see him any longer, but went on his way rejoicing.
> 40 But Philip was found in Azotus, and as he passed through he kept preaching *the good news* to all the cities, until he came into Caesarea.
>
> * The best manuscripts omit v. 37, which contains the eunuch's confession of faith in Jesus as the Son of God.

After **they had testified** to the truth of the Gospel, **the Word of the Lord, they returned to Jerusalem, preaching** the Gospel **to many villages of the Samaritans** as they went. The Lord had said they would be His witnesses in Samaria (1:8), and so it was.

God had other plans, however, for Philip. Rather than continuing his work among the Samaritans or returning to Jerusalem, he was to push the boundaries of the Gospel further into the non-Jewish world. Luke patterns the story after stories of the Old Testament prophets, since the age of the prophetic Spirit had begun (2:17f). **An angel of the Lord spoke to Philip** and directed him to go in a certain way. This mention of angelic direction recalls the angelic assistance given to the apostles in 5:19f, and also echoes the prophetic angel of the Lord who spoke to Israel in Judges 2:1f. Luke mentions it to stress it is God who directs His Church as they expand into new territory.

Philip seems to have traveled with Peter and John as they returned south to Jerusalem, parting from them when they reached **the road going down from Jerusalem to Gaza**. This angelic direction was important, for if Philip had taken the coastal road to Gaza and not the road that led south through the **wilderness**, he would have missed his God-appointed meeting with the **Ethiopian eunuch**.

This man was probably a Jewish proselyte of the Diaspora. (It is unlikely that Philip would have so readily baptized a Gentile who had not converted to Judaism—even Peter needed the help of visions and the proof of Gentiles speaking in tongues before he was willing to do so; 10:1f.) Eunuchs, however, were forbidden full membership in Israel in Deuteronomy 23:1, and though this stricture was being loosened, it is possible that the man's status as a eunuch made his Jewishness somewhat suspect.

He was also a **court-official of Candace** (the hereditary title of Ethiopian queen mothers), and he had **come to Jerusalem to worship**. He was now **returning** home, **sitting in his *traveling*-chariot** (probably a kind of covered wagon) as it lumbered south, and **reading the prophet Isaiah**. Philip overtook him as they headed south and heard him reading (for reading was done aloud at that time). **The Spirit** within him told him to **join the *traveling*-chariot**, and Philip obeyed, politely making contact and offering his company by asking the stranger if he **knew** and understood **what** he was **reading**. The man accepted Philip's offer of company by professing need of his help to understand the sacred text, **calling Philip to come up to sit with him** in his carriage as it rode along.

Luke presents his readers with **the scripture** the man **was reading**, expecting his Christian readers to see in it the providence of

III. The Church Spreads to Judea and Samaria   Acts 8:25–40

God. For the Scripture was Isaiah 53:7–8, a vivid prophecy of Jesus. It was Jesus who **was led as a sheep to the slaughter** on the Cross, and who stood **as a** mute **lamb before its shearer** when He refused to defend Himself before Pilate. It was Jesus who in His **humiliation** had **his judgment** and the justice due Him **taken away**. It was Jesus whose **life was taken from the earth** so that He had no **generation** or descendants. The Ethiopian, however, was puzzled by the text and asked politely (**"I beseech *you*"**—or, "please" as we would say) to whom this referred—was Isaiah writing about his own experience, or about **some other**?

Here was the reason Philip was told to take this particular road and join up with this wagon. Answering the man's question, Philip **preached the *good news of* Jesus to him**, showing that Jesus fulfilled all of Israel's hopes for the Messiah. At the end of what must have been a long conversation about Jesus and how to live as His disciple, the Ethiopian was ready to convert. Though they were going through the wilderness (v. 26), **they came upon some water** (another astonishing and providential "coincidence" in the desert), and the man demanded, **"What hinders me from being baptized right now?"** Given the series of God-ordained events that led the eunuch to that moment, such was clearly the will of God, and **Philip baptized him**.

After this, **the Spirit of the Lord snatched Philip** away, so that he did not continue riding with his newfound friend southward. In ancient days, the Spirit swept Elijah away, filling him with prophetic ecstasy so that he ran from the society of men under the compulsion of divine enthusiasm (1 Kin. 18:12). In the same way, Philip, as a modern prophet, was also snatched away. The eunuch, however, did not grieve, but **went on his way** home, **rejoicing** in the goodness of God and his salvation as he headed southward.

Philip, still led by the hand of God, went northward, for when the ecstasy wore off he **was found in Azotus** (ancient Ashdod), twenty miles north of Gaza. He **kept preaching *the good news* to all the cities** of the coastal region **until he came into Caesarea**. For the conversion of the eunuch was but the beginning of further outreach and the expansion of the Gospel.

The conversion of the eunuch marked the outer edge of the Gospel's progress. It had spread through Jewish Jerusalem and Judea, and had even been accepted by the Samaritans. Now it had spread to a foreign eunuch, one normally barred from full inclusion in Israel. The only barrier left was the barrier between Jew and Gentile. And that boundary was soon to be crossed.

❧ IV ☙

THE CHURCH SPREADS TO THE GENTILES
(9:1—11:18)

§IV.1. The Conversion of Saul

9 1 Now Saul, breathing in threat and murder against the disciples of the Lord, came to the chief-priest
2 and asked for epistles from him to the synagogues at Damascus, that if he found any who were of the Way, both men and women, he might bring them bound to Jerusalem.
3 And it happened that as he went, he was *drawing* near to Damascus, and suddenly a light from heaven flashed around him;
4 and he fell to the earth and heard a voice saying to him, "Saul! Saul! Why are you persecuting Me?"
5 And he said, "Who are you, lord?" And He said, "I *Myself* am Jesus, whom you *yourself* are persecuting.
6 "But arise, and enter into the city, and it will be told you what it is necessary for you to do."
7 And the men who journeyed with him stood speechless, hearing the voice, but observing no one.

> 8 And Saul got up from the earth and having opened his eyes, he was seeing nothing, and leading him by the hand, they brought him into Damascus.
> 9 And he was three days not seeing, and he did not eat or drink.

Luke begins his story of the conversion of the Gentiles with the conversion of Saul, since, although it was Peter who would first baptize Gentile converts (10:48), it was Paul who would spearhead the Church's outreach to them.

After the stoning of Stephen, **Saul** was **breathing in threat and murder against the disciples of the Lord**—that is, the very air he breathed and the atmosphere in which he moved was filled with his malice against the Christians. With every breath he drew, he became more determined to annihilate the rest of the Christians as Stephen was annihilated. Accordingly, he **came to the chief-priest** in Jerusalem **and asked for epistles from him** (that is, letters of extradition) **to the synagogues at Damascus** in Syria. Those in Judea **who were of the Way** (an early designation of the Christian movement) and who had fled to Damascus seeking refuge were to be brought back **bound to Jerusalem** for trial.

Saul and his escort traveled north into Syria, and as **he was** *drawing* **near** to the city walls of **Damascus, suddenly a light from heaven flashed around him**, so startling and overwhelming that **he fell to the earth**. His fall to the earth reveals the judgment of God upon him: Saul had exalted himself, lifting himself up against God's Messiah, and now he was humbled, cast to the ground (see Ps. 147:6). He **heard a voice saying to him, "Saul! Saul! Why are you persecuting Me?"** The heavenly head of the Church protested on behalf of His members on the earth. Saul knew from the heavenly light that this was the voice of one of God's elect, so he responded using the honorific **lord** (Gr. *kurie*, a word meaning both "sir" and "Lord"), asking who he was. Was this Jeremiah, who appeared in a vision to Judas Maccabeus (2 Macc. 15:14), or some other saint? And why did he say Saul was persecuting him?

IV. The Church Spreads to the Gentiles Acts 9:1–9

To his horror, the One who spoke from heaven said, **"I *Myself* am Jesus, whom you *yourself* are persecuting"** (the pronouns **I** and **you** are emphatic—"*you* are persecuting *Me*"). The hated Nazarenes were right after all! Their Lord did not speak at length to Saul, but in response to his inquiry as to what He wanted from him, simply told him to **"arise and enter into the city, and it will be told you what it is necessary for you to do."** Further instructions would be given later.

Luke relates that **the men who journeyed with** Saul **stood speechless**, not knowing what to say as they struggled to their feet, for they were **hearing the voice, but observing no one**. Luke reports Paul as elaborating upon their experience in 22:9, saying that his companions saw the heavenly light, but did not hear the voice of the One speaking to Saul. Luke, who reports both versions of this event, evidently saw no contradiction between the two accounts. Probably what he means to report here is that Saul's traveling companions were amazed because they heard the voice *of Saul*, but could not see whom he was speaking to. That is, they were stunned because they could discern only the earthly half of the conversation. Whom was Saul speaking to?

For his part, **Saul got up from the earth** and, though he **opened his eyes** wide, **he was seeing nothing**. His physical blindness reflected his previous spiritual blindness. It was also a part of Christ's merciful healing of Saul's heart, for he was humbled and had no choice but to acknowledge his own helplessness before Christ. He needed assistance to continue his journey and **enter the city**, so that they were **leading him by the hand** as blind beggars were led. It was thus that they **brought him into Damascus**. He had thought to stride into the city in pride, armed with epistles from the mighty chief-priest and making the Christians tremble before him. Instead, he had to be led by the hand, humbled and helpless. He spent **three days** in the house of a friend (probably his prearranged contact there), and **did not eat or drink**, mourning his sins, unable to take any food and growing ever weaker. He had thought to serve God by annihilating the Nazarenes, and instead he had been fighting against God.

> ❧ ❧ ❧ ❧ ❧
>
> 10 Now there was a certain disciple at Damascus named Ananias; and the Lord said to him in a vision, "Ananias!" And he said, "Behold, *here* I *am*, Lord."
> 11 And the Lord said to him, "Arise and go to the street called Straight, and seek in the house of Judas for *a man* from Tarsus named Saul, for behold, he is praying,
> 12 "and he has seen in a vision a man named Ananias come in and lay his hands on him, that he might see again."
> 13 But Ananias answered, "Lord, I have heard from many about this man, how many wicked *things* he did to Your saints at Jerusalem;
> 14 "and here he has authority from the chief-priests to bind all those who call upon Your Name."
> 15 But the Lord said to him, "Go, for this one is a chosen vessel to Me, to bear My Name before the Gentiles and kings and the sons of Israel;
> 16 "for I *Myself* will show him how much it is necessary for him to suffer for My Name."
> 17 And Ananias departed and entered into the house, and after laying his hands upon him, said, "Brother Saul, the Lord sent me, Jesus, the One who appeared to you on the way by which you were coming, that you may see again, and be filled with the Holy Spirit."
> 18 And immediately there fell from his eyes *something* like scales, and he saw again, and he arose and was baptized,
> 19 and he took food and *regained* strength.

While Saul was consumed by self-loathing and reproach, the Lord undertook to act on his behalf. **There was a certain disciple at**

| IV. The Church Spreads to the Gentiles | Acts 9:10–19a |

Damascus named Ananias (by tradition, one of the seventy disciples named in Luke 10:1 and now a resident of Damascus; his feast day is October 1). Christ spoke to his prophet Ananias in a vision and told him to **go to the street called Straight and seek in the house of Judas for *a man* named Saul**. (Luke mentions the detail of the street's name, probably because he means his readers to see extra significance in this location—Saul's heart is now **straight** before God; compare 8:21.) The street was one of the main thoroughfares of the city, running east and west.

The Lord had given Saul **a vision** in response to his **praying** and fasting, in which **a man named Ananias came in and laid his hands on him that he might see again**. Ananias was sent to fulfill that vision. It is a part of Christ's mercy to Saul that He not only sends Ananias to heal him, but also prepares Saul for the visit by giving an advance vision. As Saul languished in the house of a stranger, blind, weak, and helpless, he might have feared the unknown visitor had come to hurt him in revenge for his persecution of the Christians. The vision of Ananias coming as a healer would set his heart at rest when he discovered that the stranger who had come was named Ananias.

Ananias, however, is at first reluctant to find Saul, and he protests that he had **heard from many about this man, how many wicked *things* he did to** Christ's **saints at Jerusalem**. Had he not come to Damascus for the same wicked purpose, that of **binding all those who call upon** Christ's **Name**? Ananias does not refuse, but asks for clarification. Is Christ sending him to be arrested by this man?

Christ assures Ananias that He is not sending him into danger, but that **this one** is **a chosen vessel**, for he is to **bear** His **Name before the Gentiles and** even **kings** as well as **the sons of Israel**. Christ had a special purpose for Saul, for he would go everywhere throughout the world, witnessing to Jesus' Name and honor. True, he had made Christ's saints suffer, but Christ would **show him how much** he himself would **suffer for** His **Name** and cause. Ananias could go without fear, for Saul was a changed man.

Ananias obeyed and **entered into the house** of Judas in Straight Street. Seemingly without any further explanation, he **laid his hands**

upon Saul. It was only after this healing act (perhaps as Saul's eyes burned with the grace of God?) that Ananias explained himself. Acknowledging the former persecutor as a Christian comrade and greeting him as **brother Saul**, he said that **the Lord sent** him, even **Jesus, the One who appeared** to him **on the way by which he was coming, that** Saul **may see again, and be filled with the Holy Spirit**. By this explanation, Saul was assured that this man was the one he had seen in his vision—and that his vision of Christ on the Damascus road was authentic. All was happening just as Christ had said.

In response to Ananias's laying on of hands, **there fell from** Saul's **eyes *something* like scales, and he saw again**. The darkness was pushed back, and he could see Ananias's smiling face and the world around him. Now that Saul could see (spiritually as well as physically), **he arose and was baptized**, the crown of which was the receiving of the Holy Spirit (v. 17; compare 2:38). Saul's mourning over, **he took food and *regained* strength**. (Luke the physician notes this last medical detail of renewed strength.) We note here the urgency of baptism—baptism was the way Saul could become a disciple of Jesus, and obedience to heavenly vision was his first concern, even before assuaging a three-day thirst.

---

19 Now he was with the disciples who were at Damascus for some days,
20 and immediately was heralding Jesus in the synagogues, saying, "This One is the Son of God."
21 And all those hearing him were beside *themselves* and were saying, "Is not this one he who in Jerusalem annihilated those who called on this name, and who had come here for this *reason, that* of binding them and bringing *them* before the chief-priests?"

IV. Church Spreads to Gentiles — On the Journey to Arabia

> **22 But Saul was empowered *even* more and was confounding the Jews dwelling at Damascus by proving that this One is the Christ.**

Saul would stay with the church in **Damascus for some days**. His witness to Jesus, however, began **immediately**. When the next Sabbath came, Saul joined all his fellow Jews in the local synagogue at Damascus. As an important visitor, he was welcomed to give the exposition on the readings from the Law and the Prophets during the service. As part of his talk, he was **heralding Jesus** to them, saying, **"This One is the Son of God."** It was an astonishing *volte-face*, and **all those hearing him were beside *themselves*** with amazement, saying, **"Is not this one he who in Jerusalem annihilated those who called on this name,"** and **who had come** to Damascus for the express purpose of **binding** those who spoke like this? What was going on? Saul continued his work of debating in the synagogues and was **confounding** his opponents **by proving** from the Scriptures that **this One**, Jesus, **is the Christ**.

> ### ⁜ EXCURSUS
> #### On the Journey to Arabia
>
> According to Gal. 1:15–17, Paul said that after his conversion, he did not immediately consult with the apostles in Jerusalem (so that his authority was not derived from theirs). Rather, he was soon off to faraway "Arabia" (an elastic term, probably designating Nabatea, a kingdom whose northwestern limit was just east of Damascus). This Arabian visit occurred at this time, shortly after his conversion, perhaps after his first visits to the synagogues narrated above. The duration of the Arabian visit is not specified; it probably lasted some weeks or months. He soon returned to Damascus to continue his work there for "considerable days"— a period of over two years (Gal. 1:17–18).

> ૐ ૐ ૐ ૐ ૐ
> 23 And when considerable days were fulfilled, the Jews counseled to destroy him,
> 24 but their counsel became known to Saul. And they were also observing the gates both day and night that they might destroy him;
> 25 but his disciples took him during the night and let him down through the wall, lowering *him* in a hamper.

After **considerable days** had elapsed and his Jewish opponents in Damascus continued to be bested by Saul, they **counseled to destroy him**, being as determined to wipe out the Christian heresy as were their comrades in Jerusalem. Accordingly, they were **also observing the gates** of the city **both day and night**, to seize him if he tried to escape. This plot **became known to Saul** and his friends, and **during the night**, they **let him down through** a window from a house built into **the wall, lowering *him* in a hamper**. This was a humiliating way to leave the great city, and Saul never forgot it, treasuring it ever after as an aid in his quest for humility. In 2 Cor. 11:32, Paul says this escape was "under King Aretas"—the Nabatean ethnarch who apparently had some jurisdiction in Damascus. Perhaps Saul had stirred up some Nabatean opposition during his sojourn there.

> ૐ ૐ ૐ ૐ ૐ
> 26 And when he had arrived in Jerusalem, he was trying to cling to the disciples, and they were all afraid of him, not believing that he was a disciple.
> 27 But Barnabas took hold of him and brought him to the apostles and described to them how he had seen the Lord on the way, and that He had spoken to him, and how at Damascus he had *spoken* boldly in the Name of Jesus.

IV. The Church Spreads to the Gentiles   Acts 9:26–31

> 28 And he was with them going in and going out in Jerusalem, *speaking* boldly in the Name of the Lord.
> 29 And he was speaking and debating with the Hellenistic *Jews*; but they were setting their hand to destroy him.
> 30 But when the brothers learned *of it*, they brought him down to Caesarea and sent him out to Tarsus.
> 31 The church therefore through the whole of Judea and Galilee and Samaria had peace, being built up; and going in the fear of the Lord and in the encouragement of the Holy Spirit, it was being multiplied.

When Saul **arrived in Jerusalem** and **was trying to cling to the disciples**, seeking to join them for their Christian Eucharists, they would have none of it. Most of them had not heard of his work in Damascus and still **were afraid of him**. They remembered only too well his persecution when last he was in the city. Was his desire to join them some new scheme to entrap them?

Barnabas had learned of **how** Saul **had seen the Lord on the way** to Damascus and how while there **he had *spoken* boldly in the Name of Jesus**. He believed that his conversion was genuine, and he **took hold of him and brought him to the apostles**, namely Peter and James (Gal. 1:18–19). Barnabas sponsored Saul, relating all he had heard about him. They believed Barnabas, since he was a prophet and a man of credibility, and this apostolic testimony swayed the others. Saul **was with them, going in and going out in Jerusalem** (that is, mixing with them freely), *speaking* **boldly in the Name of the Lord** there as he had in Damascus.

As he **was debating with the Hellenistic *Jews*** in the synagogues (probably in the same synagogue Stephen had debated in), the Jews there began to plot against him as had his foes in Damascus. **The brothers learned *of it*** and decided to send him home. Wherever Saul was, people were trying to **destroy him**! After fifteen days

(Gal. 1:18), they **brought him down to** the seaport of **Caesarea and sent him to Tarsus,** to the safety of his family.

After Saul's departure, the **church through the whole of Judea and Galilee and Samaria had peace** as the persecution subsided. The result was that it was **being built up** and continued to **be multiplied** by God. This expansion is described as them going forward **in the fear of the Lord and in the encouragement of the Holy Spirit**. They continued in Jewish piety as the true Israel, enjoying the encouragement and joy given by the Spirit of God. These were no heretics (as their foes alleged), but truly pious Jews.

We note that (in the best manuscripts) the word *church* here is singular, even though it refers to churches or communities in various cities. This witnesses to the unity of all the believers in Christ—though they were scattered throughout many cities, they were still one single Church, one brotherhood, one family.

§IV.2. Peter Preaches to the Gentiles

St. Luke begins his story of Peter preaching to the Gentiles by describing the providential circumstances that led to it. That is, he narrates how Peter was healing a paralytic at Lydda, then raising a woman from the dead in Joppa, showing by these two stories how Peter was led by God to be at Joppa and then at Caesarea. Peter's acceptance of the Gentiles at Caesarea was therefore not his idea, but part of God's leading.

Peter at Lydda

> 32 Now it happened that as Peter was passing through all those *regions*, he came down also to the saints dwelling at Lydda.
> 33 And there he found a certain man named Aeneas, who had been lying down on a pallet eight years, who was paralyzed.
> 34 And Peter said to him, "Aeneas, Jesus Christ

IV. The Church Spreads to the Gentiles   Acts 9:36–43

> cures you; arise and make your *bed*." And immediately he arose.
> 35 And all those dwelling at Lydda and Sharon saw him and turned to the Lord.

After Peter's return to Jerusalem (8:25), he set out on a preaching tour, passing through all Judea, Galilee, and Samaria. He **came down also to the saints dwelling at Lydda** (the Old Testament town of Lod), a town about ten miles from the coast, northwest of Jerusalem. It was probably evangelized by Philip on his way from Azotus to Caesarea (8:40). One of the believers there was **a certain man named Aeneas, who had been lying down on a pallet eight years**, for he **was paralyzed**. As Peter heals the man, he ascribes the power to Jesus—it is **Jesus Christ** who cures him, Jesus who does His works through the Church, His Body. Aeneas is told to **arise** and **make** his bed. He may put his pallet away now, for he will no longer need it.

All those dwelling at Lydda saw Aeneas as he walked among them, and heard the news of how the paralyzed man had been restored—as did those in **Sharon**, the surrounding coastal plain. Not surprisingly, they **turned to the Lord** and were received into the Church. Peter began his journey to the Gentiles of Caesarea in the fullness of Christ's blessing, being guided by Him every step of the way.

Peter at Joppa

> 36 Now in Joppa there was a certain disciple named Tabitha (which interpreted means "Gazelle"); this one was full of good works and almsgiving which she was doing.
> 37 And it happened in those days that this one became sick and died; and having washed her, they laid her in an upper room.

> 38 And since Lydda was near Joppa, the disciples, having heard that Peter was in it, sent two men to him, urging him, "Do not delay to come to us."
>
> 39 And Peter arose and went with them. And when he had arrived, they brought him into the upper room; and all the widows stood beside him weeping, and showing off all the shirts and garments that Gazelle was making while she was with them.
>
> 40 But Peter cast them all outside and fell on *his* knees and prayed. And turning to the body, he said, "Tabitha, arise." And she opened her eyes, and when she saw Peter, she sat up.
>
> 41 And he gave her his hand and raised her up; and calling the saints and widows, he presented her alive.
>
> 42 And it became known throughout the whole of Joppa, and many believed on the Lord.
>
> 43 And it happened that he remained considerable days in Joppa with a certain Simon, a tanner.

It was while Peter was at Lydda that a woman in nearby Joppa **became sick and died**. Her name was **Tabitha** (Luke translates it as meaning **Gazelle**—in Greek, Dorcas). She **was full of good works and almsgiving**, for she would make shirts and outer garments which she gave to the poor and the widows as part of her church visitation. The pious women of the church **washed** her body as was customary and **laid her in an upper room**. Normally burial would have followed immediately, but **since Lydda,** where Peter was staying, **was near Joppa** (a mere three-hour foot journey), **the disciples** decided to ask Peter if he would come to raise her. They **sent two men to him, urging him** insistently, "**Do not delay to come to us.**" Let Peter please come to them that same day, not waiting until tomorrow before setting out, for if he was unwilling, the burial must follow quickly.

IV. The Church Spreads to the Gentiles   Acts 9:36–43

Peter obliged them, walking the three hours to Joppa, and arrived at the house where the dead woman lay. **They brought him into the upper room**, where **all the widows** who were recipients of Tabitha's charity **stood beside him, weeping and showing off all** the clothing that their Gazelle (Dorcas, as they would have called her) had made for them. ("She was so kind—she made this shirt here, this very one!")

Peter wanted quiet to pray, and so he **cast all** those weeping and wailing **outside and fell on *his* knees and prayed**. This was fervent prayer indeed, for the usual posture for prayer was standing, and one only prayed on one's knees in times of great emotion (compare Luke 22:41). Being a Hebrew, Peter used the Aramaic form of her name, saying to her, **"Tabitha, arise."** Christ was with His apostle in Joppa as He had been in Lydda, and **she opened her eyes, and when she saw Peter, she sat up** in surprise. This miracle **became known throughout the whole of Joppa, and many believed on the Lord**. This led to Peter staying for **considerable days** there, lodging with **a certain Simon, a tanner**.

We note in passing Luke's eye for detail and his interest in people: He notes that Saul stayed with Judas (9:11), that Peter stayed with Simon, a tanner by trade (9:43), and that Paul and company stayed with Philip and his daughters (21:8–9) and then with Mnason of Cyprus (21:16). Hospitality is no small gift, and Luke mentions by name those who provided it.

Peter Comes to the Gentiles at Caesarea

The story of how the first Gentiles were received into the Church on equal terms with the Jews is so important that all the miraculous details are repeated twice (10:1–6 and 30–32; 10:9–16 and 11:5–14). By receiving the Gentiles as full members of the Church without requiring that they be circumcised, the Church was making an effective break with Judaism, and with centuries of tradition going back to Abraham. Up until then, the Christian movement could have been considered just another Jewish sect; now it was apparent that it was something entirely different. The divine credentials of

Judaism were established. If the Church was going to define herself as different from Judaism, it was crucial that she establish her own credentials now too—thus the importance of demonstrating that this move had the divine approval.

> 🙠 🙠 🙠 🙠 🙠
>
> **10** 1 Now there was a certain man in Caesarea named Cornelius, a centurion of a cohort, the *one* called *the* Italian *cohort*,
> 2 pious and fearing God with all his house, doing much almsgiving to the people, and beseeching God continually.
> 3 He plainly saw in a vision, around about the ninth hour of the day, an angel of God coming in to him and saying to him, "Cornelius!"
> 4 And staring at him, and becoming afraid, he said, "What is it, lord?" And he said to him, "Your prayers and almsgiving have gone up for a memorial before God.
> 5 "And now send men to Joppa, and send for a certain Simon, who is called Peter;
> 6 "this *one* is lodging with a certain Simon, a tanner, whose house is by the sea."
> 7 And when the angel who was speaking to him had departed, he called two of his house-*slaves* and a pious soldier of those who were attached to him,
> 8 and after he had explained everything to them, he sent them into Joppa.

The story begins with the divine initiative. Peter had providentially been brought to Joppa (9:32–43), and **in Caesarea**, a largely Gentile town to the north, there was **a certain man named Cornelius**. He was **a centurion** of the **Italian** *cohort*, an auxiliary cohort, like the one stationed in Palestine, normally consisting of a

IV. The Church Spreads to the Gentiles   Acts 10:9–23a

thousand men. (The name *Italian* means simply that originally the cohort consisted of Italian citizens; by this time, however, it consisted of provincials, not citizens.) It is possible that Cornelius was retired from active service.

Whatever his military status, he had excellent religious credentials (for a Gentile). He was **pious and feared God with all his house**. That is, he was a "God-fearer," a Gentile who kept all the Jewish Law but had not taken the step of circumcision so as to become a Jew. Moreover, he did **much almsgiving to the people** of Israel and spent his time **beseeching God continually**, observing the daily times for prayer.

Around about the ninth hour of the day, one of the set hours for prayer, as Cornelius was praying, he **plainly saw in a vision an angel of God coming in to him and saying to him, "Cornelius!"** (Luke stresses that he **plainly** saw this—this was no dream.) His immediate reaction was one of terror (the word rendered *afraid* is the Greek *emphobos*, "terrified," a stronger word than *phobos*, the usual word for fear). The angel assured him that he had not come for judgment, but rather for reward.

Using strongly sacrificial language, the angel informed him that his **prayers and almsgiving** had **gone up for a memorial before God** (compare Lev. 2:2 LXX). God accepted this sacrifice, and now gave him this in return: he should **send men to Joppa and send for a certain Simon, who is called Peter**. It was understood that Peter would declare God's prophetic Word to Cornelius, whereby he would be blessed. Cornelus obeyed, sending **two of his house-slaves and a pious soldier** to protect them on the way (by **pious** is meant one who was a God-fearer like Cornelius). Since the angel appeared at the ninth hour (that is, 3:00 P.M.), they would have left first thing the next morning, Joppa being thirty miles to the south.

༃ ༃ ༃ ༃ ༃

9   And on the next day, as those who were journeying *drew* near to the city, Peter went up onto the housetop to pray about the sixth hour.

10 And he became hungry and was wanting to eat; but while they were preparing *the meal*, an ecstasy came upon him

11 and he observes the heaven opened, and a certain vessel like a great sheet coming down, let down by four corners upon the earth,

12 in which were all quadrupeds and reptiles of the earth and birds of the heaven.

13 And a voice came to him, "Arise, Peter, slaughter and eat!"

14 But Peter said, "Certainly not, Lord, for I have never eaten anything common or unclean."

15 And a voice *came* to him again a second *time*, "What God has cleansed, you *yourself* are not to *consider* common."

16 And this happened three *times*, and immediately the vessel was taken up into the heaven.

17 Now while Peter was perplexed in himself as to what the vision which he had seen might be, behold! the two men sent by Cornelius, having asked *the way* for Simon's house, stood at the gate;

18 and calling out, they were inquiring whether Simon, the one called Peter, was lodging there.

19 And while Peter was pondering about the vision, the Spirit said to him, "Behold, three men are seeking you.

20 "But arise, go down and go with them without disputing, for I *Myself* have sent them."

21 And Peter went down to the men and said, "Behold, I *myself* am *the one* you are seeking; for what reason have you come?"

22 And they said, "Cornelius, a centurion, a righteous and God-fearing man, witnessed to by the whole nation of the Jews, was *divinely*

IV. The Church Spreads to the Gentiles — Acts 10:9–23a

> directed by a holy angel to send for you *to come* to his house and hear words from you."
> 23 And therefore he called them in and lodged them.

As Cornelius's men were approaching the Jewish house of Simon the tanner in Joppa, God was preparing Peter to receive them. Jews would never lodge in the house of a Gentile or eat with them, considering them to be unclean. In order to welcome these men and accede to their request to go and lodge with Cornelius, Peter needed to have his Jewish conditioning overcome.

About **the sixth hour** (that is, noon), **Peter went up onto the housetop to pray**, probably keeping the customary time for noon prayer. The housetops of such homes were flat places where one could rest or pray. They were reached by stairs outside the house, and often covered by an awning as protection from the heat.

During this time, **an ecstasy** or trance (Gr. *ekstasis*) **came upon him**. Since he had become **hungry** while waiting for the meal **and was wanting to eat**, the vision God used took the form of food.

In this vision, he **observes the heaven opened, and a certain vessel like a great sheet coming down, let down by four corners upon the earth**. When the sheet touched the earth and the four corners were lowered too, Peter saw that the bundle contained **all quadrupeds and reptiles of the earth and birds of the heaven**, clean and unclean creatures all mixed in together, as in some horrible Gentile food bazaar. **A voice came to him,** saying, **"Arise, Peter, slaughter and eat!"** That is, the Voice was suggesting that he kill and eat whatever he found there, regardless of Jewish food laws prohibiting the eating of unclean animals and birds.

Was this a test to see if he would obey even when hungry? If so, he would not fail. Like a good Jew, Peter instinctively answered, **"Certainly not, Lord, for I have never eaten anything common** or defiled (Gr. *koinos*) **or unclean."** To his surprise, the Voice does not commend him for this, but reproves him, saying, **"What God has cleansed, you *yourself* are not to *consider* common** (Gr. *koinos*)."

To confirm this as God's will, **this happened three *times*** before the **vessel was taken up into the heaven** from whence it came.

What did the vision mean? How had God cleansed what was previously unclean? And why was Peter being told this now? Were his hosts going to offer him unclean food for the noon meal? As if in answer to these questions, **the men sent by Cornelius stood at the gate** and began **calling out, inquiring whether Simon, the one called Peter, was lodging there**. (The suddenness of their appearance is indicated by **behold!**) They were obviously Gentiles. Peter's initial apprehension was overcome as **the Spirit said to him, "Behold, three men are seeking you. But arise, go down and go with them without disputing, for I *Myself* have sent them."** This inner voice was confirmed as being truly that of the Spirit when Peter went down by the outer stairs and found there were indeed **three men** seeking him. This was further confirmed by their tale of Cornelius receiving an angelic visitation that mentioned Peter by name and gave his location. Peter therefore welcomed them in and **lodged *them*** in the same house as himself.

The providential arrival of the men had revealed to Peter the meaning of his vision. The Jewish food laws were not ends in themselves, as if the prohibited foods could actually defile a person spiritually (see Rom. 14:14). Rather, these food laws were primarily aimed at forbidding social intercourse with pagans and keeping Israel separate from its Gentile neighbors (for such mixing usually took place over meals, and all meals had a religious component). By declaring all food clean, God was clearing the way for all social intercourse, even between Jew and Gentile. Peter was being shown that he should not call anyone common or unclean (v. 28)—even Gentiles like the ones at his gate.

The Holy Spirit Poured Out upon the Gentiles

> 23 And on the next day he arose and went out with them, and some of the brothers from Joppa went with him.

IV. The Church Spreads to the Gentiles   Acts 10:23b–33

> 24 And on the next day, he entered into Caesarea. Now Cornelius was expecting them, having called together all his relatives and his close friends.
> 25 And it happened that when Cornelius met him, he fell at his feet and worshipped.
> 26 But Peter raised him, saying, "Stand up, I *myself* also am a man."
> 27 And as he conversed with him, he entered, and finds many people assembled.
> 28 And he said to them, "You *yourselves* know how wanton it is for a Jewish man to join or come to a foreigner; and God has shown me that I should call no one common or unclean.
> 29 "For this reason I came when I was sent for without even objecting. And therefore I inquire for what reason you have sent for me."
> 30 And Cornelius said, "Four days ago to this hour, I was praying in my house at the ninth hour; and behold! a man stood before me in bright garb,
> 31 "and he says, 'Cornelius, your prayer has been heard and your almsgiving has been remembered before God.
> 32 "'Send therefore to Joppa and send for Simon, who is called Peter; he is lodging at the house of Simon, a tanner, by the sea.'
> 33 "Immediately therefore I sent for you, and you did well to arrive. Now therefore, we *ourselves* are all present before God to hear all that you have been commanded by the Lord."

After resting the night, Peter **arose and went out with** the three men back to Caesarea. Despite the vision, he still felt unsure about the whole affair, and so brought **some of the brothers from Joppa with him** (six in number, as we learn from 11:12; Peter evidently felt the need of support). Their trip was perhaps more leisurely, so that they had to find lodging that night someplace between Joppa and Caesarea, and it was not until **the next day** that Peter **entered into Caesarea**.

Cornelius was expecting them, and he **had called together all his relatives and his close friends** to hear what the Jewish prophet would say to them. The devout centurion hastened to welcome Peter, and as Peter stepped into his home, **he fell at his feet and worshipped**, offering obeisance as he would to a superior (compare Gen. 33:3). Peter, however, would have none of that. He **raised him** up, saying, "Stand up, I *myself* also am a man." The apostles, despite their authority, were determined to refer all things to Jesus Christ.

They **conversed** together while on the way to the large central room. Peter **entered** the room with his host and **finds many people assembled**—all of them Gentiles! (The historic present—**finds**—is used, and we can almost see Peter's surprise at finding such a large audience.) By way of introduction, Peter acknowledges that as **a Jewish man**, it was considered **wanton** to **join or come** visit **a foreigner**. He had come nonetheless, for **God** Himself had **shown** him that **no one** was to be considered **common** (that is, defiled) or **unclean**.

The words used by Peter here are very strong. The word rendered *wanton* is the Greek *athemitos*, meaning unlawful, forbidden, disgusting. It is the same word used in 1 Peter 4:3 to describe pagan idolatry. It might almost be translated "taboo." The word rendered *foreigner* is the Greek *allophulos* (literally, "another tribe"), and in a Jewish context it has a derogatory meaning of "pagan, heathen." It is used in 1 Samuel 14:19 to designate the uncircumcised Philistines. In bringing Peter into a roomful of Gentiles, God was overcoming the deepest and most ingrained of Jewish feelings.

In response to Peter's natural question of why they sent for him, Cornelius rehearses fully the story of the appearance of the angel four days before (by inclusive reckoning). Peter's arrival at the very **hour** at which the angel first appeared to Cornelius is considered by the centurion to be another providential sign that God has engineered their meeting. He politely thanks Peter for coming (literally, **you**

IV. The Church Spreads to the Gentiles   Acts 10:34–43

did well to arrive), and with open hearts, offers himself and the gathering as **present before God to hear** Peter's words.

> ॐ ॐ ॐ ॐ ॐ
>
> 34 And opening his mouth, Peter said, "In truth I grasp that there is no respect of persons with God,
>
> 35 "but in every nation the one who fears Him and works righteousness is acceptable to Him.
>
> 36 "*You know* the Word which He sent to the sons of Israel, preaching *the good news* of peace through Jesus Christ (this *One* is Lord of all)—
>
> 37 "you *yourselves* know the thing which happened through the whole of Judea, starting from Galilee, after the baptism which John heralded.
>
> 38 "*You know of* Jesus of Nazareth, how God anointed Him with the Holy Spirit and power, who went about doing good, and curing all who were overpowered by the devil, for God was with Him.
>
> 39 "And we *ourselves* are witnesses of all *the things* He did both in the region of the Jews and in Jerusalem, whom they also destroyed, hanging Him upon a tree.
>
> 40 "This One God raised on the third day, and gave Him to be revealed,
>
> 41 "not to all the people, but to witnesses who were preappointed by God, to us, who co-ate and co-drank with Him after He arose from the dead.
>
> 42 "And He ordered us to herald to the people and testify that this One is the One appointed by God *as* Judge of the living and the dead.

> 43 "Of this One all the prophets witness that through His Name everyone who believes in Him receives forgiveness of sins."

Faced with the fact that God has indeed evidently engineered the present situation, Peter confesses the truth he just lately has **grasped**—that **there is no respect of persons with God**, no partiality or favoritism. Until that hour he had thought (as all Jews did) that the prayers and good deeds of Gentiles would not be rewarded by God, but that He only accepted good deeds done by Jews. Now he sees that **in every nation the one who fears Him and works righteousness** (such as prayer and almsgiving) **is acceptable to Him** and might be saved.

Having confessed his recent inward revolution, Peter begins by telling them the story of Jesus' ministry. The Greek sentence structure of his sermon is rather awkward—a sign that Peter's Greek was not that good (or possibly that he spoke in Aramaic and was rather literally translated by someone present). The substance of the sermon concerned **the Word** or message God **sent** to His covenant people, **the sons of Israel, preaching peace** and forgiveness to them **through Jesus Christ**. (Peter adds parenthetically that **this** Jesus **is Lord of all**, exalted by God to sit at His right hand.)

Peter refers to events they surely already knew about, for although **starting from Galilee**, it spread **through the whole of Judea** (that is, all Palestine). In an important capital and military center like Caesarea, they knew of **Jesus of Nazareth, how God anointed Him with the Holy Spirit and power** at His baptism and how He **went about doing good.** The word translated *doing good* is the Greek *euergeteo*, cognate with the *euergetes*, the title used by kings and sometimes translated "benefactor" (Luke 22:25). Christ was a Benefactor to His people, dispensing divine favors and **curing all who were overpowered by the devil.**

Peter vouches for all these miracles, saying he and the other apostles are **witnesses of all *the things*** Jesus did. This Jesus the Jews in Jerusalem **destroyed, hanging Him upon a tree** and crucifying

IV. The Church Spreads to the Gentiles — Acts 10:44–48

Him. This is the same Jesus whom **God raised on the third day**. And God **gave Him to be revealed, not to all the people, but to witnesses who were preappointed** for this task—namely, to the apostles. That was why His Resurrection was not a matter of public knowledge. But the apostles were witnesses of His Resurrection even as they were of His public ministry.

And this was no fleeting glimpse of the Master, as if they could somehow have been mistaken. On the contrary, they **co-ate and co-drank with Him after He arose from the dead**, spending time with their risen Lord. (The verbs translated *co-eat* and *co-drink*—Gr. *sunesthio* and *sumpino*—indicate intimate fellowship.) Before His Ascension, Jesus **ordered** them to **herald to the people and testify** that He is **the one appointed by God *as* Judge of the living and the dead**—all will stand before Jesus of Nazareth on the Last Day to give an account of their lives and be judged by Him.

Let all take care, therefore, to become His disciples. For if anyone would **believe in Him**, he would **receive forgiveness of sins** through His Name (that is, by calling on His Name in baptism). This promise was sure and certain, for **all the prophets** of the Hebrew Scriptures **witness** to this.

ॐ ॐ ॐ ॐ ॐ

44 While Peter was yet speaking these words, the Holy Spirit fell upon all those hearing the Word.

45 And the faithful of the circumcision, as many as had come with Peter, were beside *themselves*, because the gift of the Holy Spirit had been poured out even upon the Gentiles.

46 For they were hearing them speaking with tongues and magnifying God. Then Peter answered,

47 "Can anyone refuse the water for these to be baptized who received the Holy Spirit as we *ourselves* also *did*?"

> **48 And he commanded them to be baptized in the Name of Jesus Christ. Then they asked him to remain on for some days.**

Peter had not yet finished his message. It is interesting to speculate whether or not he would have suggested they be baptized. Perhaps he would have dealt with them as with the Samaritans—baptizing them but not laying on hands for the gift of the Spirit. But God was not waiting for Peter's decision. Cornelius and his friends were accepting everything Peter was saying as he said it, and when Peter spoke of believing in Jesus (v. 43), they opened their hearts to receive Him.

It was then that **the Holy Spirit fell upon all those hearing the Word** as He once fell upon the apostles. The **faithful of the circumcision**, the Jews whom Peter had brought with him, **were beside *themselves*** with amazement, **for they were hearing** the Gentiles **speaking with tongues and magnifying God**. What else could this mean but that **the gift of the Holy Spirit had been poured out even upon the Gentiles**? This was the same work of Jesus He had done on Pentecost (Luke uses the same vocabulary to describe it also; on both occasions, those who heard it were "beside themselves"—2:12; 10:45).

Usually the gift of the Holy Spirit was given *after* baptism, through the laying on of hands. But Christ had responded to the Gentiles' faith by not waiting for them to be baptized, but giving them the gift of the Spirit immediately, even before baptism. This was to make it undeniably clear to Peter that the Gentiles were to be accepted as full members of the Church. What else could Peter do?

He asks his Jewish comrades the rhetorical question, **"Can anyone** here **refuse the water for these to be baptized?"** For they **received the Holy Spirit** just as the apostles once did. On his authority, then, **he commanded them to be baptized in the Name of Jesus Christ** (that is, with Christian baptism). And when they invited him to accept their hospitality and **remain on for some days**, he accepted. Normally a Jew would never lodge with a Gentile, but Christ was evidently tearing down the old barrier between Gentile and Jew.

IV. The Church Spreads to the Gentiles   Acts 11:1–18

§IV.3. Jerusalem Blesses the Gentile Mission

11 1 Now the apostles and the brothers throughout Judea heard that the Gentiles also had welcomed the Word of God.

2 And when Peter went up to Jerusalem, those who were circumcised disputed with him,

3 saying, "You entered *a house* having uncircumcised men and co-ate with them."

4 But Peter began and set forth to them successively, saying,

5 "I *myself* was in the city of Joppa praying; and in an ecstasy I saw a vision: a certain vessel coming down like a great sheet let down by four corners from the heaven; and it came to me,

6 "into which I stared. I was considering *it* and I saw the quadrupeds of the earth and the beasts and the reptiles and the birds of the heaven.

7 "And I also heard a voice saying to me, 'Arise, Peter, slaughter and eat.'

8 "But I said, 'Certainly not, Lord, for common or unclean *things* have never entered into my mouth.'

9 "But a voice from heaven answered a second time, 'What God has cleansed, you *yourself* are not to *consider* common.'

10 "And this happened three *times*, and everything was drawn up into the heaven.

11 "And behold, immediately three men stood at the house in which we were, having been sent to me from Caesarea.

12 "And the Spirit told me to go with them without disputing. And these six brothers

> also went with me, and we entered into the man's house.
> 13 "And he declared to us how he had seen the angel standing in his house and saying, 'Send to Joppa, and send for Simon who is called Peter;
> 14 "'and he will speak words to you by which you *yourself* will be saved, and all your house.'
> 15 "And as I began to speak, the Holy Spirit fell upon them, just as upon us also in the beginning.
> 16 "And I remembered the word of the Lord, how He was saying, 'John baptized with water, but you *yourselves* will be baptized in the Holy Spirit.'
> 17 "If God therefore gave to them the same gift as to us also, having believed on the Lord Jesus Christ, who was I that I could refuse God?"
> 18 And when they heard these *things*, they were quiet and glorified God, saying, "Then to the Gentiles also God has given the repentance to life."

News of Peter's bold baptism of a whole roomful of Gentiles had spread **throughout Judea**, and those in Jerusalem **disputed with him** when he **went up to Jerusalem**. They were scandalized that he **entered *a house*** having uncircumcised men and even **co-ate with them**, sharing intimate table fellowship. Besides, such un-Jewish behavior was sure to enrage their fellow Jews, and thus could jeopardize the credibility of the whole Christian movement.

Though Peter was the leader of the apostles, Christ's promise of infallible guidance was made to the Church as a whole, not to any one person. Accordingly, Peter was answerable to the Church and felt bound to justify his actions when he returned home.

In his reply, Peter does not rely upon his personal authority to sway them, but simply **sets forth to them successively** the events

IV. The Church Spreads to the Gentiles — Acts 11:1–18

that led up to the baptisms, leaving nothing out. Peter's account of his vision differs somewhat from the account given by Luke in 10:9–16 in that Peter's account contains certain vivid eyewitness touches absent from Luke's account. Thus Peter says the great sheet **came to me,** being let down right in front of him, and that he **stared** into it. Also, Peter does not simply say that he had never eaten anything common and unclean, but the more emphatic **common or unclean *things* have never entered into my mouth.** Peter also stresses that he was not alone in this matter, but that **six brothers also went with** him. (Luke's earlier account of 10:23 says only that "some brothers went with him"—Peter is at pains to stress the large number of them.)

Peter's ultimate defense is that this was not his decision, but Christ's. Before Peter had a chance to make any decision about the status of these Gentiles, and as he merely **began to speak, the Holy Spirit fell upon them, just as** He did upon the apostles **in the beginning**. It was God who decided these Gentiles should be given **the same gift** of the Spirit as soon as they inwardly **believed on the Lord Jesus Christ**. So, **who** was Peter that he **could refuse God?** The decision to include them fully was God's, not Peter's!

When those present **heard these *things*, they were quiet**, having nothing to say in reply. They could only **glorify God** for His unexpected graciousness, saying that, unlikely as it seemed, **to the Gentiles also God has given the repentance** that leads **to life** eternal. They would not have guessed that God would give the unclean Gentiles the opportunity to repent and receive His forgiveness, but so it was. The Church in Jerusalem thus gave its blessing to the practice of giving to Gentiles the fullness of Christian baptism.

❧ V ☙

THE CHURCH FOUNDED AT GENTILE ANTIOCH
(11:19—15:35)

§V.1. Jerusalem Blesses the Church at Antioch

The church at Antioch was significant, for it was not only the church that sent out Barnabas and Paul to spearhead the controversial mission to the Gentiles (13:1f), it was also the first church containing a high percentage of Gentile believers. It was, in fact, the prototype of the mixed Gentile-Jewish church that would soon come to predominate the Roman world. In blessing the work at Antioch, the mother church in Jerusalem was setting the direction the Christian movement would take for years to come.

> ☙ ☙ ☙ ☙ ☙
>
> 19 **Therefore those who were dispersed from the tribulation that happened because of Stephen went to Phoenicia and Cyprus and Antioch, speaking the Word to no one except to Jews alone.**
> 20 **But there were some of them, men of Cyprus and Cyrene, who came to Antioch and were speaking to the Greeks also, preaching** *the good news* **of the Lord Jesus.**
> 21 **And the hand of the Lord was with them, and a large number who believed turned to the Lord.**
> 22 **And the word was heard in the ears of the church in Jerusalem, and they sent out Barnabas to Antioch.**

> 23 Then when he arrived and had seen the grace of God, he rejoiced and was exhorting them all to remain resolute of heart to the Lord,
> 24 for he was a good man, and full of the Holy Spirit and faith. And a considerable crowd was added to the Lord.
> 25 And he left for Tarsus to seek out Saul;
> 26 and when he had found *him*, he brought *him* to Antioch. And it happened that for a whole year they were assembled with the church, and taught a considerable crowd. And in Antioch the disciples were first called "Christians."

The work in Antioch began with **those who were dispersed from the tribulation** and persecution **that happened because of Stephen** (see 8:1). The Jews of Jerusalem (mostly Hellenistic Jews) traveled afar to the coastal strip of **Phoenicia** north of Palestine, and even northwest from there to the island of **Cyprus**. They also went north from Phoenicia into pagan **Antioch**, the metropolis in Syria, where there was a large Jewish community. They confined themselves to **speaking the Word** of the Gospel **to no one except to** their fellow **Jews alone**.

Some of those who were scattered came from **Cyprus** and **Cyrene** (Cyrene being a city on the north coast of Africa). In the wake of Jerusalem's decision to accept Peter's baptisms of the Gentiles of Caesarea, they were speaking to the Greeks of Antioch as well as the Jews there. **The hand of the Lord was with them** (Luke uses this Old Testament phrase—compare Is. 66:14—to indicate the continuity of God's work under the Law and in the Gospel). **A large number** of the Gentiles of Antioch **turned to the Lord**.

Word of this new development **was heard in the ears of the church in Jerusalem, and they sent out Barnabas to Antioch** to investigate, even as they had sent out Peter and John to inspect the new development in Samaria (8:14). Barnabas was a man of sound reputation, and he had proven himself to be a man of vision when

V. The Church Founded at Gentile Antioch   Acts 11:19–26

he welcomed the newly converted Saul of Tarsus. He was also from Cyprus himself, like those who helped form the church in Antioch. He was therefore the perfect choice to judge this work also.

When he had seen **the grace of God** in the lives of these new believers and had judged them truly converted, he **rejoiced**, setting his apostolic seal upon this new development, and **was exhorting them all to remain resolute of heart to the Lord**. The "son of exhortation" (4:36) was true to his name. By the phrase *exhorting them*, Luke probably refers to prophetic words of encouragement, in which Barnabas urged the new converts to resist the temptations of the pagan world around them. Luke adds that **he was a good man, and full of the Holy Spirit and faith**, for it was only the wickedly suspicious and unspiritual who could fail to see in this new church the manifest grace of God.

The work at Antioch grew mightily, and **a considerable crowd was added to the Lord**. Barnabas discerned in this the need for another teacher like himself and immediately thought of Saul. Accordingly, he **left for Tarsus to seek out Saul**, whom he had left there (9:30). After he had **brought *him* to Antioch, for a whole year** he and Saul **were assembled with the church**, meeting with them and becoming part of their community. Together they **taught a considerable crowd**, and Saul gained a reputation for teaching and preaching.

St. Luke adds a final note, saying that **in Antioch the disciples** of Jesus **were first called "Christians."** The Greek for *Christian* is *Christianos*. It meant "partisan of Christ," just as the word *Herodianos* meant "partisan of Herod." The people of Antioch were infamous for their satiric wit, and it appears that the title *Christianos* was intended in a dismissive and derogatory way, rather like the modern title "Jesus freaks." The label caught on. The disciples of Jesus themselves, however, were not ashamed of the stigma of wearing their Master's Name, but gloried in it (1 Pet. 4:16). Luke mentions the origin of the title as connected with Antioch because by the time of his writing, the title was in universal use, and he means to show by this how the Antiochene model of a Gentile church is properly universal as well.

§V.2. Antioch Sends Aid to Judean Poor at Time of Persecution

> ৯৭ ৯৭ ৯৭ ৯৭ ৯৭
>
> 27 Now in these days, prophets came down from Jerusalem to Antioch.
> 28 And one of them named Agabus arose and was signifying through the Spirit that a great famine was about to occur in the whole world. (And this happened in the *time* of Claudius.)
> 29 And as any of the disciples had means, each of them appointed to send for the service of the brothers dwelling in Judea,
> 30 which they also did, sending *it* to the elders through the hand of Barnabas and Saul.

In further showing the validity of this new Jewish-Gentile church, Luke relates an example of charitable aid which that church sent. Jewish **prophets came down from Jerusalem to Antioch**, and **one of them named Agabus arose** to prophesy. He began **signifying through the Spirit that a great famine was about to occur in the whole world**—striking the poor brethren in Jerusalem also. (The universality of the famine is mentioned to show that the Church's concern is with the whole world.) Luke adds that **this** famine did indeed **happen in the *time* of** the Emperor **Claudius**, whose reign was from AD 41 to 54. The famine itself probably was that which began in Judea in around 44.

The church in Antioch, being truly one with their fellow believers in Jerusalem, decided to do something. **As any of the disciples** of Antioch **had means, each of them appointed to send** money to their Jewish **brothers dwelling in Judea**, for they knew they were impoverished and would feel the effects of the famine worse than others. The word rendered **service** is the Greek *diakonia* (cognate with *diakon*, "deacon"). It is the word usually used for such charitable work as that administered by the deacons (see 6:1). This work of gathering money began around AD 43, the plan being to **send**

V. The Church Founded at Gentile Antioch — Acts 12:1–5

the money **to the elders** of Judea **through the hand of Barnabas and Saul** (who possibly did not complete their mission until 45).

This important work not only demonstrated the spiritual unity of Antiochene Gentile with Judean Jew. It also proved that these Gentiles were truly a part of the original apostolic Church, an integral part of the commonwealth of Israel.

---

12 1 Now during that time Herod the king laid hands to mistreat some of those from the church.
2 And he killed James the brother of John with a sword.
3 And when he saw that it was pleasing to the Jews, he proceeded to take Peter also. Now *this* was *during* the days of Unleavened *Bread*.
4 And when he had taken hold of him, he put him in prison, delivering him to four squads of soldiers to guard him, intending after the Passover to bring him *before* the people.
5 Therefore Peter was kept in the prison, but prayer was being made fervently by the church to God about him.

St. Luke next relates the persecution of the churches in Judea that took place about this time. **Herod the king** (Herod Agrippa, grandson of Herod the Great) **laid hands to mistreat some of those from the church**, most probably the apostles in Jerusalem and other prominent Christians. His motivation was mainly political, for Jesus was considered by the authorities to be a risk to the political status quo (John 11:47–50), and His movement was considered a similar risk. Moreover, the recent decision of the Jerusalem church to ignore the distinction between Jew and Gentile (Acts 11:18) would have enraged the Jewish community in the city even more. Another wave of persecution therefore swept over the Church in Jerusalem (probably beginning in AD 42 or 43).

As part of this persecution, Herod had **James the brother of John** arrested and **killed with a sword**. Why James was specially chosen is not stated; perhaps an outspoken utterance of his provided the occasion. Afterward, **when** Herod **saw that** this **was pleasing to the Jews** (and therefore politically advantageous to him), **he proceeded to take Peter also,** imprisoning him perhaps in the Tower of Antonia, in the northwest corner of the Temple, where Roman troops were garrisoned. Peter was the leader of the movement, and doubtless Herod felt his removal would deal the movement a deathblow. The year was 44.

His arrest was ***during* the days of Unleavened *Bread***, the week following Passover. When the Paschal feast was over, Herod **intended to bring him *before* the people** for trial and execution. Perhaps Herod delayed because of the popular feeling that executions were incompatible with the sacred season.

Until then he was kept **in prison**, guarded by **four squads** (literally, four *quaternions*, squads of four men each), one squad for each of the four watches of the night. Two men from each squad stood guard outside the prison cell door, while another two guarded the prisoner in the cell, one chained to each of the prisoner's arms. Luke mentions the four squads to show that Peter was well guarded. Humanly speaking, rescue was impossible. But all was possible for the God of the Christians, and **prayer was being made fervently by the church to God about** Peter while he waited in prison.

༄ ༄ ༄ ༄ ༄

6 And when Herod was about to bring him forward, on that night Peter was sleeping between two soldiers, bound with two chains; and the guards before the door were keeping *watch over* the prison.

7 And behold! an angel of the Lord stood over *him*, and a light shone in the room; and he struck Peter's side and raised him, saying, "Arise quickly." And his chains fell off his hands.

V. The Church Founded at Gentile Antioch   Acts 12:6–11

> 8 And the angel said to him, "Gird *yourself* and put on your sandals." And he did thus. And he says to him, "Clothe yourself with your garment and follow me."
> 9 And he went out and was following *him*; and he did not know that what was happening through the angel was true, but thought he was seeing a vision.
> 10 And when they had passed the first guard and the second, they came upon the iron gate that leads into the city, which opened for them by itself; and they went out and went along one lane, and immediately the angel left him.
> 11 And when Peter came to himself, he said, "Now I know truly that the Lord has sent out His angel and taken me out from the hand of Herod and from all the expectation of the Jewish people."

In response to the church's prayer, God acted. As often is the case, He delayed until the last moment (compare the rescue of Israel from the Egyptians at the last moment; Ex. 14:10). On the night before Herod was about to bring Peter forward for execution, God sent His angel to bring His apostle to freedom. The account of the escape is replete with details only an eyewitness (namely Peter) could provide.

Luke stresses this escape was entirely the work of God by showing how Peter was entirely passive throughout. Indeed, so far from planning escape, **Peter was sleeping**, so that the **angel of the Lord** had to **strike Peter's side** to **raise him** from sleep. The angel's detailed instructions to Peter—**"Gird *yourself* and put on your sandals . . . clothe yourself with your** (outer) **garment and follow me"**—also show how passive Peter was in this matter, for he was not even dressed. Indeed, it was not until Peter and the angel had **passed the first guard and** then **the second** and **came upon the iron gate that leads into the city** that **Peter came to himself** and truly believed that he had not simply been **seeing** another **vision**.

139

(Up until that time, he had thought this was a vision like the one he had seen in 10:10–16.)

The supernatural nature of his escape is shown by the fact that the guards knew nothing of what was happening, that Peter's **chains fell off his hands,** and that the iron gate **opened for them by itself**. Luke means his Roman audience to realize God is with the Christians, so they would be wise not to persecute them.

> ꙮ ꙮ ꙮ ꙮ ꙮ
>
> 12 And when he knew *this*, he came upon the house of Mary, the mother of John who was also called Mark, where considerable *numbers* were gathered together and were praying.
> 13 And when he knocked at the door of the gate, a servant-girl named Rhoda came up to listen;
> 14 and when she recognized Peter's voice, because of her joy she did not open the gate, but ran in and declared that Peter was standing before the gate.
> 15 And they said to her, "You are raving!" But she was insisting that *it* was thus. And they were saying, "It is his angel."
> 16 And Peter continued knocking; and when they had opened *the gate*, they saw him and were beside themselves.
> 17 And motioning to them with his hand to be silent, he described to them how the Lord had led him from the prison. And he said, "Declare these *things* to James and the brothers." And he departed and went to another place.

When Peter realized his escape was real, he went to **the house of Mary, the mother of John who was also called Mark**. This was a large and wealthy house, used as a gathering place for the local Christians, and was probably the place where Jesus had gathered

V. The Church Founded at Gentile Antioch   Acts 12:12–17

with His disciples for the Last Supper. (If this is so, it explains the ancient tradition that the young man who followed the apostles to the Garden of Gethsemane and then fled away from there naked was John Mark himself; see Mark 14:15, 51–52.)

Luke narrates Peter's arrival there for maximum humorous effect, showing also that the Jerusalem Christians were not the ones responsible for the jailbreak. They were so far from planning Peter's escape, they would scarcely believe he had escaped even when he stood knocking at the door!

The church there was still **praying** for Peter and his release **when he knocked at the door of the gate. A servant-girl named Rhoda came up to listen** to the sound, **and when she recognized Peter's voice**, she was so overcome with **joy** she forgot to let him in! (We note in passing Luke's concern for names; perhaps Rhoda was Luke's source for the story.) Instead, she **ran in** to the others and **declared that Peter was standing before the gate**. The assembled people refused to believe a mere servant-girl, however, and simply said, **"You are raving!"** When she continued **insisting that *it* was thus** (leaving poor Peter still speechless at the door), they responded, **"It is his angel."** Agreeing at length that she had seen something, they still could not believe it was Peter. One's guardian angel was evidently thought to resemble the person guarded—perhaps it was simply that she had seen a vision of Peter's angelic guardian.

The debate was resolved when **Peter continued knocking** and insisted on being let in. He chose to knock rather than to shout that it was he, for he was, after all, a wanted man. When **they saw him** standing there in the flesh, **they were beside themselves** with shock and joy and led him in. All the crowd began talking at once, so that Peter had to **motion to them with his hand to be silent**, not being able to make himself heard above the happy din. When he could be heard, **he described to them how the Lord had led him from the prison** through His angel. Herod's men would soon be searching for him, and his presence there was a danger to them. He could not linger, nor report to **James**, the leader of the Jerusalem church, or **the brothers**, his fellow elders. He therefore told them to **declare** to them that he had been freed by the Lord, and **departed**.

Where did he go from there? Luke will only say that it was **another place**; it sounds as if he is deliberately concealing the location. One tradition suggests Rome. It was well outside Herod's jurisdiction, and a wanted man could lose himself among its teeming crowds. If this is so, Peter went to Rome then not to preach or to do his apostolic work, but simply to lay low for a few weeks or months.

> 18 Now when day came, there was not a little commotion among the soldiers *as to* what then had become of Peter.
> 19 And when Herod had sought after *him* and had not found him, he investigated the guards and ordered them to be led away. And he went down from Judea to Caesarea and was spending *time there.*

St. Luke relates the aftermath in a few words. In a wonderful understatement, he says, **when day came, there was not a little commotion among the soldiers *as to* what had become of Peter.** Guards were responsible for their prisoners at the cost of their lives, and each would blame the others for Peter's escape. The squad guarding him, evidently made insensible by the hand of God, could not give a satisfactory answer for Peter's escape, but neither could any of the other guards keeping the gates. Each doubtless accused the other of having been bribed and of letting Peter go.

Herod, furious at losing his securely kept prey at the last moment, **sought after *him***, scouring the city, but could not find him. He must have concluded that the guards had indeed been bribed by the Christians, and so **ordered them to be led away** to execution. After this, **he went down from Judea** to his capital city and principal residence at **Caesarea**. Herod is an image of the world, mystified at the mighty acts of the God of the Christians, and powerless to oppose Him. As one who opposes God, he is also destined for the divine judgment.

V. The Church Founded at Gentile Antioch   Acts 12:20–24

> ꙮ ꙮ ꙮ ꙮ ꙮ
>
> 20 Now he was furious with the Tyrians and the Sidonians; and with the same-impulse they came to him, and having persuaded Blastus, who was over the king's bedchamber, they were asking for peace, because their region was fed by the royal *one*.
> 21 And on an appointed day Herod, having clothed himself in his royal garb, and having sat upon the judgment-seat, was *giving* a public address to them.
> 22 And the people were calling out, "The voice of a god and not a man!"
> 23 And immediately an angel of the Lord struck him because he did not give the glory to God, and having become worm-eaten, he died.
> 24 But the Word of the Lord continued to grow and be multiplied.

Luke concludes his story of Peter's escape by narrating the death of Herod, who slew John and was intent on slaying Peter, as a warning to those who would persecute the Church of God. The tale of Herod's end is told also by Josephus in his *Jewish Antiquities,* 19, 8.

The cities of Tyre and Sidon, though not part of Herod's kingdom, were part of a **region** that was **fed by the royal** region of Herod, since they relied upon Galilee for food supplies. Those cities had done something to offend Herod, and **he was furious** with them, withholding their supply of grain. As famine threatened the whole land, they decided to **ask for peace** and publicly apologize. They did this by first **having persuaded Blastus** (that is, having bribed Blastus), the official who **was over the king's bedchamber**, to grant them an audience.

The **appointed day** for this public reconciliation was that of the public shows in honor of Caesar (probably the emperor's birthday on August 1). On the second day of the celebrations, Herod **clothed**

143

himself in his royal garb, a garment of silver, which reflected the sun's rays with piercing brilliance. He **sat upon the judgment-seat**, the rostrum used for such public appearances, and began *giving* **a public address to them**, declaring himself appeased. Eager to flatter and please, **the people** began **calling out, "The voice of a god and not a man!"** Though a Jew who should have known better than to accept such blasphemous praises, he did not rebuke them, but proudly basked in the impious praise and **did not give the glory to God**.

Immediately, he was **struck** down in pain and collapsed, dying five days later. A medical diagnosis of a ruptured hydatid cyst has been offered as the physical cause, but Luke was able to discern a blow from the **angel of the Lord** as the ultimate source of Herod's demise. Luke mentions the detail that Herod had **become worm-eaten** to stress that this was truly the judgment of God.

By contrast to Herod's ignominious and disgusting death, the Church which he had thought to destroy continued to live and thrive. **The Word of the Lord continued to grow and be multiplied**, as the Church went from strength to strength despite Herod's persecution.

> ৯৽ ৯৽ ৯৽ ৯৽ ৯৽
> 25 And Barnabas and Saul returned from Jerusalem when they had fulfilled this service, taking with them John, who was also called Mark.

As a final note, Luke returns to the story of **Barnabas and Saul**. They had been sent from Antioch to Jerusalem (arriving with the Antiochene offerings perhaps in AD 45, after Herod's death), and then **returned from Jerusalem when they had fulfilled this service** (Gr. *diakonia*). They returned with **John, who was also called Mark**, son of the Mary whose house the Jerusalem Christians were using.

If this John was the same young man mentioned in Mark 14:51–52, he was evidently eager for apostolic adventure. It seems he accompanied Barnabas and Saul back to Antioch because they had persuaded him to join him in their work of preaching. (Or did

V. The Church Founded at Gentile Antioch Acts 13:1–3

he persuade *them* to allow him to join them?) He was soon to accompany them on their first missionary journey—though he would find this was more adventure than he had in mind (see Acts 13:5, 13).

§V.3. First Missionary Journey of Paul

A new section begins with the story of Paul's missionary journeys, as the main focus of Luke's narrative now shifts from Peter to Paul. Paul was to spearhead and embody the Church's mission to the Gentiles, and his presence in Rome at the end of Acts is a portent that the Church will take root in Rome and in all the Gentile world.

Departure

> **13** 1 Now there were in Antioch, in the church that was *there*, prophets and teachers: Barnabas, and Simeon who was called Niger, and Lucius the Cyrenian, and Manaen the intimate-friend of Herod the tetrarch, and Saul.
> 2 And while they were offering *worship* to the Lord and fasting, the Holy Spirit said, "Separate for Me Barnabas and Saul for the work to which I have called them."
> 3 Then, when they had fasted and prayed and laid *their* hands *on* them, they sent them out.

Paul's missionary journeys begin in Antioch, the center of Gentile Christianity at that time. In the church at **Antioch**, there were a number of such **prophets and teachers**. The **prophets** were those who received words and insight from the Holy Spirit to share authoritatively with the Church so that all might discern the will of God. The **teachers** were men responsible for transmitting the authoritative teaching of the Church to its members. Like the rabbis of Palestine, the teachers also carried a measure of authority, so that the offices of teacher and ruler (or shepherd) often tended to overlap (see Eph. 4:11; 1 Tim. 2:12; 5:17).

Their presence is mentioned here by St. Luke to show Antioch is able to bless the Gentile mission of Barnabas and Paul with prophetic authority, and to spread its divine teaching throughout the world. Some may have thought the Gentile mission involved a repudiation of the Jewish inheritance, but the presence of such men in Antioch blessing the mission showed that this mission was truly the will of God.

The church at Antioch was a truly international body, consisting of believers from many lands. The Cypriot **Barnabas** comes first in the list of prophets and teachers, since it was he who first came from Jerusalem to inspect and bless the church there at the beginning (11:22–23). Then comes **Simeon who was called Niger** (or "the Black"), who possibly came from Africa. **Lucius the Cyrenian** is probably one of the original founders of the Antiochene church mentioned in 11:20. **Manaen** is described as **the intimate-friend of Herod the tetrarch** in Palestine. The word rendered here *intimate-friend* is the Greek *suntrophos*—literally "co-fed," someone brought up with another from childhood. It is sometimes used to indicate a foster brother. It is possible that he was a friend of Chuza, Herod's steward mentioned in Luke 8:3. Lastly, **Saul** is mentioned, whom Barnabas fetched from his home in Tarsus (11:25).

It was during the regular eucharistic worship that God spoke to the church there. (The word translated **offering** *worship* is the Greek *leitourgeo*, used in the Greek Septuagint to indicate the formal ministry of the priests; compare Ex. 28:35 LXX.) This worship was accompanied that day by a special time of **fasting**, doubtless because the church was seeking to know God's will from the prophets there regarding whether or not to send out Barnabas and Saul on their missionary journey at that time. God responded through one of the prophets there, as **the Holy Spirit** told them to **separate for** Him **Barnabas and Saul for the work to which** He had already **called them.**

It would seem that Barnabas and Saul believed this was God's will for them, Saul especially having been already told by Christ that

V. The Church Founded at Gentile Antioch — Acts 13:4–12

he was to go to the Gentiles (22:21; 26:17–18). This special time of prayer and fasting was to confirm that this was the appointed time for such a mission. The Church there obeyed this prophetic word. They **fasted and prayed** again for the missionaries (at a later date, after having made the necessary travel arrangements) and **laid *their* hands *on* them**, commissioning them and authorizing their mission. The work of Barnabas and Saul therefore was no private endeavor, but represented the will of the entire Antiochene church. Since all was done in obedience to the prophetic word, they were **sent out** not just by men, but also **by the Holy Spirit** (v. 4).

Cyprus

> 4 Therefore, being sent out by the Holy Spirit, they went down to Seleucia, and from there they sailed to Cyprus.
> 5 And when they were in Salamis, they were proclaiming the Word of God in the synagogues of the Jews; and they also had John *as* their attendant.
> 6 And when they had gone through the whole island as far as Paphos, they found a certain man, a magus, a Jewish false-prophet whose name was Bar-Jesus,
> 7 who was with the proconsul, Sergius Paulus, a man of insight. This one called Barnabas and Saul to *himself* and sought to hear the Word of God.
> 8 But Elymas the magus was withstanding them (for thus his name is translated), seeking to turn the proconsul away from the Faith.
> 9 But Saul, who was also *called* Paul, having been filled with the Holy Spirit, stared at him,
> 10 and said, "You who are full of all guile and crime, you son of the devil, you enemy of all

> righteousness, will you not cease to *make* crooked the straight ways of the Lord?
> 11 "And now behold! the hand of the Lord *is* upon you, and you will be blind and not see the sun for a time." And immediately a mistiness and a darkness fell upon him, and he went around seeking those who would lead him by the hand.
> 12 Then the proconsul, having seen what had happened, believed, being thunderstruck at the teaching of the Lord.

The missionaries **went down to Seleucia**, a town that served as the port for Antioch, just sixteen miles away. They made first for **Cyprus**, where Barnabas was born (4:36) and where others in Antioch also had roots (11:20). They arrived in Salamis, a Greek city on the east coast of the island, probably because it had a large Jewish settlement with not just one but several **synagogues**. This was the obvious place to start, because they could expect a welcome—and a hearing—from their fellow Jews. They probably also hoped the God-fearers of the synagogues would be especially receptive to their message.

In all this work, **they also had John** Mark *as* **their attendant**. As mentioned above, this young man seemed eager for spiritual adventure. It is possible that he asked to go with them, especially since Barnabas was his cousin (Col. 4:10).

They traveled westward across the island **as far as Paphos**, the capital city under Roman administration. There they soon **found a certain man, a magus**. By describing him as a **magus**, Luke identifies him as a cheap charlatan, a religious huckster (see comments on 8:9f). Luke further describes him as **a Jewish false-prophet**, someone who claimed a spiritual authority and a role he did not truly possess. His name was **Bar-Jesus** (i.e. son of Jesus, or *Yeshua*). This man was the local celebrity, just as Simon was in Samaria (8:9f). It would seem he gave himself the title **Elymas**—perhaps the Greek version of the Semitic word for "dream interpreter" (Aramaic

V. The Church Founded at Gentile Antioch   Acts 13:4–12

holoma). Luke explains that the title Elymas was the equivalent of "magus" (v. 8).

As a local celebrity, Bar-Jesus **was with the proconsul, Sergius Paulus**. It is doubtful that he was part of the proconsul's staff. Rather, the Jewish self-promoter seems to have attached himself to the proconsul as the local Roman authority, hoping thereby to increase his own popularity. The proconsul **called Barnabas and Saul to *himself* to hear the Word of God** they were preaching in his territory. Though motivated by a desire to learn the truth (that seems to be why Luke lauds him as **a man of insight**), no doubt he also wanted to discover if the message of these two foreigners was in any way a threat to Rome.

Elymas, however, **was withstanding them**, contradicting their message and **seeking to turn the proconsul away from the Faith**. Perhaps the false-prophet saw in his two compatriots a threat to his own popularity on the island. **Saul** (who like many Jews had a second name, in this case **Paul**, used for dealings with the Gentile world; here possibly his Roman cognomen, Paulus) turned on Elymas, the true prophet rebuking the false one. **Having been** just **filled with the Holy Spirit** (compare such a fresh prophetic anointing in 4:8), he pronounced God's sentence on His adversary. Paul **stared at him**, as if allowing the divine judgment to take aim.

The divine sentence was swift. Paul denounced the liar as **full of all guile and crime**, as a **son of the devil**, as an **enemy of all righteousness**. Rhetorically he demanded to know when Elymas would **cease to *make* crooked the straight ways of the Lord**, opposing God. He then pronounced sentence upon him: **the hand of the Lord** was **upon** him in judgment, so that he would **be blind and not see the sun for a time**. No sooner had Paul spoken these words than God acted and a **mistiness and a darkness fell upon** Elymas, so that he was reduced to going about seeking someone to **lead him by the hand**. The false-prophet had claimed to see into the future, but now was unable to see anything!

The proconsul, not surprisingly, was **thunderstruck** by this demonstration of divine power. Luke identifies this miracle as **the teaching of the Lord**, since it confirmed the apostles' words to the

Acts 13:13–16 THE BOOK OF ACTS

proconsul. Accordingly, the Roman **believed** the apostles' word, though nothing is said about actual conversion or baptism. For Luke, it is enough to report that the proconsul approved of the apostolic message and did not disallow it as seditious or dangerous.

Pisidian Antioch

> 13 Now those around Paul put out *to sea* from Paphos and came to Perga of Pamphylia; and John left them and returned to Jerusalem.
> 14 But going on from Perga, they arrived at Pisidian Antioch, and on the Sabbath day they entered into the synagogue and sat.
> 15 And after the reading of the Law and the Prophets, the synagogue-rulers sent to them, saying, "Men, brothers, if there is among you any word of exhortation for the people, say *it*."
> 16 And Paul arose, and motioning with *his* hand, he said, "Men of Israel, and you who fear God, hear!

Paul now assumes center stage for the duration of Luke's narratives—in 13:7 it was "Barnabas and Saul"; now that the journey to Gentile towns is underway it becomes "Paul and Barnabas" (13:42). Barnabas remained the leader (being likened to Zeus, the head of the pantheon), but Paul was the main speaker (likened to Hermes, the god of oratory and inventor of speech; 14:12).

Leaving the island of Cyprus, **those around Paul** (i.e. Paul and his companions) **came to Perga of Pamphylia**, sailing north of Cyprus to the coast of Asia Minor. When they reached shore, **John** Mark **left them and returned to** his home in **Jerusalem**. Reasons for his giving up are not stated. It would seem he was not as ready for adventure as he had thought. Paul and Barnabas continued their journey, leaving the town of **Perga** (probably after landing at the port

V. The Church Founded at Gentile Antioch   Acts 13:17–25

town of Attalia twelve miles away), and entering **Pisidian Antioch**. This town (a different town from Antioch in Syria) was the civil and military center of the region. There was also a good Jewish population there, with their own synagogue, who could be relied upon to give them a hearing. This would include the Gentile "God-fearers" who attended the synagogue services. Accordingly, **on the Sabbath day they entered into the synagogue and sat** down in the seats reserved for distinguished guests to pray with their compatriots.

The synagogue service consisted of prayers and **the reading of the Law and the Prophets**. After this, it was customary for a distinguished rabbi or guest to expound on the meaning of the Scriptures that had been read. Paul and Barnabas were perhaps already known as leaders in the Christian movement, and the people would have been interested to hear their message firsthand. **The synagogue-rulers** (those responsible for assigning parts of the service to those present) **sent** a message **to them**, saying that if there was **among** them **any word of exhortation for the people**, they might now **say it**. Did either of them want to expound on the Scriptures? Paul did. He **arose** (a somewhat unusual posture; teaching was delivered while sitting in Palestine; compare Luke 4:20). His standing posture perhaps indicated the special importance of his message—he had come to announce news, not just to teach! **Motioning with *his* hand** for silence (were the people abuzz with excitement, wondering what the controversial visitors would say?), he called them to **hear** his news.

ॐ ॐ ॐ ॐ ॐ

17 "The God of this people Israel chose our fathers and exalted the people during their sojourn in the land of Egypt, and with a high arm He led them out from it.

18 "And for a time of about forty years He put up with them in the wilderness.

19 "And when He had brought down seven nations in the land of Canaan, He gave their land as an inheritance—*this took* about four hundred and fifty years.

> 20 "And after these *things* He gave *them* judges until Samuel the prophet.
> 21 "And then they asked for a king, and God gave them Saul son of Kish, a man from the tribe of Benjamin, *for* forty years.
> 22 "And after He had removed him, He raised up David for a king for them, to whom He also witnessed *and* said, 'I have found David the *son* of Jesse, a man after My heart, who will do all My will.'
> 23 "From the seed of this *one*, according to promise, God has brought to Israel a Savior, Jesus,
> 24 "after John had preheralded before the presence of His entry a baptism of repentance to all the people of Israel.
> 25 "And while John was fulfilling his course, he was saying, 'What do you suppose that I am? I *myself* am not *He*. But behold! He is coming after me, the sandals of whose feet I am not worthy to loose.'

His message consisted of a rehearsal of the mighty acts of God in Israel's history, placing Jesus within that divine history. God had given many gifts to His People: He **chose our fathers and exalted them during their sojourn in Egypt** by making them numerous, and **with a high arm** (that is, with a show of power) **He led them out from it** through the Red Sea. He patiently **put up with them in the wilderness**, caring for them despite their rebellion. **When He had brought down seven nations in the land of Canaan** by conquering them through Israel, **He gave their land as an inheritance** to His people. Thus He cared for His Israel for **about four hundred and fifty years** (counting the four hundred years in Egypt, the forty years in the wilderness, and ten years for the conquest of Canaan), so that His mercy stretched out from generation to generation.

Even then He continued to give gifts to His people. **He gave**

V. The Church Founded at Gentile Antioch — Acts 13:26–41

them **judges until Samuel the prophet**, and when they **asked for a king**, He **gave them Saul son of Kish**. (Paul cannot help adding that this first king was **from the tribe of Benjamin**—Paul's own tribe.) After blessing them for another **forty years** through Saul, **after He had removed him**, God **raised up David for a king for them**. God's gifts were continuous and unrelenting.

Jesus is presented as the crown of these gifts. He was not simply a controversial celebrity, as some may have supposed—He is the fulfillment of all salvation history. **According to** the **promise** God had made to David, **God brought to Israel** the Messianic **Savior** and deliverer, **Jesus**, David's descendant. It was in this way that David would **do all** God's **will**, for his **seed** would provide the final Messiah.

All of the Jews in the synagogue had heard of John and accepted him as a prophet (Luke 20:6). Paul builds on this belief, saying that John's movement was not an end in itself, but that John **preheralded** Jesus before He came through his **baptism of repentance**. John's baptismal ministry had no other goal than preparing Israel to receive Jesus. And John himself explicitly denied that he was anything more than the Forerunner of the Messiah, the One **the sandals of whose feet** he confessed he was **not worthy to loose**. If they accepted John, they should accept Jesus as well, for John pointed to Him.

ॐ ॐ ॐ ॐ ॐ

26 "Brothers, sons of Abraham's race, and those among you who fear God! To us the word of this salvation was sent out.

27 "For those who dwell in Jerusalem, and their rulers, not knowing this *One* nor the voices of the prophets which are read every Sabbath, fulfilled *these words* by judging *Him*.

28 "And though they found no cause for death, they asked Pilate that He be destroyed.

29 "And when they had finished all the things written about Him, having taken Him down from the tree, they laid Him in a tomb.

30 "But God raised Him from the dead;

31 "who was seen for many days by those who came up with Him from Galilee to Jerusalem, who now are His witnesses to the people.

32 "And we *ourselves* preach to you *the good news* of the promise made to the fathers,

33 "that these *things* God has fulfilled to us their children, in that He raised up Jesus, as it is also written in the second psalm, 'You *Yourself* are My Son; today I *Myself* have begotten You.'

34 "And that He raised Him from the dead, no longer about to return to decay, He has spoken thus: 'I will give You the holy faithful *blessings* of David.'

35 "Therefore He also says in another *psalm*, 'You will not give *over* Your holy one to see decay.'

36 "For David, after he had served the intention of God in his own generation, fell asleep, and was gathered to his fathers, and saw decay;

37 "but He whom God raised did not see decay.

38 "Therefore let it be known to you, brothers, that through this *One* forgiveness of sins is proclaimed to you,

39 "and through this *One* everyone who believes is justified from all things which you were not able to be justified through the Law of Moses.

40 "See therefore that the thing spoken of in the Prophets may not come upon *you*:

41 "'Behold, you despisers, and marvel and perish; for I *Myself* am working a work in your days, a work which you will never believe, though someone should describe *it* to you.'"

Paul now comes to his point, calling to his Jewish **brothers** and **those** Gentiles **among** them **who fear God** (the so-called "God-fearers"; see commentary on 10:1f). It was to them, as the **sons of**

V. The Church Founded at Gentile Antioch   Acts 13:26–41

Abraham, that **word of this salvation** in Jesus was now **sent out**. God had given them many gifts throughout their history and was giving them one more.

Recent events in **Jerusalem** bore this out. The Jewish **rulers** in the Sanhedrin did **not know** that Jesus was the Messiah, nor understand **the voices of the prophets** even though they were **read every Sabbath**. The prophets had predicted that Jesus would come as a lamb to the slaughter (e.g. Is. 53:7), but the rulers failed to see this. Ironically, they therefore **fulfilled** those very words **by judging** Jesus worthy of death and **asking Pilate that** Jesus **be destroyed. When they had finished all the things written about Him** in the prophets (perhaps the very readings read in the synagogue that day?), the rulers **laid Him in a tomb**, thinking that was the end of Him. **But God raised Him from the dead**, overturning their verdict and proving that Jesus was His Messiah.

This can be known, Paul says, because Jesus **was seen for many days by those who came up with Him from Galilee to Jerusalem** and who could thus recognize Him—including the Twelve who are even **now His witnesses to the people** of His resurrection. Paul and Barnabas are standing there (the **we** is emphatic) to announce that **the promise** God **made to** their **fathers** to send the Messiah He had now **fulfilled** to them, the father's **children**. For God had indeed **raised up Jesus** (i.e. brought Him to the public eye; compare such a use of "raised up" in v. 22) and given Him to Israel as King, manifesting Him publicly at His baptism.

That is what God promised in **the second psalm** when He said, **"You *Yourself* are My Son; today I *Myself* have begotten You."** The image of begetting in Psalm 2:7 was an image of divine adoption. It refers to the anointing of David's descendant as king, when the king was adopted as God's son and heir. This was fulfilled in Jesus, when the eternal Son was anointed by God at His baptism and manifested as messianic King (compare 10:38).

And that God **raised** the Messiah **from the dead, no longer to return to decay**, is proven by the prophecy in Isaiah 55:3, **"I will give You the holy faithful *blessings* of David"**—that is, "all that I promised to David, I will give to You." And what did God promise to David? That He would **not give *over*** His **holy one to see decay** (Ps. 16:10). David himself indeed **fell asleep** and **saw decay**, so that the fullness of that blessing was not fulfilled in him personally, but in his messianic descendant, for **He whom God raised**, Jesus, **did not see decay**.

Therefore, Paul concludes, let them all know that **through this very *One***, Jesus, **forgiveness of sins** was **proclaimed** and offered to Israel. Through **the Law of Moses** they could have earthly cleansing and justification, for the Law dealt with earthly purification (see Heb. 9:13). But through Jesus **everyone who believes** and becomes His disciple **is justified from all things**, receiving the heavenly and eternal acquittal, cleansing and freedom not before available. Let them take care to accept this word, **that the thing spoken of in the Prophets may not come upon** them.

Habakkuk had spoken of God **working a work** that they would **never believe** (Hab. 1:5). In his day, Habakkuk's words described the Chaldean invasion, saying that the scoffing **despisers** of truth would not repent of their hardheartedness even though Habakkuk was describing the invasion in advance and warning them of it. The prophets were replete with such warnings to repent. Let Paul's hearers take care lest the doom pronounced by Habakkuk on the scoffers fall on them today. Paul had **described** God's work in Jesus to them; let them see to it that they did not **marvel** at it as too miraculous and so **perish** along with the scoffers of all ages.

One final word might be added about Luke's redaction. Though of course Luke gives us only the gist of the sermon (it is quite unlikely Paul only spoke for about two and a half minutes, the length of time it takes to read vv. 16–41), he didn't have to record any of the sermon at all. He need only have said something like "and Paul preached Jesus to them" (compare 8:35). But Luke gave a fairly long sample of Paul's preaching, even as he gave similarly long samples of Peter's preaching (2:14f; 3:12f; 7:2f). It seems that part of his motivation is to let Theophilus and his Roman readers know the substance of the Christian message, so that they could see for themselves that it was not seditious, but only had to do with matters of the Jewish Law and its fulfillment (see 18:15), and eternal life.

V. The Church Founded at Gentile Antioch — Acts 13:42–52

❧ ❧ ❧ ❧ ❧

42 And as they were going out, they were urging them that these words be spoken to them the next Sabbath.

43 Now when the synagogue had broken up, many of the Jews and of the worshipping proselytes followed Paul and Barnabas, who, speaking to them, were persuading them to continue on in the grace of God.

44 And the coming Sabbath nearly all the city was assembled to hear the Word of God.

45 But when the Jews saw the crowds, they were filled with jealousy and were contradicting the things spoken by Paul, reviling.

46 And Paul and Barnabas *spoke* boldly and said, "It was necessary that the Word of God be spoken to you first; since you push it aside and judge yourselves not worthy of eternal life, behold! we turn to the Gentiles.

47 "For thus the Lord commanded us: 'I have put You for a light to the Gentiles, that You should be for salvation to the end of the earth.'"

48 And when the Gentiles heard *this*, they were rejoicing and glorifying the Word of the Lord; and as many believed as had been appointed to eternal life.

49 And the Word of the Lord was spreading through the whole region.

50 But the Jews incited the worshipping women of prominence and the leading *men* of the city; and they stirred up a persecution against Paul and Barnabas, and cast them out from their areas.

51 But they shook off the dust of their feet against them and came to Iconium.

> **52 And the disciples were being filled with joy and the Holy Spirit.**

As Paul and Barnabas **were going out** of the synagogue afterwards, the people there **were urging them** that they tell them more about this **the next Sabbath**. They were electrified by their message, and would not wait until next week to hear more. After **the synagogue** meeting **had broken up, many of the Jews and the worshipping proselytes** (i.e. Gentile converts to Judaism) **followed Paul and Barnabas** to their private lodging to hear more. We may imagine these times of instruction continued long into the night, as the apostles **were persuading them to continue on in the grace of God** by continuing to accept the Gospel with open hearts. By *the grace of God*, Luke means the Kingdom of God and eternal life, now freely poured out on any and all who would receive it. Such a mixed crowd of the receptive was a sign and image of the future Church, which would contain both Jew and Gentile.

When **the coming Sabbath** arrived, word had spread to all the Gentile population so that **nearly all the city was assembled to hear the Word of God. The Jews** of the synagogue had never seen such Gentile **crowds** openly excited about hearing their own words about Judaism. They were therefore **filled with jealousy** at the sight (especially so since they probably had their own misgivings about Paul's message) and began **contradicting the things spoken by Paul, reviling** him as one who was distorting the Scriptures and misrepresenting God. (The Greek *blasphemeo* can be used both of blasphemy when referring to God, and reviling when referring to men. I would suggest translating it as "revile," since Paul seems to be the focus of the passage—though rejecting and reviling Paul as a heretic also involves blasphemy against Jesus as a false Messiah, so that perhaps *blasphemeo* here includes a bit of both.)

Paul and Barnabas were not content to continue dialogue with men who blasphemed their beloved Lord. They ***spoke* boldly** in reply, rejecting their censure outright and repudiating their authority. It was **necessary** in God's providence and covenant **that the Word of God be spoken** to them **first**, since they were the Chosen

V. The Church Founded at Gentile Antioch   Acts 13:42–52

People, and the promises were made first of all to them. But if they were determined to **push it aside** and judge Paul and Barnabas as heretics, the apostles would not accept this. (Synagogues considered themselves competent to discipline Jews for such things.) By rejecting the apostles' words, the rulers had not judged *them*, but simply **judged** *themselves* **not worthy of** the **eternal life** the apostles were offering them.

Did these Jewish authorities think the apostles would accept the decisions of the synagogue about the Gospel? On the contrary—they would persevere in their work and **turn to the Gentiles**. They were following what **the Lord** had **commanded**, as witnessed to in Isaiah 42:6; 49:6—Messiah was to be **a light to the Gentiles**, and His **salvation** would extend **to the end of the earth**. In the prophecies of Isaiah, God had revealed that His Messianic Servant would not only enlighten and bless His own People, but would shine on the whole world. Those prophecies formed the marching orders and set the program for Paul and Barnabas. In beginning to focus more exclusively on the Gentiles, they were not being disloyal Jews, but simply fulfilling the ancient prophecies of their people's Scriptures.

When the Gentiles heard the apostles' determination to welcome them, they began **rejoicing and glorifying the Word of the Lord** by accepting it. And **as many believed as had been appointed to eternal life**. We note here that Paul's words are styled **the Word of God** (vv. 44, 46) and **the Word of the Lord** (vv. 48, 49). In the view of the Jews of Pisidian Antioch, the apostolic proclamations and interpretations of the Scriptures were simply their own opinions, the word of men. But for Luke and the Church, their message was nothing less than the Word of God, so that to reject it was not to reject merely the word of another man but that of God Himself (see Luke 10:16; 1 Thess. 2:13).

Luke's point about the Gentiles being **appointed to eternal life** has nothing to do with their individual predestination after the fashion of Calvin. Such appointment, whether for Jew or Gentile, was made on the basis of the individual's humble and open heart, not on the basis of an arbitrary decree outside of time, for God appointed that all who responded to His Christ would have eternal life and be conformed to the image of His Son (Rom. 8:29). Luke mentions that some of these Gentiles had been **appointed to eternal life** to show that God's choice of such humble men to be heirs of the age to come *now included Gentiles as well as Jews.*

With this success among the Gentiles of the city, **the Word of the Lord** began **spreading through the whole region**. This was intolerable to the jealous Jews, and they **incited the worshipping women of prominence** in the synagogue to get their husbands to use their influence with **the leading *men* of the city**, the official magistrates. The substance of the charges is not given; presumably the apostles were charged with being rabble-rousers and disturbers of the peace. **A persecution** was **stirred up** against them, and they were **cast out from their areas**.

Paul and Barnabas were not downcast, thinking this a defeat. As Christ had commanded in such situations (Luke 9:5), **they shook off the dust of their feet** for a witness **against them** on the Last Day and **came to Iconium**, ninety miles southeast of Pisidian Antioch, to proclaim the Word there. **The disciples** left behind also were not downcast, but continually **were being filled with joy and the Holy Spirit**—a sign of the Kingdom of God.

Iconium

> **14**1 And it happened in Iconium that together they entered into the synagogue of the Jews, and spoke thus that a great multitude believed, both of Jews and of Greeks.
> 2 But the Jews who disobeyed stirred up the souls of the Gentiles and embittered them against the brothers.
> 3 Therefore they spent considerable time *speaking* boldly, *relying* upon the Lord, who was witnessing to the Word of His grace, giving

V. The Church Founded at Gentile Antioch   Acts 14:1–7

> that signs and wonders occur through their hands.
> 4 But the multitude of the city was split; and some were with the Jews, and some with the apostles.
> 5 And when an attempt was made by both the Gentiles and the Jews with their rulers to abuse and stone them,
> 6 they having become aware *of it*, they fled-away to the cities of Lycaonia, Lystra, and Derbe, and the surrounding-country;
> 7 and there they were preaching *the good news*.

The apostles' experience at Iconium was similar. They **entered into the synagogue of the Jews** there to offer the Gospel first to their Jewish compatriots, as was their usual custom. So persuasive were they that a **great multitude believed, both of Jews and of Greeks**, the God-fearers attached to the synagogue. **The Jews** there **who disobeyed** God's call through the apostles were jealous of the newcomers' success, and they **stirred up the souls of the Gentiles and embittered them**. Like the Jews of Pisidian Antioch, they used their influence to convince the Gentile rulers of the city that the apostles were dangerous charlatans.

Despite the apostles' initial success, therefore, all of Iconium did not immediately receive their Word. Paul and Barnabas **spent considerable time *speaking* boldly**, striving to overcome the opposition and turn the tide, even working **signs and wonders**. As the apostles preached, the city became polarized into two mutually antagonistic camps, for **some were with the Jews, and some with the apostles**.

Tensions continued to escalate, and the Jewish opposition again grew deadly. **An attempt was made**, concocted by both **the Gentiles** who ruled the city and **the Jews with their rulers** in the synagogue, to resolve the city's division by getting rid of the troublesome pair. A lynch mob was arranged to **abuse and stone** the apostles, perhaps as they left their lodgings. The apostles **became aware of it**, however (through a sympathizer in the enemy camp?), and **they fled-away** from Iconium before the plot could be carried out, going to the cities of **Lystra and Derbe**, towns in the entirely pagan area of **Lycaonia**. Lystra was about eighteen miles southwest of Iconium, and Derbe just to the east of Lystra.

Among those who sided with the apostles, tradition records Thekla, a young woman influenced by Paul's preaching to devote herself entirely to Christ. Her story is told in an embellished second-century document, *The Acts of Paul*. She remains a great saint in the Church. Her feast day is September 24.

Lystra

> 8 And a certain man was sitting at Lystra, powerless in his feet, lame from his mother's womb, who had never walked.
>
> 9 This *one* heard Paul speaking, who, having stared at him, and having seen that he had faith to be saved,
>
> 10 said with a great voice, "Stand aright upon your feet!" And he leaped and was walking.
>
> 11 And when the crowds saw what Paul did, they raised their voice, saying in the Lycaonian *tongue*, "The gods have become like men and have come down to us!"
>
> 12 And they were calling Barnabas Zeus, and Paul Hermes, because he was the leader of the speech.
>
> 13 And the priest of Zeus Before-the-City brought bulls and wreaths to the gates and wanted to sacrifice with the crowds.
>
> 14 But when the apostles, Barnabas and Paul, heard of it, they tore their garments and leaped into the crowd, crying out
>
> 15 and saying, "Men, why are you doing these

V. The Church Founded at Gentile Antioch — Acts 14:8–18

> *things?* We *ourselves* also are men of the same nature as you, and preach *the Gospel* to you that you should turn from these useless *things* to a living God, who made the heaven and the earth and the sea and all things in them.
> 16 "And in the generations gone by He allowed all the nations to go their ways;
> 17 "And yet He did not leave Himself without witness, doing good and giving you rains from heaven and seasons of fruit-bearing, filling *you* with food and your hearts *with* gladness."
> 18 And saying these *things*, they with difficulty restrained the crowds from sacrificing to them.

Once the apostles had reached **Lystra**, they began speaking to the pagan crowds in the marketplace, possibly in Greek (the international language). Among the hearers was **a certain man,** a beggar who sat wherever crowds gathered, hoping for alms. He was **powerless in his feet, lame from his mother's womb**, so that he **never walked**. By the way he looked at Paul, the apostle could tell he was accepting his message and **had faith to be saved**. Led by the Spirit, St. Paul said to the man in a loud voice, **"Stand aright upon your feet!"** even though the cripple had never before done so. The lame man **leaped** up and began **walking** about, crying (we may think) with joy.

The effect on the multitude was immediate. They were primitive pagans, for whom the dividing line between gods and men was ill-drawn. They perhaps knew the Greek story of Philemon and Baucis, an elderly couple who welcomed the gods Zeus and Hermes when they came down to earth in the likeness of men and gave them hospitality when all others refused them. According to the story, this aged couple alone was spared for their act of hospitality, while the others who refused the gods were destroyed. The Lycaonians were not about to repeat the mistake and refuse hospitality again when **the gods became like men and came down** to them! For that was evidently who these two strangers were—how else could they perform such a divine work? **Barnabas** they identified as **Zeus**, the king of the gods (since Barnabas was apparently the leader), and **Paul** they identified as **Hermes**, the messenger of the gods, since Paul was **the leader of the speech**, the chief speaker.

News of the divine visitation spread like wildfire through the town, but because the locals were speaking excitedly **in the Lycaonian** *tongue*, the apostles had no idea what the excitement was about. Perhaps they were simply excited about the healing and about the Lord Jesus.

The priest of Zeus Before-the-City (that is, whose temple was outside the city) **brought bulls** adorned with woolen **wreaths to the gates** of the temple and wanted to sacrifice the bulls in honor of the newly arrived gods, Zeus and Hermes. **The crowds** present also were enthusiastic, and perhaps went to fetch the gods. **The apostles**, though not knowing the Lycaonian language, could see only too clearly from the adorned bulls what was going on, and, as good Jews, they were aghast. In horror at the impending catastrophe of idolatry, **they tore their garments and leaped into the crowd, crying out** in protest.

Their hasty and impassioned speech was a model of Jewish apologetic. They protested first of all that the Lycaonians should not do this—Barnabas and Paul were not gods at all, but **men of the same nature** as themselves. Their whole message to them was that they **should turn from these useless** *things* (that is, from pagan sacrifices to the gods) **to a living God**, the One who **made the heaven and the earth and the sea and all things in them**.

In the generations gone by He allowed all the nations to go their ways and indulge in such useless things. But no more. Now they must repent, turn from their old dead gods, and embrace the true and living God. They must not fear to do this, as if they were choosing a god they had never known, and thus being ungrateful to the gods who had cared for them. It was the true God who had really cared for them. And even though He allowed them to go their own

V. The Church Founded at Gentile Antioch   Acts 14:19–20

way, **He did not leave Himself without witness** that He was their true God and benefactor. For He **did good** to them, **giving** them **rains from heaven and seasons of fruit-bearing, filling** them with food and their **hearts *with* gladness**. Their bounty did not come from the pagan gods, but from the One God. He had always cared for them—let them turn to Him now! Despite such fervent pleas, it was only **with difficulty** that they **restrained the crowds from sacrificing to them**.

> ॐ ॐ ॐ ॐ ॐ
>
> 19 But Jews came from Antioch and Iconium, and having persuaded the crowds, they stoned Paul and dragged him outside the city, supposing him to be dead.
> 20 But while the disciples encircled him, he arose and entered into the city. And the next day he went out with Barnabas to Derbe.

That was not the end of the tale, however. **Jews came from Antioch and Iconium**, stalking the apostles, intent upon their harm. They **persuaded** the pagan **crowds** that the apostles were deceivers after all. (Luke means us to see the folly of the pagan Lycaonians, who so easily went from regarding the apostles as gods to regarding them as villains.) Their would-be devotees now **stoned Paul and dragged *him* outside the city, supposing him to be dead**, leaving him there and returning to town.

Those converted at Lystra did not so quickly abandon their apostle. The new **disciples encircled him**, perhaps grieving and thinking of honorable burial. But God was with His servant, and Paul **arose** with new strength and **entered into the city**. Though he did not actually die, he was still an image of the Church, able to arise as if from death, surviving all persecutions by the power of God. **The next day**, Paul **went with Barnabas to Derbe**, a journey of some sixty miles to the southeast—a long road for one so recently injured as Paul.

Return to Antioch

> ꙮ ꙮ ꙮ ꙮ ꙮ
>
> 21 And after they had preached *the Gospel* to that city and had made considerable disciples, they returned to Lystra and to Iconium and to Antioch,
> 22 establishing the souls of the disciples, exhorting *them* to remain in the Faith, and *saying*, "It is necessary for us to enter into the Kingdom of God through many tribulations."
> 23 And when they had ordained elders for them in every church, having prayed with fastings, they committed them to the Lord in whom they had believed.

After they had preached *the Gospel* in Derbe, the apostles did not proceed further east to Paul's native Cilicia. Instead, they decided to consolidate their gains by **returning to Lystra and to Iconium and to Antioch** of Pisidia. The tribulations and persecutions they had sustained perhaps made them worry for their new converts, and they wanted to encourage them to persevere. Despite the risk to themselves from revisiting places where they had so recently been attacked, they courageously retraced their steps. At each of the new Christian communities, they were **establishing the souls of the disciples**, steeling them for whatever trials might come, by **exhorting them to remain in the Faith** despite the certainty of persecution. The gist of their message was that it was inevitable they would **enter into the Kingdom of God** on the Last Day only **through many tribulations** and persecutions. Let them expect such trials, and not be taken unawares. These apostolic words to their new converts were to prove true for the entire Church throughout all ages.

Before the apostles **committed them to the Lord in whom they had** newly **believed** and left them to whatever trials might come, they **ordained elders** (Gr. *presbuteros*, "presbyters") **for them in every church**, having first **prayed with fastings**. The word

V. The Church Founded at Gentile Antioch   Acts 14:24–28

translated *ordained* is the Greek *cheirotoneo*, meaning originally "to stretch out the hand." It was used for the act of election, wherein a group chooses someone by a show of hands, and thus also means "to appoint or designate" (compare such a use in 2 Cor. 8:19). Here it is used for the act of installing someone in an office in conformity with Jewish customs for transmitting authority, where hands were laid on the candidate to bestow authority and blessing. The Church continues this practice in ordaining men as deacons, presbyters (or priests), and bishops.

It is significant that these ordinations form part of the earliest apostolic provisions for the local churches. Though not mentioned elsewhere in Acts, similar ordinations can be assumed to have taken place in other communities. Luke mentions it here to show that the churches formed as part of Paul's first missionary journey were fully formed churches, equal in function and dignity to the church in Antioch, which also had teachers (13:1). These were not defective Christian communities. The phenomenon of Gentile churches, begun in Antioch, was beginning to spread throughout the world.

We note in passing how quickly the church established an indigenous ministry for its newly formed missionary communities. There was no talk of the new converts not being ready to govern themselves, so that their churches should be ruled from afar, like so many colonies of Antioch or Jerusalem. Rather, the apostles trusted in the power of the Holy Spirit to sustain the new churches created by the Spirit's power and **committed them to the Lord**, believing that His grace was sufficient for them—and their newly ordained presbyters.

---

24 And having gone through Pisidia, they came into Pamphylia.
25 And having spoken the Word in Perga, they went down to Attalia;
26 and from there they sailed to Antioch, from which they had been delivered to the grace of God for the work that they had fulfilled.

> 27 And when they had arrived and assembled the church, they were announcing what God had done with them and how He had opened a door of faith to the Gentiles.
> 28 And they were spending not a little time with the disciples.

The progress through **Pisidia** and **Pamphylia** to the south, to **Perga** and the coastal town of **Attalia** presumably went without incident. From Attalia they **sailed to Antioch**, from which starting point they **had been delivered to the grace of God for the work that they had** indeed **fulfilled**. This delivering refers to their original blessing and commission, mentioned in 13:3. Luke mentions this here to show that all the apostles had done, even the formation of Gentile churches, had been according to God's will. These accomplishments were not those of the apostles, but of God.

That is why, after they **assembled the church** and **were announcing** to them all their adventures, they ascribed all to God. It was not a matter of what they had done for God, but rather of what **God had done with them**. The initiative belonged to God, not to Paul and Barnabas. That **a door of faith** and an opportunity to become God's children had **opened to the Gentiles** was entirely His doing. Those who would soon oppose the Gentile mission (see 15:1f) would be setting their faces against God Himself.

§V.4. Jerusalem Council Vindicates Gentile Mission

> **15**1 And some *men* came down from Judea and were teaching the brothers, "If you are not circumcised according to the custom of Moses, you are not able to be saved."
> 2 And when Paul and Barnabas had not a little strife and debate with them, they appointed that Paul and Barnabas and some others of

V. The Church Founded at Gentile Antioch   Acts 15:1–3

> them go up to Jerusalem to the apostles and elders about this debate.
> 3 Therefore, being sent forth by the church, they were going through both Phoenicia and Samaria, describing the turning of the Gentiles, and were bringing great joy to all the brothers.

After Paul and Barnabas's return to Antioch, **some *men* came down from Judea** and its center, Jerusalem. They spent a long time in Antioch and **were teaching the brothers** there, saying, **"If you are not circumcised according to the custom of Moses, you are not able to be saved."** In Galatians 2:4, Paul would later refer to them as "false-brothers," men who had "sneaked-in to spy out their freedom in Christ" in order to "enslave" them. That is, although these were confessing Christians, their ultimate allegiance was to the Law, not to Jesus, and in their minds, Jesus was subordinate to the Law. They could not conceive of anyone being saved apart from Judaism's Law, since (for them) the Jesus movement was simply another branch of Judaism. Although they had claimed to come to Antioch in order to fellowship with their brethren, they had actually come to see if it was true that these Gentiles were claiming to be true Christians while remaining uncircumcised. In Paul's eyes, these Judeans were like enemy spies sent on a reconnaissance mission, intent on overthrowing those into whose midst they came. They had not come to help their Antiochene brothers, but to judge them and change them.

Doubtless they heard with alarm the news of the Gentiles at Caesarea being allowed into the Church without circumcision (11:18) and hoped that it would prove the sole exception to their rule of all Christians first becoming Jews. The mission of the Antiochene church through Paul and Barnabas proved that the concept of Gentile Christians was spreading. In their minds, they had to take a stand and cut off this heretical innovation at its source.

Accordingly, once they had inveigled their way into the Antiochene church and gained credibility, they began teaching that Gentile Christians must be circumcised if they hoped to be saved on the

Last Day. Without this, they taught, Christ would certainly disown the uncircumcised disciples as pagans.

This teaching struck at the heart of Paul's ministry and his apostolic calling. He and Barnabas therefore **had not a little strife and debate with them**. (The word here rendered *strife* is the Gr. *stasis*, rendered as "riot" in Luke 23:19—quite a loud debate indeed!) This debate threatened to divide the whole Antiochene church, so the church there **appointed that Paul and Barnabas and some others** of their church **go up to Jerusalem** to get this debate resolved. Jerusalem was the center of the Jewish (and Christian) world, and their judgment would be sufficient to resolve everything. (Paul would later clarify that he went up to this synod not simply as an Antiochene delegate, as if he had no apostolic authority of his own, but also because he had a vision from Christ, telling him to go; Gal. 2:2.)

Luke records that as they traveled southward for the 250-mile journey through **both Phoenicia and Samaria**, their stories of **the turning of the Gentiles** to God brought **great joy to all the brothers** who heard it. This joy was a sign that their work was indeed of God, and would therefore be confirmed by the church in Jerusalem.

> ॐ ॐ ॐ ॐ ॐ
>
> 4 And having arrived in Jerusalem, they were welcomed by the church and the apostles and the elders, and they announced what God had done with them.
> 5 But some of the sect of the Pharisees who had believed rose up, saying, "It is necessary to circumcise them and to order them to keep the Law of Moses."
> 6 And the apostles and the elders were assembled to see about this word.

After they **arrived in Jerusalem, they were welcomed by the church** there and by **the apostles and elders** (not frozen out as innovators and heretics, as their enemies said they were), and they shared their story of **what God had done with them** on their first

V. The Church Founded at Gentile Antioch   Acts 15:7–12

missionary journey. (We note that Paul spoke of his results among the Gentiles not as his ideas but as what God had willed and accomplished.) This was immediately contradicted by **some of the sect of the Pharisees who had believed** (that is, Pharisees who were now confessing Christians). These did not want to suggest that God had *not* won these Gentiles (Paul's accompanying miracles were evidence enough that He had). But they insisted that it was now **necessary to circumcise** these new converts and to **order them to keep the Law of Moses**—in other words, to finish their conversion by making them Jews. **The apostles and elders assembled to see about this word** and matter and to decide where the truth lay, gathering together with all the believers in the city.

---

7 And after much debate had occurred, Peter, having arisen, said to them, "Brothers, you *yourselves* understand that from the old days God chose among you, that by my mouth the Gentiles should hear the Word of the Gospel and believe.

8 "And God, the Knower of hearts, witnessed to them, giving them the Holy Spirit just as *He* also *did* to us;

9 "and He discerned nothing between us and them, cleansing their hearts by faith.

10 "Now, therefore, why do you test God by placing upon the neck of the disciples a yoke which neither our fathers nor we have been able to bear?

11 "But we believe that we will be saved through the grace of the Lord Jesus, in the same way as they also *are*."

12 And all the multitude was silent, and they were hearing Barnabas and Paul as they were explaining what signs and wonders God had done through them among the Gentiles.

After much debate occurred (possibly between Paul and his Pharisaical opponents), **Peter arose** to add his voice. Not only was he the leader of the Twelve, but his own credibility was directly involved, since he also baptized Gentiles into the Church without requiring circumcision (10:48). This event took place perhaps ten years earlier, but Peter's memory of it was vivid.

In speaking of **the old days** when **God chose** Peter from **among** them so that it would be **by** his **mouth** that **the Gentiles should hear the Word of the Gospel and believe**, he was referring to the vision he received at the household of Simon the tanner in Joppa and its aftermath in the house of Cornelius (10:9f). That is, Peter was not stressing his leading role in the affair so much as he was reminding his hearers of the miraculous events surrounding it. **God, the Knower of hearts**, knew that the secret hearts of those Gentiles at Caesarea had been **cleansed by** their **faith** in Peter's message, and He **witnessed** to this by **giving them the Holy Spirit just as He also did** to the Jewish disciples on the Day of Pentecost. The speaking in tongues proved that these uncircumcised Gentiles had received the Spirit, and that therefore God had **discerned nothing between** the Jews and the Gentiles—both were equally acceptable to God through their faith alone.

To require circumcision of Gentiles would therefore be to contradict this verdict, and thus to **test God**, as Israel sinfully tested God in the wilderness, to their own destruction. The **yoke** of complete submission to all the oral Law which the Pharisees then required of simple people (compare Matt. 23:4) was something **neither** their **fathers** nor they were **able to bear**—why **place** this **upon the neck of** these new **disciples**? As for Peter and the Twelve, they **believed** that they would **be saved through the grace of the Lord Jesus** and through His mercy, not through obedience to the Jewish Law—just as these Gentiles Paul was describing would be.

This was evidently the signal for **Barnabas and Paul** to describe afresh their experiences. (We note that in Jerusalem, Barnabas takes the lead, since it is his home church, and thus his name here comes before that of Paul.) They told the whole assembled multitude of believers in Jerusalem **what signs and wonders God had done**

V. The Church Founded at Gentile Antioch — Acts 15:13–21

through them among the Gentiles during their last mission—clear evidence of the truth of their teaching.

> ৵ ৵ ৵ ৵ ৵
>
> 13 And after they were silent, James answered, saying, "Brothers, hear me!
> 14 "Simeon has explained how God first looked at *and* took from among the Gentiles a people for His Name.
> 15 "And with this the words of the Prophets agree, just as it is written,
> 16 "'After these *things* I will return, and I will rebuild the fallen Tent of David, and I will rebuild the things which were razed, and I will restore it,
> 17 "'so that the rest of men may seek out the Lord, even all the Gentiles over whom My Name has been called,
> 18 "'says the Lord, making these *things* known from of old.'
> 19 "Therefore I *myself* judge that we do not trouble those who are turning to God from among the Gentiles,
> 20 "but that we write to them that they abstain from the pollutions of idols and from fornication and from what is strangled and from blood.
> 21 "For Moses from old generations has in every city those who herald him, since he is read in the synagogues every Sabbath."

The multitude listened respectfully to Barnabas and Paul until they were finished, and only **after they were silent** did anyone speak. The first speaker was **James**, brother of the Lord, bishop of the Jerusalem community and the local leader. He called for attention and endorsed what **Simeon** (i.e. Peter) had said. (We note that he diplomatically does not side with Paul and Barnabas explicitly, since they were controversial. Rather, he refers to Simeon, whose authority and prestige were unquestioned.)

Simeon Peter's experience, James said, was confirmed by **the words of the Prophets**, such as Jeremiah 12:15 and Amos 9:11–12. Jesus had not given any teaching about this question of whether or not converting Gentiles must be circumcised, but the Scriptures were consistent with the experience of Simeon. That is, God would one day **return** to Israel to rebuild and resettle them (Jer. 12:15). **The Tent of David**, the royal house and messianic hope that had been **razed** and fallen into ruins, God would **rebuild** and **restore**, so that Israel would be rebuilt from the ground up. In this radical rebuilding, the **rest of men would seek out the Lord, even all the Gentiles over whom** God's **Name had been called**. (This reference to calling God's Name over the Gentiles clearly is being applied to the baptismal invocation.) The Gentiles, *as Gentiles*, therefore had a share in this new Israel.

This being the case, James for his part (the **I** is emphatic) **judged that** they should **not trouble those who were turning to God from among the Gentiles** by insisting they become Jews. Israel had always said Gentiles were not bound by the Law of Moses but by the so-called "Covenant of Noah"—the universal requirements binding all those descended from the sons of Noah and mentioned in Genesis 9:4. It would be enough if these new Gentile Christians kept those traditional requirements. That is, if they were to abstain from the **pollutions of idols** (i.e. from food offered to idols), **from fornication** (universally accepted in the pagan world), from what is **strangled** (i.e. from eating food with the blood in it), and from eating **blood** in any form. (The prohibition against eating blood continued in the Church and was mentioned in later canons.) The dietary part of these requirements was especially important if the Gentiles were to have table fellowship with the Jewish brothers in Christ without scandalizing them.

This ruling that Gentile Christians need not keep all the Mosaic Law would do no harm to the dignity of the Law (as the Pharisees feared), **for Moses had in every city** of the Empire **those who herald**

him, and his Law was **read in the synagogues** not just occasionally, but **every Sabbath**. There was thus no danger that the Law would disappear from the world!

ॐ ॐ ॐ ॐ ॐ

22 Then it seemed *good* to the apostles and the elders, with the whole church, to choose men from them to send to Antioch with Paul and Barnabas—Judas called Barsabbas, and Silas, leading men among the brothers,

23 through their hand, having written: "The brothers, *both* the apostles and elders, to the brothers throughout Antioch and Syria and Cilicia who are from the Gentiles, greetings.

24 "Since we have heard that some from us to whom we *gave* no orders have shaken you with words, plundering your souls,

25 "it seemed *good* to us, having become of the same-impulse, to choose men to send to you with our beloved Barnabas and Paul,

26 "men who have delivered up their souls for the Name of our Lord Jesus Christ.

27 "Therefore we have sent Judas and Silas, who themselves will also declare the same things by word *of mouth*.

28 "For it seemed *good* to the Holy Spirit and to us to lay upon you no greater burden than these necessary *things*:

29 "that you abstain from things sacrificed to idols, and from blood, and from *things* strangled, and from fornication; if you keep yourselves from these, you will do well. Farewell."

This judgment **seemed** *good* to the apostles and the elders, and indeed to **the whole church** assembled in Jerusalem. (The

Pharisees of v. 5 who opposed Paul and Barnabas no doubt were silenced by the overwhelming consensus of the others.) The church in **Antioch,** which had appealed to the mother church in Jerusalem for clarification about this issue, was to be informed of the result. When **Paul and Barnabas** returned there, **leading men** from the Jerusalem church were to accompany them, bringing the epistle, whose contents they could confirm **by word *of mouth*.** The assembly chose **Judas called Barsabbas**, possibly the brother of Joseph Barsabbas, who was put forward as a candidate for the Twelve in 1:23 (his twin?—the name "Barsabbas" means "son of the Sabbath," indicating their shared birthdate). With him, the assembly chose **Silas** (whose name here is a contraction of the Roman name Silvanus). The presence of such men would lend weight to the account of Paul and Barnabas, and put an end to any possible division in Antioch about this matter.

The epistle was addressed not just to the church in **Antioch**, but also to the churches throughout **Syria and Cilicia** in the surrounding area, for the controversy had spread beyond the confines of the Syrian capital itself. (We note in passing that the simple opening of **greetings** is found elsewhere only in the Epistle of James 1:1—a confirming sign of authenticity.)

The church at Jerusalem stressed that those who came from them to spread the teaching that the Antiochene Gentiles must be circumcised (15:1) were in no way acting under orders, however much those teachers implied the contrary. The apostles and elders *gave* **no orders** like that to them, and were in fact sorry that these unauthorized men had **shaken** them up **with words, plundering** and devastating their **souls**. The apostles and elders had investigated this matter and **had become of the same-impulse** and of one united mind about it—a sure sign that their decision was from God. They had completely vindicated the teaching of **Barnabas and Paul** (commended as **our beloved** and as men **who delivered up their souls for the Name** of the Lord, men who had risked their lives for Him). Barnabas and Paul could tell them all about the events in Jerusalem, and their words would be confirmed by **Judas and Silas**.

In summary, the synod at Jerusalem had decided on the

following. They need not be circumcised, but need only observe **these necessary** *things*, in order not to offend their Jewish brothers: they must **abstain from things sacrificed to idols, and from blood, and from** *things* **strangled, and from fornication**. This decision is described not just as what seemed best to the synod at Jerusalem, but firstly as what **seemed** *good* **to the Holy Spirit**, for the Spirit worked through that human assembly. To contradict this ruling was therefore to oppose God Himself.

> 30 Therefore, when they were dismissed, they went down to Antioch; and having assembled the multitude, they delivered the epistle.
> 31 And when they had read *it*, they rejoiced because of the exhortation.
> 32 And Judas and Silas, also being prophets themselves, exhorted and strengthened the brothers with a lengthy word.
> 33 And after they had spent time, they were dismissed from the brothers in peace to those who had sent them.
> 35 But Paul and Barnabas stayed in Antioch, teaching and preaching, with many others also, the Word of the Lord.

The returning delegation was **dismissed** and sent out from Jerusalem **to Antioch**, where they **delivered the epistle**. When the Antiochene church **read** *it*, **they rejoiced** at its contents—another sign that the decision was from God, for joy is a sign of the Kingdom. Consistent with this Spirit-inspired decision contained in the letter, **Judas and Silas**, who were **prophets themselves, exhorted and strengthened the brothers with a lengthy word**, doubly confirming the divine truth of Jerusalem's decision with their prophecies. Judas and Silas **spent** a long **time** there before they were **dismissed** by the Antiochenes **in peace**. Luke means us to see the **peace** in which they departed as evidence of the unity of the Spirit, preserved by the decision of Jerusalem. Satan had meant to shake the unity of the Church by the work of those who opposed Paul and Barnabas, but that unity remained. **Paul and Barnabas stayed in Antioch**, triumphantly vindicated, **teaching and preaching** as they had always done.

⁌ EXCURSUS
On the Confrontation with Peter in Antioch

According to Galatians 2:11f, Paul said that when Peter came to Antioch (presumably after the Synod whose results were reported in Gal. 2:1–10), he had to oppose him to his face. It was Peter's custom to eat with the Gentile Christians there, but after certain men came from James (that is, from the Jerusalem church), he changed this custom and would no longer eat with Gentiles, but with Jews alone. It would seem that Peter's visit to Antioch and his confrontation by Paul are to be dated to this time following Paul's return from the Jerusalem synod.

Some might think it strange that Peter should act in this way so soon after the synod. But the synod was not dealing with the specific question of whether Jews might eat with Gentiles, but with the question of whether or not Gentiles must be circumcised. To cool-headed theological hindsight, the two questions are obviously interrelated. But Peter was not always known for cool-headedness (see Matt. 16:22; 26:69–75). It would seem that the arrival of his friends from Jerusalem temporarily overcame his better judgment, so that he acted inconsistently with his own convictions and his previous actions (see 11:3). In this he was justly rebuked by Paul, and no doubt he immediately saw Paul's point. For ourselves, we may take encouragement from the fact that even the Prince of the Apostles may experience lapses in judgment and failures of nerve, for that means there is hope for us too.

VI

PAUL'S FURTHER JOURNEYS
(15:36—21:16)

§VI.1. Second Missionary Journey of Paul

Departure

> 36 And after some days Paul said to Barnabas, "Let us return and visit the brothers throughout every city in which we proclaimed the Word of the Lord, *to see* how they are."
> 37 And Barnabas was intending to take along also John, called Mark.
> 38 But Paul was insisting that they should not take along him who had withdrawn from them in Pamphylia and had not gone with them to the work.
> 39 And there arose a provocation so that they left one another, and Barnabas took along Mark and sailed to Cyprus.
> 40 But Paul departed, having selected Silas, being delivered to the grace of the Lord by the brothers.
> 41 And he was going through Syria and Cilicia, strengthening up the churches.

After some days (a period probably of several months or more), Paul's pastoral heart was concerned for the new converts they had made about three years earlier, on their first missionary journey. He therefore proposed **to Barnabas** that they **return and visit** those newly founded churches *to see* **how they were**. Were they still walking in faith? Had they been duped or seduced by heresy or worldliness? Had fear of persecution caused them to fall away? **Barnabas** immediately agreed to this suggestion and **was intending to take along also John, called Mark**, as they had on their trip. He was Barnabas's cousin (see Col. 4:10), and since John Mark was desirous of going, Barnabas felt it was only right he should go.

For Paul, however, this was out of the question, and he kept **insisting that they should not take along him who had withdrawn from them in Pamphylia** (13:13). He had deserted them once, and, as far as Paul was concerned, had proven himself unsuited for the rigors of mission work in hostile areas. Had not Solomon warned of the folly of trusting a faithless man in time of trouble (Prov. 25:19)? Barnabas, for his part, was willing to trust Mark's expression of readiness. His cousin had doubtless repented of his former loss of nerve and was eager to try again. Surely he should be given the chance?

With the candor that characterizes all the New Testament writers, Luke does not gloss over these differences, for he was serving the Lord of Truth. He records that **there arose a provocation** between Paul and Barnabas. (It is possible too that Paul's recent confrontation with Peter did nothing to help his working relationship with Barnabas, for he had to oppose Barnabas then also; see Gal. 2:13f.)

The word rendered *provocation* is the Greek *paroxusmos*, from which we derive the English word "paroxysm." This was quite a quarrel indeed, with many sharp words—so much so **that they left one another**, since neither would give in. **Barnabas took along Mark and sailed to** his native **Cyprus**, to work among his kinsmen there. **Paul departed, having selected Silas**, who probably came from Jerusalem to Antioch at Paul's invitation.

Silas was the perfect selection—like Paul, he was a Roman citizen (see 16:37), as his Roman name Silvanus witnesses. (Silas is a contraction of Silvanus.) As such, they both shared a certain dignity in the eyes of their audience, which would lend credibility to their message. He was also part of the mother church in Jerusalem and

VI. Paul's Further Journeys — Acts 16:1–3

thus able to confirm Paul's account of the recent synod there, should anyone challenge them.

Paul and Silas were **delivered to the grace of the Lord by the brothers**, being prayed for with the laying on of hands as Paul and Barnabas had once been (13:3; 14:26). (The fact that no such commendation is recorded for Barnabas and Mark perhaps means that most of the Antiochene church agreed with Paul. Certainly his was the "official" mission of that church.)

Though Paul had first envisioned a return to Cyprus (since this was a part of the first missionary journey), he left that work to Barnabas and Mark, a natural division of labor since Barnabas was a Cypriot (4:36). Paul instead headed north to his own native **Syria and Cilicia**. Though he had quarreled with Barnabas, he still did not consider himself his rival, but left him to work for Christ as seemed good to him. Thus, their personal difficulties were not allowed to harm their mutual work. Would that all Christian jurisdictions today could learn that apostolic lesson!

---

16 1 **And he came also to Derbe and to Lystra. And behold! a certain disciple was there, Timothy by name, the son of a faithful Jewish woman, but his father *was* Greek,**
2 **who was witnessed to by the brothers in Lystra and Iconium.**
3 **This one Paul wanted to depart with him; and he took him *and* circumcised him because of the Jews who were in those places, for everyone knew that his father was a Greek.**

Having traveled without notable incident through Syria and Cilicia (which included Paul's hometown of Tarsus), Paul **came also to Derbe and to Lystra**, the scene of so much tumult on their first journey. There a surprise awaited them (signaled by the word **behold!**)—**a certain disciple, Timothy by name**, who wanted to join them in their adventures. He was **the son of a faithful Jewish woman**, even though **his father *was* Greek**. That is, his mother, Eunice by name (2 Tim. 1:5), was no apostate, even though she had married a Gentile, and Timothy had been raised as a pious Jew. His piety and zeal were **witnessed to by the brothers in** his hometown of **Lystra**, and even by the neighboring church in **Iconium**. (Derbe was too far off to know Timothy very well.)

Paul was quite willing to have the young man accompany them. However, there was a problem. Although to Gentile eyes Timothy was a Jew, as far as the Jews themselves were concerned he was still a Gentile, for **everyone knew that his father was a Greek**, and that therefore Timothy had never been circumcised. This fact presented a strategic difficulty, for the presence of a Gentile among apostles meant that the Jews to whom they went would not offer them table fellowship—or a hearing. Paul therefore **took him *and* circumcised him** to remedy this. This was no inconsistency on Paul's part. Though he was adamant that one should not receive circumcision if it was offered as a condition of salvation (15:1–2; Gal. 5:2), he also knew that, of itself, the rite was neutral (Gal. 6:15). Paul was willing to become all things to all men—including a Jew to the Jews (1 Cor. 9:20)—and he included his young protégé as part of this strategy.

Before they left Lystra, the elders there laid their hands on Timothy, ordaining him and blessing him for this work (1 Tim. 4:14). A prophecy was given at that time, perhaps one encouraging him to speak boldly for the Lord and not be intimidated by his youth.

> ৵ ৵ ৵ ৵ ৵
> 4 Now while they were passing through the cities, they were delivering the decrees for them to keep which had been judged by the apostles and elders in Jerusalem.
> 5 Therefore the churches were being strengthened in the Faith, and were increasing in number daily.
> 6 And they went through the Phrygian and

VI. Paul's Further Journeys — Acts 16:4–10

> Galatian region, having been forbidden by the Holy Spirit to speak the Word in Asia;
> 7 and when they had come to Mysia, they were trying to go into Bithynia, and the Spirit of Jesus did not permit them;
> 8 and passing by Mysia, they came down to Troas.
> 9 And *there was* a vision during the night: there appeared to Paul a certain Macedonian man who was standing and urging him, and saying, "Come over to Macedonia *and* help us!"
> 10 And when he saw the vision, immediately we sought to depart into Macedonia, concluding that God had called us to preach *the Gospel* to them.

Having taken along another companion, they continued **passing through the cities** of Lycaonia for some time, perhaps using the large city of Iconium as a base. (It seems likely they revisited Pisidian Antioch at this time too.) As they went, they **were delivering the decrees** for the new converts to keep **which had been judged** and decided upon **by the apostles and elders in Jerusalem**. Although addressed nominally to the Gentile converts of neighboring Syria and Cilicia (15:23), these decrees obviously applied to all Gentiles, including those of Lycaonia, and Paul did not want his Judaizing detractors to stir up trouble for these spiritual children either. As further indication that this Jerusalem decision was pleasing to God, Luke records that, having received the decrees, **the churches were being strengthened in the Faith and were increasing in number daily**. This blessing was a sign that the "experiment" of Gentile churches was the will of Christ.

When the time came to leave, after revisiting the cities they had previously evangelized, Paul and his company had to decide where to go next to begin a fresh work. They considered heading directly west through the province of Asia, with its capital of Ephesus. But the prophets in the churches of the Lycaonian cities told them not to make Asia their next preaching destination, **the Holy Spirit** using them to guide the apostles and **forbidding** this proposed course of action. Accordingly, they headed north **through the Phrygian and Galatian region**, preaching to the peoples there, perhaps including such cities as Pessinus (of ancient renown as a cult center for Cybele, the Great Mother goddess) and Ancyra (the capital of the province). In Galatia they received a warm welcome: Paul was later to write that they welcomed him as an angel of God, as Christ Jesus Himself (Gal. 4:14).

From there they thought to head northwest, **into Bithynia**, where there were colonies of Jews. But this proposed itinerary too was forbidden them: **the Spirit of Jesus did not permit them** to go to this destination. Instead they were to **pass by Mysia,** which lay southeast of Bithynia, without preaching there, and hurry down **to Troas** near the coast of the Aegean Sea.

St. Luke refers to these last prophetic utterances as coming from **the Spirit of Jesus** to show that it is through His prophets that the risen Jesus continues to guide and direct the apostles. The actions of the apostles, including their very itinerary, are directed by Christ, and it is Jesus who causes His Church to grow and prosper. Despite what men thought, Jesus was very much alive (compare 25:19).

It was while they were in Troas that Paul had **a vision during the night**. In his vision, **a certain Macedonian man** was **standing** in a posture of urgent entreaty (possibly with outstretched hands) **and urging him and saying, "Come over to Macedonia *and* help us!"** This, Paul concluded, was why the prophets had not permitted him to go west into Asia or northwest into Bithynia—they were to head further west across the Aegean Sea into Macedonia. That was where Christ wanted them to preach the Gospel next.

Why Macedonia? One can only speculate. But it seems the Lord was driving the apostles ever westward. The Gospel was not just to flourish on the Asian continent, but on the European as well. The apostles were to set their sights constantly outward, pushing the boundaries as far as they could go.

We note a change of pronoun in verse 10. Previously Luke had narrated the story in the third person, saying, "*they* were passing

VI. Paul's Further Journeys — Acts 16:11–15

through the cities" (v. 4); now he uses the first person plural, saying, "*we* sought to depart into Macedonia." From this it is apparent that Luke joined them in Troas and was their traveling companion from this point.

Philippi

> ❧ ❧ ❧ ❧ ❧
>
> 11 Therefore, sailing before the wind from Troas, we ran a straight course to Samothrace, and on the following *day* to Neapolis;
> 12 and from there to Philippi, which is a first city of the district of Macedonia, a *Roman* colony; and we *ourselves* were spending *time* in this city for some days.
> 13 And on the Sabbath day we went outside the gate beside a river, where we were supposing a *place of* prayer to be; and we sat and were speaking to the women who had come together.
> 14 And a certain woman, Lydia by name, from the city of Thyatira, a seller of purple cloth, a worshiper of God, was hearing *us*; and the Lord opened-up her heart to pay attention to the things spoken by Paul.
> 15 And when she and her house had been baptized, she urged *us*, saying, "If you have judged me to be faithful to the Lord, enter into my house *and* remain." And she prevailed upon us.

Fair winds must have attended the voyage **from Troas** to **Neapolis** (via the island of **Samothrace**), for it was accomplished in two days, whereas the journey from Neapolis to Troas (recorded in 20:6) took five days. From the port of Neapolis, the apostles went **to Philippi**, ten miles away.

Philippi was the **first city of the district of Macedonia**—that is, a city of some importance. It was also a ***Roman* colony**, modeling itself after Rome and using Roman law. It had many Roman citizens, who prided themselves upon being Roman, spoke Latin, dressed like Romans, and kept this Roman connection in the center of their lives. Paul and his companions stayed here **for some days**, recognizing the city's strategic importance.

It was Paul's custom to go to the local synagogue and offer the Gospel to the Jews first. This being such a Roman city, there was not enough of a Jewish population to have a synagogue. However, the apostles heard about **a *place of* prayer**, a spot where pious Jewish women met to pray every Sabbath, **outside the gate** of the city **beside** the **river** Gangites. **On the** next **Sabbath day**, the apostles went there, **sat** down to teach (sitting was the posture for teachers), and began **speaking to the women who had come together** there to pray.

One of the women, **Lydia by name**, came from **the city of Thyatira** in Asia Minor. Thyatira was famous for the manufacture of purple dye, and it had a Jewish population. It would seem that Lydia (named perhaps for the Lydian kingdom in which Thyatira then lay) became a **worshiper of God** in that town, a Gentile who nonetheless worshipped only the Jewish God. She now lived in Philippi as **a seller of purple cloth**. As Paul spoke to her about the Lord Jesus, **the Lord opened-up her heart to pay attention** to Paul's message, and **she and her house** (consisting perhaps mostly of slaves) were **baptized**. Being a woman of wealth, she **urged** Paul and his companions to **enter into** her **house** and **remain** with them, allowing her to support them. The apostles agreed, and her home became their base of operations in Philippi.

Luke mentions her conversion to show that it was not simply slaves and the uneducated who accepted the message of the apostles (compare 1 Cor. 1:26), but also higher-class women such as Lydia.

---

16 And it happened that as we were going to the *place of* prayer, a certain servant-girl having a

VI. Paul's Further Journeys — Acts 16:16–24

pythonic spirit met us, who was bringing her lords much profit by *giving an* oracle.

17 This one, following Paul and us, was crying out, saying, "These men are slaves of the Most High God, who are proclaiming to you a way of salvation!"

18 And this she was doing for many days. But Paul was annoyed, and turned and said to the spirit, "I order you in the Name of Jesus Christ to come out of her!" And it came out at that same hour.

19 But when her lords saw that their hope of profit had come out, they took hold of Paul and Silas and dragged them into the marketplace before the rulers,

20 and when they had brought them to the praetors, they said, "These men are shaking up our city, being Jews,

21 "and are proclaiming customs which it is not permitted for us to welcome or do, being Romans."

22 And the crowd rose up together against them, and the praetors, having torn off their garments, were ordering to beat *them* with rods.

23 And when they laid many blows upon them, they cast them into prison, ordering the prison-guard to keep them securely;

24 and he, having received such an order, cast them into the inner prison and secured their feet in the stock.

St. Luke next relates the circumstances of the apostles leaving Philippi. One Sabbath, as was their custom, as the Christians were **going to the *place of* prayer** by the river (probably about a mile and a half west of the city, near a gate marking the city border), **a certain servant-girl having a pythonic spirit met** them. This girl was supposed to possess a gift for ***giving an*** **oracle** from the god Apollo, and people would pay to hear what she said. Apollo was the god of prophecy and oracles, and the python was sacred to him. (Serpents were associated with wisdom in the ancient world.) Some who gave oracles from Apollo were socially significant (such as the oracle at Delphi); others were drawn from the lower classes and were little better than imposters and lunatics. This servant-girl was among the latter. She was a slave, jointly owned by two men, and she **brought her lords** or masters **much profit** as people paid to hear her ravings.

This unfortunate woman began following Paul and his companions as they made their customary way out of the city and down to the riverside. All the way she kept shrieking and **crying out**, screaming her message, **"These men are slaves of the Most High God, who are proclaiming to you a way of salvation!"** This was true enough, but it brought disrepute to the Christians to be associated with and commended by such a lunatic. It gave the populace the impression that Paul and the Christians were charlatans, on the same level as this poor woman and her exploiting masters.

Paul put up with this for **many days**, doubtless praying for the poor slave-girl. Finally, he **was annoyed** and distressed past endurance, grieved that their holy work was being hindered by this demon spirit who was tormenting the girl. He **turned** on her and **said to the spirit, "I order you in the Name of Jesus Christ to come out of her!"** The demon **came out at that same hour** (i.e., that very moment). We may imagine the demon shrieking as it left her, leaving the girl exhausted, at peace, and relieved.

But though the woman may have been relieved at being delivered from the demonic presence, **her lords** and masters were not. It was not merely the demonic spirit that had **come out of her**, it was also **their hope for profit** which **had come out**! They could no longer exploit the wretched girl, and they were furious at being deprived of their source of income. They roughly **took hold of Paul and Silas** (the leaders of the group) **and dragged them into the marketplace** (the place where courts were held) **before the rulers**. The case was heard by the local magistrates (Gr. *strategos*, translating the Latin

VI. Paul's Further Journeys Acts 16:16–24

praetor, the popular term the Philippians would have used. Their official title was *duoviri*, the "two men").

The slave-owners, of course, could hardly state the true nature of their complaint—exorcism was not a crime. They therefore fastened on the obviously Jewish looks of Paul and Silas and twisted the truth about their message. Jews were unpopular, especially in Roman colonies like Philippi, since the Jews had lately been expelled from Rome (compare 18:2). The slave-owners therefore accused Paul and Silas of **shaking up** their **city** (i.e. the crime of disturbing the civil peace)—just what one would expect from **Jews**—and **proclaiming** that all should abandon their religion and adopt Jewish **customs**, which it was **not permitted** for **Romans to welcome** or accept. Those born Jews might practice Judaism, but Roman conversion to Judaism was quite another matter. It was untrue that Paul and Silas had shaken up and disturbed the civic peace, simply by praying in a private house and by a riverside outside the city, and so far Paul's outreach had only extended to Jews and God-fearers. But these things the accusers did not mention—all that mattered to them was retaliation for their financial loss.

The locals, however, supported what the men were saying, partly perhaps out of the common dislike of foreigners (and especially Jews), and also because mobs love violence. **The crowd rose up together**, shouting and screaming that something be done. (Such popular participation was not then uncommon.) The **praetors** therefore decided to act swiftly to avoid a riot, dispensing with the formality of a trial. The accused were not Romans, they thought, but Jews, who were disturbing the peace with their inane superstition, and civic peace was more important than the formalities of a trial, especially when there was such social disparity between accusers and accused and when the accused were so obviously guilty. They therefore gave the order for the lictors (the local police attendants) to **tear off their garments** as preparation for **beating *them*** with the **rods** the lictors usually carried.

The lictors carried out their orders and **laid many blows upon them**. The praetors then **cast them into prison**, giving **the prison-guard** the **order** to **keep them securely**, lest they escape and inflict more mischief. The jailer interpreted this order according to the maximum cruelty, for he **cast them into the inner prison, and secured their feet in the stock**. The **inner prison** was a damp and cold dungeon cell, separated from the usual cells, far from any light, where men rotted in the darkness. The **stock** in which their legs were put was built in such a way as to stretch the legs beyond endurance. This was not simple confinement, but a kind of punishment as well. There the apostles were confined, unfed, their wounds still bleeding and untended.

> ॐ ॐ ॐ ॐ ॐ
>
> 25 But about midnight Paul and Silas were praying, *singing* hymns to God, and the prisoners were listening to them;
> 26 and suddenly a great earthquake happened, so that the foundations of the prison-house were shaken, and immediately all the doors were opened and everyone's chains were unfastened.
> 27 And when the prison-guard was roused, and had seen the doors of the prison opened, he drew his sword and was about to destroy himself, supposing that the prisoners had fled away.
> 28 But Paul cried with a great voice, saying, "Do yourself no harm, for we are all here!"
> 29 And having asked for lights, he leaped in and, trembling, he fell down before Paul and Silas,
> 30 and having brought them outside, he said, "Lords, what is it necessary for me to do to be saved?"
> 31 And they said, "Believe on the Lord Jesus, and you will be saved, you and your house."
> 32 And they spoke the Word of the Lord to him, with all those in his house.
> 33 And he took them that *very* hour of the night

VI. Paul's Further Journeys — Acts 16:25–34

> and washed their wounds, and immediately he was baptized, he and all that were his.
> 34 And having brought them into his house, he set a table before *them* and exulted, having believed in God with his whole house.

The apostles, however, rejoiced. Sleeping while confined in the stocks was out of the question. They began **praying**, therefore, giving thanks at receiving the privilege of suffering for their Lord. Their prayer turned to praise as they began *singing* **hymns to God**. These hymns were doubtless the psalms (compare the same verb, *umneo*, used in Matt. 26:30 to refer to Ps. 115—118). We cannot know which psalms they sang—perhaps the Great Hallel, Ps. 113—118, sung every Passover, or Ps. 107:10f, which spoke of God releasing the prisoners who dwelt in darkness, in misery and chains. Whatever their hymns, the other **prisoners** (probably contained in the inner prison with them for the night, for security reasons) **were listening to them**, astonished. No others who had been so beaten and confined had lifted up their voices in joy in that dreadful place. Who were these strange men? Were they really the slaves of the Most High God, come to proclaim the way of salvation, as was rumored?

As if to confirm this suspicion, **suddenly a great earthquake happened, so that the foundations of the prison-house** (i.e. the cell) **were shaken, and immediately all the doors were opened and everyone's chains were unfastened**. (The doors were secured by wooden bars, and the chains secured to the walls; the earthquake would have dislodged both, moving the bars aside and ripping the chains from the walls.) The apostles did not flee themselves, and they seem to have shouted out to the other prisoners that they should not flee either. Such was the regard the prisoners now had for Paul and Silas that they obeyed the orders from these strange slaves of the Most High God and remained in their cells.

The earthquake had, of course, **roused the prison-guard** from sleep. His own quarters were evidently just above the cells, and he knew only too well what such an earthquake could do to those cells. Accompanied by his distressed family, he ran down to the cells, and when he had **seen the doors of the prison opened**, he assumed **the prisoners had fled away**. Under Roman law, he was responsible for those prisoners with his own life, which he supposed was now forfeit. In a fit of panic, he **drew his sword and was about to destroy himself**.

Paul could see the jailer's form in the light above, and he **cried with a great voice, saying, "Do yourself no harm, for we are all here!"** The jailer laid aside his sword, **asked for lights** to explore the cells, and **leaped in** to that underground to confirm that this was so. **Trembling**, he fell down in obeisance **before Paul and Silas**, fearful at having inflicted such punishment upon those who after all had proven to be the special servants of the Most High. He brought them outside into the courtyard, and having secured the cells again, said to them, **"Lords** (or "sirs," Greek *kurioi,* a term of profound respect), **what is it necessary for me to do to be saved?"** He had been party to a shameful sacrilege by harming God's servants, who had come to show all the way of salvation—what must he do to win that salvation for himself? What great deed must he do to atone for his sins, what sacrifice must he offer to the offended Deity?

Paul and Silas looked at the man, surrounded by his trembling family. They responded, **"Believe on the Lord Jesus, and you will be saved, you and your house."** From this beginning, **they spoke the Word of the Lord to him, with all those in his house**, telling them of the necessity of repentance, righteous living, holy Baptism, and living as disciples of Jesus in His Church.

The jailer and his family responded immediately. **That *very* hour of the night**, the jailer **washed their wounds** (an expression of penitence for the harm inflicted), and **immediately** after this **he was baptized, he and all that were his**. Baptism was the way of becoming a disciple of Jesus, and in his joy, the jailer would not wait until morning. It was only after this that he **brought** Paul and Silas **into his house and set a table** of food **before *them***, to restore their strength and offer hospitality to the servants of God. The gladness of Paul and Silas at the providence of God was eclipsed, we may think, by the joy of the jailer and his family as they **exulted, having believed in God**.

VI. Paul's Further Journeys Acts 16:35–40

> ৩৭ ৩৭ ৩৭ ৩৭ ৩৭
>
> 35 Now when day came, the praetors sent the lictors, saying, "Dismiss those men."
> 36 And the prison-guard declared these words to Paul, "The praetors have sent that you may be dismissed. Now therefore, come out and go in peace."
> 37 But Paul said to them, "They have beaten us publicly, uncondemned, men who are Romans, and have cast *us* into prison—and now they are casting us out secretly? No indeed! But let them come themselves and lead us out."
> 38 And the lictors declared these words to the praetors. And they were afraid when they heard that they were Romans.
> 39 And they came and urged them, and when they had led them out, they were asking them to go out from the city.
> 40 And they went out from the prison and entered *the house of* Lydia, and when they saw the brothers, they exhorted them and went out.

All of this, however, occurred without the knowledge of the praetors. As far as they were concerned, the troublesome foreigners had been punished enough for their insolence and were unlikely to stir up any more trouble. The **praetors** therefore **sent the lictors** word that they could now **dismiss those men** and send them away. The lictors gave this message to **the prison-guard**, which he in turn **declared to Paul, "The praetors have sent that you may be dismissed. Now therefore, come out and go in peace."**

When Paul received this verbatim message from his new friend, he was indignant. The praetors had **beaten** them **publicly, uncondemned, men who** were **Romans, and** had **cast** them **into**

193

prison—and now they were **casting** them **out secretly?** After such an outrage of Roman justice, did they think they could just eject Paul and Silas—Roman citizens like the praetors themselves—and they would simply slink away, as if they were indeed criminals? **No indeed!**

In refusing to do this, Paul was doubtless motivated not only by moral indignation at the injustice done to himself and Silas, but also by a desire to sustain the newly founded church. The public must not be left with the impression that the Christians were indeed criminals and seditious, for that would endanger the new converts. Paul and Silas must be publicly vindicated if the church was to continue unmolested. The praetors must **come themselves and lead** them **out** by way of public apology, that all could see the Christians had been unjustly condemned. It was intolerable that, being **publicly** humiliated (v. 37), they should be **secretly** exonerated. Let their exoneration and restoration of honor be as public as their humiliation!

When the praetors heard this, **they were afraid when they heard that** Paul and Silas **were Romans**, for to beat and imprison a fellow citizen without trial was a major offense, one with serious consequences for themselves. With great cost to their own public honor, they therefore **came** quickly and **urged them** to come forth, **asking them** humbly **to go out from the city** for the sake of public peace. They had no right to expel them, but would Paul and Silas please leave on their own?

The apostles were pleased to comply. Having left the prison compound (we may imagine they spent the rest of the night in the jailer's home), they **entered** *the house of* Lydia to give news to **the brothers**, the church in Philippi that met in her house. Having **exhorted them** to remain steadfast, they **went out** of the city, as they promised the praetors they would. Their work in Philippi was done. They stayed at Lydia's house only long enough to instruct the new converts and (more especially) to make plain to the watching citizens of Philippi that they were not being expelled from the city but were leaving of their own accord.

It may be asked why Paul and Silas did not assert their Roman citizenship before they did, for this would certainly have averted the infliction of a violent beating and imprisonment before a trial. While no certainty about this is possible, I would suggest that it had to do with the good of their mission work. To have proven their citizenship might have required a long delay, as witnesses traveled from Tarsus to Philippi (the production of "papers" by him, the *testatio*, might not have been sufficient in those circumstances), and Paul could not afford a lengthy stay in Philippi (at his own expense) while he awaited the end of his trial. And more importantly, such an assertion of immunity through Roman citizenship would have had a disastrous effect for his new converts, who could produce no such immunity. By claiming to be Romans, Paul and Silas would have avoided persecution for themselves, but would have left their non-Roman converts at the mercy of the persecution they had managed to avoid—not a secure foundation on which to build a church of future converts. Better to accept persecution for the sake of the Name, leaving an example for their fledgling flock.

Thessalonica

17 1 Now when they had gone through Amphipolis and Apollonia, they came to Thessalonica, where there was a synagogue of the Jews.
2 And according to Paul's custom, he went to them, and for three Sabbaths discussed with them from the Scriptures,
3 opening-up and pointing out that it was necessary for the Christ to suffer and arise from the dead, and *saying*, "This *One* is the Christ, Jesus, whom I *myself* am proclaiming to you."
4 And some of them were persuaded and were joined to Paul and Silas, both a great

multitude of the God-fearing Greeks and not a few of the leading women.
5 But the Jews, becoming jealous and taking along some evil men from the marketplace, formed a crowd and *set* the city *in* an uproar; and coming upon the house of Jason, they were seeking to bring them out to the people.
6 And not finding them, they were dragging Jason and some brothers before the politarchs, shouting, "These *men* who have upset the world have come here also;
7 "and Jason has welcomed them, and these all act against the decrees of Caesar, saying that there is another king, Jesus."
8 And they stirred up the crowd and the politarchs who heard these things.
9 And when they had received a pledge from Jason and the rest, they dismissed them.
10 And the brothers immediately sent Paul and Silas out by night to Berea; who when they arrived, went into the synagogue of the Jews.
11 Now these were more well-born *than* those in Thessalonica, for they welcomed the Word with all readiness, investigating the Scriptures daily, *to see* whether these things were thus.
12 Many of them therefore believed, as well as not a few prominent Greek women and men.
13 But when the Jews from Thessalonica knew that the Word of God had been proclaimed by Paul in Berea also, they came there as well, shaking and stirring up the crowds.
14 And then immediately the brothers sent Paul out to go as far as the sea; and Silas and Timothy remained on there.
15 Now those who conducted Paul brought him

VI. Paul's Further Journeys   Acts 17:1–15

> as far as Athens; and receiving a commandment for Silas and Timothy to come to him as quickly *as possible*, they departed.

Paul and Silas then left Philippi to travel the Via Egnatia about thirty miles southwest to **Amphipolis**. (Luke apparently stayed behind in Philippi, since he writes here, "*they* had gone through Amphipolis," not "*we* had gone.") Staying in Amphipolis overnight, they continued about another thirty miles to **Apollonia**, spending the night there as well. The following day they traveled the thirty-seven miles to **Thessalonica**. Unlike the Roman colony of Philippi, Thessalonica held **a synagogue of the Jews**, and it was thence Paul resorted upon arriving in the city, as was his **custom**.

As a distinguished guest, Paul was given the opportunity by the local synagogue rulers to expound on the Scriptures at their Sabbath services, and **for three Sabbaths** he did so, **opening-up** the Scriptures and **pointing out** the passages that proved it **was necessary for the Christ to suffer and arise from the dead**. This was the controversial part, for Jewish expectation was of a conquering Messiah, not a dying one. Doubtless St. Paul appealed to such passages as Psalm 22 and Isaiah 53, showing how they were fulfilled in the life of **Jesus, whom** Paul was even then **proclaiming** (the I in v. 3 is emphatic).

He and Silas had great success, for a **great multitude of God-fearing Greeks were persuaded** (that is, Gentiles who lived as Jews but had not taken the step of circumcision), and **not a few of the leading** Jewish **women**. Presumably Jason (v. 6) was one of the God-fearers (whose name was a Hellenized version of the Hebrew Joshua), as well as Aristarchus and Secundus (20:4). We learn from 2 Thessalonians 3:8 that the apostles worked hard at secular employment also, making tents in order to earn their daily bread. Even so, when the money was insufficient, Paul had to accept some help from his friends in Philippi (Phil. 4:16).

As at Pisidian Antioch, however, their success created problems among those who were not yet persuaded. **Becoming jealous**, some

Jews gathered a crowd of evil loafers who hung about **the marketplace** and **formed a crowd**. This mob *set* **the city** *in* **an uproar**, yelling accusations about Paul and his teaching and inciting others to join them. From his later letters to the Thessalonians, it appears that Paul spoke much about Jesus as bringing the Kingdom at His Second Coming (compare 1 Thess. 1:10; 3:13; 4:13—5:11; 2 Thess. 1:5–10; 2:1f), and it was this emphasis on the kingship of Jesus that Paul's foes were able to distort into a charge of sedition.

The mob, **coming upon the house of Jason** (where Paul and Silas were lodging), **were seeking to bring them out** for trial **to the people** (Gr. *demos*, the public assembly). Paul and Silas were absent from the house when the mob stormed it, and so, **not finding them**, the mob began **dragging Jason and some** other **brothers** who were there **before the politarchs**, the local civic rulers. The crowd **shouted** out their accusations while their representatives made the formal complaint: **"These *men* who have upset the world have come here also; and Jason has welcomed them, and these all act against the decrees of Caesar, saying that there is another king, Jesus."** That is, Paul and those with him were accused of sedition, of conspiring to overthrow Roman might (against Jews, this accusation always carried weight), supporting Jesus as a rival king to Caesar. The riots and controversy that attended their previous visits to other cities (compare 14:4, 19; 16:19f) would give substance to the charges.

The politarchs showed themselves good rulers. Since Paul and Silas were not there to be interrogated, they could not convict them of sedition. It was apparent, however, that the strangers were threats to public peace, as the presence of the howling mob proved. They therefore **received a pledge from Jason and the rest**, a sum of money guaranteeing the good behavior of their guests Paul and Silas, including probably their word that Paul and Silas would leave the city without protest. Having gotten this, **they dismissed them**.

Paul and Silas were now in an impossible situation, for they could not stay without compromising their friend Jason and the others. For a while anyway (at least during the term of office of those politarchs), it was impossible for them to remain in Thessalonica. It is possible

VI. Paul's Further Journeys   Acts 17:1–15

this continued opposition was part of Satan's hindrance Paul refers to in 1 Thessalonians 2:18. The **brothers** therefore **immediately sent Paul and Silas out by night to Berea**, some sixty miles away, before the mob could find them and create another disturbance.

On their arrival in Berea, Paul and Silas once again went into the synagogue of the Jews. These Jews, however, **were more well-born**, more noble-minded *than* **those in Thessalonica**. Instead of becoming jealous over any possible loss of popularity in favor of the Christian movement, **they welcomed the Word with all readiness**, for they cared more for truth than for their own entrenched authority. They spent their time **investigating the Scriptures daily** *to see* **whether** the things Paul and Silas were saying **were thus**, with the result that **many of them believed**, including **not a few prominent Greek women and men** who were attached to the synagogue as God-fearers. (That the women are mentioned first indicates they took the lead, perhaps bringing their husbands with them.) Among the converts were Sopater son of Pyrrhus (20:6).

After some weeks, however, the jealous Jews of Thessalonica got news of Paul's success in the neighboring town, and they were determined to chase him out of there too. **They came there as well, shaking and stirring up the crowds**, using the same tactics that had proven so effective in Thessalonica. Reluctantly, St. Paul concluded that he must leave Berea as well, and his plans of returning somehow to Thessalonica were not going to be fulfilled (in this, Paul saw the work of Satan; 1 Thess. 2:18). The brothers **conducted** Paul to the seaport, where he parted from **Silas and Timothy**, who **remained** behind.

He would have liked to keep Silas and Timothy with him, but the need of the churches was pressing, and Paul always cared more for his beloved converts than for his own peace of mind. He therefore sent Timothy back to check on the Thessalonians (1 Thess. 3:1–2), for Jason's pledge seems to have involved only Paul and Silas, not Timothy. He also sent Silas back to care for the Bereans. Paul himself, the storm center of controversy, was **brought as far as Athens**, where he stayed alone. He did, however, give **a commandment for Silas and Timothy to come to him as quickly** *as possible*. Even an apostle can find himself in need of moral support—especially in so pagan a place as historic Athens.

Athens

> ॐ ॐ ॐ ॐ ॐ
>
> 16 Now while Paul was waiting for them at Athens, his spirit was being incited within him as he was observing the city being idol-ridden.
> 17 Therefore he was discussing in the synagogue with the Jews and the God-fearing ones, and in the marketplace every day with those who happened to meet there.
> 18 And also some of the Epicurean and Stoic philosophers were conversing with him. And some were saying, "What would this charlatan want to say?" Others *said*, "He seems to be a proclaimer of strange deities"—because he was preaching Jesus and Resurrection.
> 19 And they took him and brought him to the Areopagus, saying, "May we know what this new teaching is which you are speaking?
> 20 "For you bring some strange *things* to our hearing; we intend to know therefore what these things are."
> 21 (Now all the Athenians and the strangers visiting there used to spend time in nothing other than saying or hearing something newer.)

Paul began **waiting** in **Athens** for his companions to come, visiting first of all the local Jewish **synagogue**, where he was **discussing with the Jews and the God-fearing** Gentiles there about Jesus. As Luke does not mention any results from these discussions, perhaps they did not yield much. This would in itself make Paul the Jew feel all the lonelier in pagan Athens.

Athens was world famous as the city of philosophy, oratory,

VI. Paul's Further Journeys — Acts 17:16–21

and culture. A Gentile would be delighted to find himself in such historic surroundings. But Paul was not a Gentile but a Jew, and had a Jewish aversion to idolatry. Wherever he went, he could not help **observing** that the whole city was **idol-ridden**. Near the Areopagus (or Hill of Ares), there was a shrine to Ares, the Greek god of war for whom the hill was named. There were in the city also idols of Bacchus, Asclepius, Venus, and other gods. The Council House of Athens housed statues of Apollos and Zeus, with an altar of Vesta. The theater was dedicated to Bacchus. No wonder Paul's **spirit was being incited within him**. (The Greek word rendered *incited* is *paroxuno*, from which the English "paroxysm" is derived; Paul was evidently quite distressed.)

In the **marketplace** (Gr. *agora*), the civic center of life and discourse, he would discuss his own "philosophy" **every day with those who happened to meet there**. Chief among Paul's disputants were **some of the Epicurean and Stoic philosophers**, whose systems represented the Church's chief philosophical rivals of the day.

The Epicureans were followers of Epicurus (341–270 BC), who taught that the gods took no interest in the affairs of men. Accordingly, men must make their own way, taking what pleasure they could in an otherwise meaningless life. They aimed at a life of tranquility, free from angst and pain and disturbing passions, and free from fear—including the fear of death.

The Stoics took their name from the painted porches (Gr. *stoa*) where their founder Zeno taught, who died in 265 BC. The Stoics stressed the role of reason and the importance of being self-sufficient. They were pantheistic, regarding God as the world's soul. They were morally earnest and dedicated to duty and virtue.

These Epicureans and Stoics listened to Paul with a mixture of fascination and incomprehension. **Some were saying, "What would this charlatan want to say?"** dismissing Paul as a mere carpetbagger. The word rendered *charlatan* is the Greek *spermologos*—literally, "seed-picker." Just as a gutter sparrow picked up seeds where it could, so some worthless opportunists would pick up scraps of philosophy wherever they could and peddle them to the unsuspecting. Some dismissed Paul as simply another one of these.

Others *said*, "He seems to be a proclaimer of strange deities." Paul had spoken of **Jesus** and the **Resurrection**—in the Greek, *Iesous* and *Anastasis*—speaking of Christ and the final judgment (compare 17:31; 24:25). These people seem to have misheard Paul, thinking that he was proclaiming two healing deities, one named *Ieso* (the Greek word for healing is *iasis*, which sounds like Iesous, and *Ieso* is the Ionic form of the goddess of health), and another one named *Anastasis*, a god of restoration.

To them it was all foreign and exotic—and interesting. As Luke adds, **all the Athenians and the strangers visiting there used to spend time in nothing other than saying or hearing something newer** than before. That is, their desire to hear more from Paul did not spring from hearts eager for the truth (as was the case with the Bereans; 17:11), but from shallow curiosity. The reader is therefore prepared for the rough reception Paul would receive. The Athenians **brought** Paul **to the Areopagus**, where he could expound his ideas more fully.

The Areopagus was the name given to the court of men who had jurisdiction over such matters. The name derived from the fact that they used to meet in the Areopagus (or Hill of Ares), even though they now met in the Royal Porch on the city marketplace. Visitors facing inquiry would speak their piece in this town hall.

ॐ ॐ ॐ ॐ ॐ

22 And Paul stood in the midst of the Areopagus and said, "Athenians, I observe how religious *you are* in everything.

23 "For while I was going through and examining the objects of your worship, I also found an altar on which had been inscribed, 'To *the* Unknown God.' What therefore you show piety to in ignorance, this I *myself* proclaim to you.

Paul stood in the midst of this venerable and august assembly and presented his philosophy for their consideration. He begins

VI. Paul's Further Journeys   Acts 17:24–25

like a master tactician, complementing them on being **religious in everything** (that is, dedicated to acts of piety), and saying how he was impressed by one of their local altars. For while he was **going through** the city and **examining the objects of worship**, their altars and statues, he **found an altar on which had been inscribed, "To *the* Unknown God."** This altar had apparently been erected in times of past crisis in hopes of placating a god who otherwise had no altar specifically for itself—the Athenians were not leaving anything to chance, but wanted to cover all their bases!

Paul uses this as his starting point because it is something he and his hearers had in common. The Athenians themselves acknowledged there was an element of the unknown about their worship; Paul was not so much contradicting their worship as taking them to the next step. The Athenians worshipped a deity **in ignorance**, acknowledging they did not know much about Him—**this** same reality Paul himself was now to **proclaim** to them. For the Greek mind, ignorance was a great sin. Paul was therefore offering to rescue them from an acknowledged folly.

> ଓ ଓ ଓ ଓ ଓ
>
> 24 "The God who made the world and all things in it, this One being Lord of heaven and earth, does not dwell in sanctuaries made-with-hands;
> 25 "neither is He served by human hands, as if He needed anything, since He *Himself* gives to all life and breath and all things;

Having established a commonality between them, St. Paul now builds upon this by proclaiming the Jewish God. This **God** is the One who **made the world and all things in it**—and being **Lord of heaven and earth**, He **does not dwell in sanctuaries made-with-hands; neither is He served by human hands, as if He needed anything**. Unlike popular paganism, which conceived of their gods as locally dwelling in the sanctuaries men made for them, Paul teaches the true God is not so localized, but is above **heaven and earth**. And unlike popular paganism, which thought of their gods as being served and nourished by human hands through the sacrifices of animals, the true God does not need any sacrifices to be sustained. Rather, it is *He* who sustains *us*, **giving to all** on earth **life and breath and all things** needed. In asserting this, Paul is not yet saying anything of which his hearers would disapprove, for the Epicureans taught the gods did not need anything from men, and the Stoics taught that God is the source of all life. Paul was playing well to his audience, building upon the truths they knew.

> 26 "And He made from one, every nation of men to dwell upon all the face of the earth, having determined appointed times, and the fixed-boundaries of their dwellings,
> 27 "that they should seek God, if perhaps they might feel *for* Him and find *Him*, though He is not far from each one of us;
> 28 "for in Him we live and move and are, as even some of the poets among you have said, 'For we also are His descendants.'
> 29 "Being then the descendants of God, we ought not to think the Divine to be like gold or silver or stone, an image formed by the skill and thought of man.

Paul proceeds to lead them on to newer truths. Greeks conceived of themselves as being fundamentally superior to all others (the Greek term for non-Greeks was *barbaraios*—"barbarian"). Against such supposed racial superiority, Paul asserts the fundamental unity of the human race—God **made from one** person, Adam, **every nation of men**, so that all men stand equally before God. All are united in a solidarity of sin and death, and are accountable to Him. It is He who **determined** the **appointed times** of nations, the periods when each nation was permitted to expand or diminish, and so determined **the fixed-boundaries of their dwellings**. Men in their pride might think their national expansion was due to their own military might,

VI. Paul's Further Journeys — Acts 17:30–34

or perhaps the favor of the gods they worshipped. But such pride was misled. It was the One God who determined the fates of nations, so that all nations were accountable to Him.

God's aim in His universal care of the nations is that they should **seek God**, so that **perhaps they might feel *for* Him and find *Him***. The word rendered *feel for* is the Greek *pselaphao*, often rendered "touch" (as in Luke 24:39). The thought is of a blind man trying to recognize someone by feeling the face. God still cared for the nations of the earth, even though He had not revealed Himself to them as He had to Israel, and this care was intended to bring the nations to Him.

This was not an impossible hope, for **He is not far from each one of us. In Him**, all men **live and move and are**, having their being in God. The life of each one is sustained every moment by God, and that life unites us to the Life-giver and calls us home to Him. In the words of Tertullian, the soul is by nature Christian; like calls to like as the Creator calls in the heart of each created human being. St. Paul shows how **even some of the poets among** them knew this (poets were thought to be in some measure divinely inspired), for the poet Aratus wrote, **"For we also are** (God's) **descendants,"** His offspring. (Aratus was born in Paul's native Cilicia in 310 BC, and that is perhaps why Paul is familiar with his writing.) Though Paul's theology was not that of Aratus, Paul pointed out that even this Greek poet acknowledged the intimate link between God and men.

Since this intimate link exists between God and men, none ought to think **the Divine** nature is **like gold or silver or stone**, so that it could be adequately seen in **an image formed by the skill and thought of man**. Obviously the statues (which abounded within sight in the marketplace where Paul spoke) were utterly misleading. The divine nature was unlike such dead materials. The whole pagan cult of idols was therefore wrong.

ॐ ॐ ॐ ॐ ॐ

30 "Therefore having overlooked the times of ignorance, God now orders all men everywhere to repent,

> 31 "because He has set a day in which He is about to judge the world in righteousness by a man whom He has appointed, having given assurance to all *by* raising Him from the dead."
> 32 Now when they heard of the resurrection of the dead, some were deriding, but others said, "We will hear you about this again."
> 33 Thus Paul went out from their midst.
> 34 But some men joined him and believed, among whom also *were* both Dionysius the Areopagite and a woman, Damaris by name, and others with them.

Paul now comes to his main point: God had **overlooked the times of ignorance** in the past when the nations had been led astray into worshipping images of gold and silver and stone. But He **now orders all men everywhere to repent, because He has set a day in which He is about to judge the world** and punish them for such sins. This judgment will be given through **a man, whom He has appointed** Judge of the living and the dead, and God has **given assurance to all** the nations that this Man is the eternal Judge *by* **raising Him from the dead**. The resurrection of Jesus is proof that He is the divinely appointed Judge, and that now is the time for the nations to repent of idolatry and come to the true and living God.

We may think that St. Paul was not finished with his speech and that he had more to say about this Jesus. But he was not allowed to finish, for **when they heard of the resurrection of the dead, some** started **deriding** Paul, hooting and laughing at such notions. For the Greek mind, the idea of corpses coming to life was ridiculous, especially since they thought the body had no eternal significance but was a barrier to spiritual progress. Paul's talk about the resurrection had just proven that his philosophy was untenable, and they were not prepared to hear any more. **Others**, however, **said, "We will hear you about this again,"** and at least left the door open for Paul to explain himself further. It was **thus** that Paul **went out**

from their midst and left the court—leaving the assembly divided between the scoffers and the interested.

It was not a total loss, however. For some **joined** Paul **and believed** his message, hearing him further in private. Indeed, one of the group that met with him for more instruction was **Dionysius**, who was one of the **Areopagite** council. Given the urbane skepticism of the thirty-odd-member Athenian court, this was a hopeful sign.

Another who joined Paul for further discussions was **a woman, Damaris by name**. Little is known about her, though she seems to have been a woman of some rank and importance. She may well have been a God-fearer from the synagogue there. (Some suggest that she was the wife of Dionysius.) Along with Dionysius **and others**, she seems to have formed the nucleus and kernel for what would later become the church in Athens. The baptisms of these interested people seem to have happened later, however, and to have been accomplished by others, for Paul would later write that his first converts in Achaia were not these Athenians but the household of Stephanas (1 Cor. 16:15). Luke mentions these few converts to show that Paul's speech before the Areopagus was not without fruit, and that the Gospel could hold its own even before the sophisticated Athenians.

❧ EXCURSUS
Lessons from Paul's Speech Before the Areopagus

Paul's speech before the Areopagite assembly might have gathered but a few converts at the time, but it has gathered many since in the history of the Church, for it abides as a masterpiece and model of apologetic before a purely pagan audience. By studying it, we can glean certain principles for our own apologetic efforts, such as the following:

1. Paul begins by appealing to the hearts and emotions of his audience, commending them for their religiosity (v. 22).

Also, he mentions some part of the local scene known to his hearers (the altar to the Unknown God; v. 23), thereby establishing another link between himself and his audience. By this strategy he builds an emotional bridge by which he hopes to win over those who hear him.
2. He respects the presuppositions cherished by his audience and does not begin by denouncing their religion as demonic. Even though as a Jew Paul knew what the Gentiles sacrificed they sacrificed to demons and not to God (1 Cor. 10:20), it would have been unwise to begin with this assertion, for it certainly would have alienated his audience and made impossible future possible learning on their part. Thus Paul states such truths as would have been accepted by the Epicureans and Stoics (vv. 24–25).
3. Paul does not quote religious texts his hearers did not regard as authoritative. Thus he does not quote Hebrew Scripture, for the Athenians did not acknowledge that Scripture as holy and true. Rather, Paul appeals to such authorities as the Athenians *did* regard as true, such as the works of their own poets (v. 28).
4. When Paul does want to make an assertion his hearers think controversial (such as the unity of the human race; v. 26), he quickly couples it with an assertion with which they agree (that in God we all live and move and exist; v. 27). This makes the new truth more palatable.
5. He does not shrink from proclaiming boldly and without compromise the heart of the Gospel (that Jesus was raised from the dead and will judge all men for their sins; vv. 30–31), even though this is regarded as folly by most of his audience.
6. Paul presents his speech in such a way as to be most acceptable to his audience, speaking their style of language. Since he is addressing a refined group of intellectuals, his speech is characterized by rhetorical sophistication and elegance. Paul uses the more elegant verb *uparcho* for "to

VI. Paul's Further Journeys — Acts 18:1–7

> be," rather than the usual *eimi* (vv. 24, 27, 29). Also, the Greek of his speech abounds in alliterations. These make his speech of a more elevated style, and therefore more likely to appeal to his audience. Were he speaking to a more working-class audience today, doubtless he would alter his style to appeal to them.

Corinth

> **18**1 After these things he departed from Athens and came to Corinth.
> 2 And he found a certain Jew, Aquila by name (a native of Pontus, having recently come from Italy), and Priscilla his wife, because Claudius had directed all the Jews to depart from Rome. He came to them,
> 3 and, because he was of the same trade, he remained with them and was working; for by trade they were tentmakers.
> 4 And he was discussing in the synagogue every Sabbath and persuading Jews and Greeks.
> 5 But when both Silas and Timothy came down from Macedonia, Paul was occupied with the Word, testifying to the Jews that Jesus was the Christ.
> 6 And when they opposed and blasphemed, he shook out his garments and said to them, "Your blood *be* upon your own heads! I am clean! From now *on* I will go to the Gentiles!"
> 7 And he passed over from there and entered into the house of a certain *man*, Titius Justus by name, a God-fearer, whose house was next to the synagogue.

After a short while, Paul **departed from Athens and came to Corinth**, which was about fifty miles west of Athens. It is possible that Paul's earlier instructions to Timothy and Silas (16:15) were that they should join him in Corinth, and that his stay in Athens was simply a brief stop along the way to the arranged rendezvous. Certainly that was where they finally met him (18:5). This would make sense, for Athens was a smaller provincial town (though one with an unparalleled cultural heritage), whereas Corinth was a bustling city and the center of government and commerce. If the Church could take root in Corinth, it could spread out from there through all Achaia.

While there, Paul **found a certain Jew, Aquila by name**. Along with his wife **Priscilla** (Luke gives the diminutive of her name; her true name was Prisca), he had **recently come from Italy, because** the Emperor **Claudius had directed all the Jews to depart from Rome**. Aquila is later found in Rome (see Rom. 16:3), and it seems that his home was in Rome.

Claudius expelled the Jews from Rome in around AD 50 (Roman historian Suetonius says) because of Jewish riots instigated by "Chrestus." It is possible this is a mistake on Suetonius's part, and what actually happened is that the Christian Jews and non-Christian Jews of Rome quarreled over Christ (Latin *Christus*), easily confused by Suetonius with the name "Chrestus." It is possible Aquila and his wife were some of these Christian Jews.

Paul **came to them** and **remained with them**, lodging in their home, not just because they were fellow Jews but also because **he was of the same trade** as they. Both Paul and Aquila were **tentmakers**, probably working in *cilicium*, a cloth of goat's hair that took its name from Paul's native Cilicia. Paul worked with his new friends daily, earning his support through this trade, and **discussing** the Gospel **in the synagogue every Sabbath**.

At length **both Silas and Timothy came down from Macedonia**, Silas coming from Berea, where Paul had left him (17:14), and Timothy from Thessalonica, where Paul had sent him (1 Thess. 3:2, 6). (The fact that Silas and Timothy came from two different cities accounts for Luke saying they came from Macedonia, rather than from a single city in Macedonia.) It would seem they brought monetary gifts from the Philippian church there (see 2 Cor. 11:8; Phil. 4:15), and this allowed Paul to be less taken up with the work of tentmaking and more **occupied with the Word**.

The work at the synagogue, however, did not go well, for the Jews there **opposed** Paul's message **and blasphemed** Christ. Paul gave up on them and **shook out his garments** in the classic gesture of violent repudiation, saying, **"Your blood *be* upon your own heads!"** If he had not told them the whole truth, and they had rejected Christ, their blood-guilt would be partly his (compare Ezek. 33:6). As it was, Paul was **clean** from such guilt, for he had told them everything. **From now *on*** he would **go to the Gentiles!** He would frequent the synagogue no longer in Corinth, since his continued striving there meant only that they further hardened their hearts. Accordingly, **he passed over from** the synagogue **and entered the house of a certain *man*, Titius Justus by name**. Henceforth his discussions would center there.

Titius Justus was a **God-fearer**, a Roman Gentile who had attended the synagogue and who had heeded Paul's message. It turned out that his **house was next to the synagogue**. That meant the Christians and Jews would often meet in the street as they entered their respective places of study, and the choice between the two would be clear. It is possible Titius Justus is to be identified with the Gaius of 1 Corinthians 1:14 and Romans 16:23 (Gaius would be the first of the customary three Roman names).

⁂ EXCURSUS
On the Epistles to the Thessalonians

It seems that when Timothy came from Macedonia (18:5), he brought news from Thessalonica, where he had been dispatched by Paul earlier (17:15; 1 Thess. 3:1–6). News from Thessalonica was mixed. Paul's foes there had slandered him, saying he did not care for the Thessalonians but abandoned them as soon as things got hot for him (compare 1 Thess.

2:18). Timothy brought news that the new converts there had not believed these slanders and were still holding fast to the Faith.

There were problems, however, for some were living in the sexual immorality that was common in the Gentile world. Also, some were grieving that some of their number had recently died. Would these departed ones miss out on the final resurrection? Further, some tended to quarrel with the newly appointed leaders (compare 1 Thess. 4:3f; 13f; 5:12). Paul therefore wrote his First Epistle to the Thessalonians to deal with these issues.

This did not end matters, though. Word soon reached Paul that his emphasis on the Second Coming was being misunderstood; some of the Thessalonians had concluded the Coming was at hand. They therefore had quit working and were sitting around idly, waiting for the Lord to return (compare 2 Thess. 2:1f; 3:6f). Paul then wrote his Second Epistle to the Thessalonians, sending it along some months after his first epistle, possibly in the year 51.

༄ ༄ ༄ ༄ ༄

8 And Crispus, the synagogue-ruler, believed in the Lord with his whole house, and many of the Corinthians, when they heard, were believing and being baptized.

9 And the Lord said to Paul in the night through a vision, "Do not be afraid, but go on speaking and do not keep silent;

10 "for I *Myself* am with you, and no one will lay *hands* on you to mistreat you, for I have many people in this city."

11 And he stayed *there* a year and six months, teaching the Word of God among them.

VI. Paul's Further Journeys — Acts 18:12–18

St. Paul's hard work began to bear fruit, as no less prominent a person than **Crispus, the synagogue-ruler, believed in the Lord with his whole house**. When others **heard** of this event, they followed his example and were also **baptized**. The church was growing. Though consisting mostly of humble folk (1 Cor. 1:26), it came to include also such people as Erastus, the city treasurer (Rom. 16:23).

Such success stirred up the Jewish opposition to a fever pitch (especially since the meeting places of the Church and of the Jews were located next to each other), and Paul began to think he would be driven out of Corinth as he had been driven out of Thessalonica and Berea. Perhaps he should leave now, lest his continued presence there bring down more persecution upon his beloved new converts? Perhaps if he continued there he would even be killed? It was while he was fretting and pondering such a move that **the Lord** spoke **to Paul in the night through a vision,** telling him to persevere and not to be afraid.

Thus Paul decided to stick it out, regardless of the intensifying persecution. He would not cease **speaking** the Word boldly, no matter what plots were hatched against him and no matter what threats were uttered. And indeed, he obediently **stayed *there* a year and six months**, his longest stay to date in one missionary location. (Doubtless this included brief trips to the surrounding area of Achaia as well, such as Cenchrea, and a return trip to Athens.)

༃ ༃ ༃ ༃ ༃

12 But while Gallio was proconsul of Achaia, the Jews with the same-impulse rose up against Paul and brought him before the judgment-seat,

13 saying, "This *man* persuades men to worship God contrary to the Law."

14 But when Paul was about to open his mouth, Gallio said to the Jews, "If it were indeed an unrighteous *deed* or an evil crime, O Jews,

> it would be reasonable for me to put up with you;
> 15 "but if it is debates about a word and names and your own Law, look after it yourselves; I *myself* do not intend to be a judge of these *things.*"
> 16 And he drove them away from the judgment-seat.
> 17 And they all took hold of Sosthenes, the synagogue-ruler, and were striking him before the judgment-seat. And Gallio was concerned about none of these *things*.
> 18 And Paul, having remained many days longer, took leave of the brothers and sailed for Syria, and with him *were* Priscilla and Aquila. In Cenchrea he shaved his head, for he had a vow.

The Jewish opposition came to a head with the arrival of **Gallio** as the new **proconsul of Achaia**. The Jews took the opportunity of Gallio's newness in Corinth to press their cause, thinking he would comply with their wishes rather than begin his term of office by antagonizing one of the local groups. They therefore **rose up against Paul** and hustled him **before the judgment-seat**, the podium where such cases were heard, to make their complaint.

Their complaint is summarized thus: **"This *man* persuades men to worship God contrary to the Law."** The charge is ambiguously phrased—was it Roman law or the Jewish Torah that Paul's teaching was contrary to? (Roman law indeed did not countenance such foreign propaganda; compare 16:21.) No doubt the ambiguity was deliberate. This was an important trial, for if Paul were forbidden to teach in Corinth, the Christian movement would be compromised throughout Achaia and the whole Roman world.

Paul did not even need to make his defense. Gallio saw through the accusations (perhaps he had heard about the events in Philippi and Thessalonica?) and knew this was simply an internal Jewish matter, a question of sectarian squabbling among the troublesome

VI. Paul's Further Journeys   Acts 18:12–18

Jews. If it were a matter of some **unrighteous *deed*** or felony, some **evil crime** or fraud, then he would happily **put up with** them (i.e. hear their case). But it was apparent to Gallio that this was a matter of debates about **a word** and interpretation of their Scriptures, of mere **names** (such as whether Jesus were a "Messiah" or not), and of other abstruse details about their **own Law**. These were not matters of public concern, and he did **not intend to be a judge** of them. So saying, **he drove them away from the judgment-seat** (Paul included), refusing to hear the case.

Gentiles from the city were close at hand, watching the public proceedings. Anti-Semitism was never far from the surface in the Roman world, and when the observers saw that Gallio would not grant special consideration to the Jews, they took the opportunity to vent their hostility against them. **They all took hold of Sosthenes, the synagogue-ruler** who replaced Crispus, and **were striking him**, even within sight of **the judgment-seat. Gallio was concerned about none of these** rough-housing tactics, and he did nothing to stop them. (If this Sosthenes is the same one as mentioned in 1 Cor. 1:1, he apparently converted to Christ at a later time.) Luke mentions this last incident to show that a fair Roman, like Gallio, could see how wicked and baseless the Jewish accusations against the Christians were. This latest plot against Paul having failed, he **remained many days longer**. (It would seem that the incident before Gallio took place early in Paul's stay in Corinth.)

After this, **Paul sailed for Syria** to return to his home base in Antioch. **With him *were* Priscilla and Aquila**, who accompanied him because the ship was going by way of Asia Minor, and the couple wanted to stay in Ephesus. The three of them left from the Aegean port city of **Cenchrea**, which was the harbor for Corinth. It was here that Paul **shaved his head, for he** previously **had a vow**. Luke mentions this to show that Paul was no renegade from the Jewish Law, as he was accused, but a truly pious Jew (see also 21:23–24).

What was this vow? It was customary for Jews to let their hair grow as an act of dedication to God in order to seek His special favor (compare the Nazirite vow; Num. 6). At the end of this time of dedication, the one who had been under a vow would cut his hair and then offer it with a sacrifice in the Temple. It seems that Paul had taken a vow asking that God protect him during his stay in Corinth, and that he cut his hair upon leaving the city after the time of his vow had ended. He would keep this hair with him to offer as part of his sacrifice when he reached Jerusalem.

Return to Antioch

> ॐ ॐ ॐ ॐ ॐ
>
> 19 And they reached Ephesus, and he left them there. And he himself entered into the synagogue and discussed with the Jews.
> 20 And when they asked him to stay for a longer time, he did not consent,
> 21 but taking leave of them and saying, "I will return to you again, God willing," he put out from Ephesus.
> 22 And when he had come down to Caesarea, he went up and greeted the church and went down to Antioch.

Ephesus was a port of call along the way, and when **they reached** there, Paul **left** Priscilla and Aquila at their intended destination. (Luke mentions this to prepare the reader for the further story of their work in Ephesus with Apollos in v. 24f.) The stay at Ephesus was not long. The Jews of Ephesus with whom Paul **discussed** the Gospel in the synagogue **asked him to stay for a longer time**, but Paul was hurrying to Jerusalem, especially so since the time was fast approaching when sea travel would be difficult. Commending his return to the will of God, he put out from Ephesus. Eventually he landed at the Palestinian port of **Caesarea**, where he **went up and greeted the church** in Jerusalem, offering his sacrifice and fulfilling his vow. (The church in Jerusalem is meant rather than the church in Caesarea, since it is said that **he went up** to the church; it is only Jerusalem to which a Jew "goes up" and "comes down.") After this, he went to his home in **Antioch**, from where he began.

VI. Paul's Further Journeys — Acts 18:23–28

§VI.2. Third Missionary Journey

Apollos at Ephesus

> ॐ ॐ ॐ ॐ ॐ
> 23 And having spent some time, he went out and went successively through the Galatian region and Phrygia, establishing all the disciples.

Paul's third missionary journey is then related, which took place after he **spent some time** in Antioch. Paul was making for Ephesus, for he had left it hurriedly, hoping to return soon (18:20–21), and he planned to stay there for some time, planting the Church in that great city. (He stayed there over two years; 19:10.) Given the priority Paul gave to work in Ephesus, it is all the more remarkable that he first **went successively through the Galatian region and Phrygia**. A sea journey from Antioch to Ephesus would have been much easier than the long thousand-mile land journey to Ephesus by way of Galatia and Phrygia. But Paul's zeal for establishing the Faith in new territories did not replace his loving pastoral care for converts already made. Thus he made the arduous trip to revisit his churches in Galatia and Phrygia, **establishing all the disciples** there and making sure they were in proper spiritual health.

> ॐ ॐ ॐ ॐ ॐ
> 24 Now a certain Jew, Apollos by name, an Alexandrian by birth, a learned man, reached Ephesus; and he was mighty in the Scriptures.
> 25 This *man* had been instructed in the way of the Lord; and boiling in the Spirit, he was speaking and teaching accurately the things about Jesus, *though he* knew only the baptism of John.
> 26 This *one* began to *speak* boldly in the synagogue. But when Priscilla and Aquila heard him, they took him aside and explained

> to him the Way of God more accurately.
> 27 And when he intended to go to Achaia, the brothers urged him *and* wrote to the disciples to welcome him; and when he had arrived, he greatly helped those who had believed through grace;
> 28 for he vigorously refuted the Jews publicly, showing by the Scriptures that Jesus was the Christ.

While Paul was making for Ephesus, a **certain Jew, Apollos by name, reached Ephesus** before him. Apollos was **an Alexandrian by birth**, and accordingly **a learned man**, for Alexandria was the great Greek city in Africa, boasting an impressive library and a love of learning. Apollos was **mighty in the Scriptures**, able to quote them by heart and explain their meaning.

In the mouth of a Christian like St. Luke, the phrase *mighty in the Scriptures* implied a Christian understanding of the Hebrew Scriptures, with an ability to **show** from them that **Jesus was the Christ**. Indeed, Apollos was a Christian, in that he **had been instructed in the way of the Lord** and knew that Jesus was the Messiah. In fact, he was **boiling in the Spirit** (compare the same phrase in Rom. 12:11), on fire with enthusiasm from the Spirit of God to share his faith with others. He was unusual, however, in that although he **was speaking and teaching accurately the things about Jesus**, he **knew only the baptism of John** the Forerunner.

How was this possible? We may only guess. It seems that he had traveled from Alexandria to Palestine and received baptism from the hands of John himself. In his travels he possibly had begun speaking with some Christian Jews about Jesus and eventually (pondering their words after his contacts with them had ended) found himself won over by their arguments. Possibly he had heard of those arguments from non-Christian Jews who had themselves been speaking with Christians. Either way, it seems he had become persuaded of the validity of the Christian message when he was at a distance from an actual Christian community, and so had never requested baptism.

VI. Paul's Further Journeys — Acts 19:1–7

Whatever Apollos's personal history, once in Ephesus, he **began to *speak* boldly in the synagogue**, proclaiming that Jesus was the Messiah. **When Priscilla and Aquila heard** him (and thereby learned that he had not yet been baptized), **they took him aside and explained to him the Way of God more accurately.** That is, they privately showed him John's baptism had a merely preparatory character, and faith in Jesus was expressed in Christian baptism. With an exquisite delicacy (born out of his concern to preserve the dignity of Apollos as much as possible), Luke does not mention that Priscilla and Aquila actually baptized Apollos, for his was an embarrassing deficiency. But it seems certain this was done, albeit discreetly and privately.

At length Apollos **intended to go to Achaia**, that is, Corinth. Priscilla and Aquila were in Ephesus at that time, and their description of their stay in Corinth piqued his interest. **The brothers** of the newly established church in Ephesus **urged him** to carry out this plan and **wrote** a letter of commendation for him to the church in Corinth. (Such letters were the usual way of commending a traveling brother; compare 2 Cor. 3:1.) Apollos was popular in Corinth, for **when he arrived** there, **he greatly helped those who had believed through grace, for he vigorously refuted the Jews publicly, showing by the Scriptures that Jesus was the Christ**. That is, in his public debates with the Jews in the synagogue, he won debate after debate, thereby adding to the prestige of the Christian community next door to them (18:7). Apollos also made a great sensation with his stirring and flowing rhetoric, which he doubtless learned in Alexandria (compare 1 Cor. 1:12; 3:4–6).

Paul at Ephesus

191 And it happened that while Apollos was at Corinth, Paul, having gone through the upper parts, came to Ephesus and found some disciples;

> 2 and he said to them, "Did you receive the Holy Spirit when you believed?" And they said to him, "But we have not even heard if there is a Holy Spirit."
> 3 And he said, "Into what therefore were you baptized?" And they said, "Into John's baptism."
> 4 And Paul said, "John baptized with the baptism of repentance, saying to the people that they should believe in Him who was coming after him, that is, in Jesus."
> 5 And when they heard this, they were baptized into the Name of the Lord Jesus.
> 6 And when Paul had laid his hands upon them, the Holy Spirit came upon them, and they were speaking in tongues and prophesying.
> 7 And there were in all about twelve men.

After **Apollos** had left Ephesus for **Corinth**, Paul **came to Ephesus** (traveling through **the upper parts** north of Ephesus, and not through the Lycus Valley) **and found some disciples**. Despite their deficiencies, they were Christians, for the term "disciple," when used alone, always refers to disciples of Jesus (compare 18:27). It is possible they had some connection with Apollos, for like him they knew only the baptism of John.

In worshipping with them, Paul suspected they did not **receive the Holy Spirit when** they **believed** and were baptized, and so he asked them if this were the case. (It is possible he was led to suspect this by their lack of spiritual gifts as they worshipped together; compare the presence of prophecy in the early Christians: Rom. 12:6; 1 Cor. 12:10; Eph. 2:20.) In response to his question, they admitted they **had not even heard if there** was **a Holy Spirit**—that is, if the Holy Spirit had been poured out upon the earth, as was promised in the Old Testament prophecies (Joel 2:28f). (As disciples of John they would have known that the Holy Spirit existed; the issue was His eschatological presence among men.)

This answer led to a further question: **"Into what therefore were**

VI. Paul's Further Journeys   Acts 19:8–10

you baptized?" for Christian baptism, which included a laying on of hands, bestowed the gift of the Holy Spirit (see Acts 2:38). When they answered that they had received only **John's baptism**, Paul told them this baptism was only a **baptism of repentance**, one which prepared **the people** for **Him who was coming after** John, that is, for **Jesus**. Therefore they must receive Christian baptism to complete their experience. **When they heard this, they were baptized into the Name of the Lord Jesus**, receiving Christian baptism in the Name of the Trinity, as Jesus commanded in Matt. 28:19. (The phrase "baptized into the Name"—*ebaptisthesan eis to onoma*—refers not to the baptismal formula used, but to the relationship into which baptism brought them. Hence to be baptized "into Moses" [1 Cor. 10:2] meant to be in a relationship with Moses as his disciple.) **When Paul had laid his hands upon them**, as the final component in the baptismal initiation, **the Holy Spirit came upon them**, as proven by the fact that they began **speaking in tongues and prophesying**.

Why does St. Luke mention this episode? In coupling this with the story of how Apollos's similar deficiency was remedied (18:25–26), Luke seems to stress that the Church is the true heir to the movement of John the Baptizer, and therefore to Israel. The work and prophetic status of John were known from afar (see 10:37; 13:24–25), and Luke is concerned to show how John's acknowledged credibility supports the claims of the Christian movement. The prophet John belongs not to the non-Christian Jews, but to the Church. The group of Ephesian disciples constituted a kind of synagogue (that is perhaps why Luke mentions **there were in all about twelve men**, for it took at least ten men to constitute a synagogue). Luke shows by this story how the Johannine synagogues were to find their true home in the Christian Church.

ॐ ॐ ॐ ॐ ॐ

8   And having entered the synagogue, he was *speaking* boldly for three months, discussing and persuading about the Kingdom of God.
9   But when some were being hardened and were disobeying, speaking-evil of the Way before

> the multitude, he withdrew from them and separated the disciples, discussing daily in the school of Tyrannus.
> 10 And this happened for two years, so that all dwelling in Asia heard the Word of the Lord, both Jews and Greeks.

St. Luke then describes the progress of the Gospel in Ephesus. Paul **entered the synagogue** there, as was his usual custom, and began *speaking* **boldly, discussing and persuading** all present **about the Kingdom of God** and the crucial role of Jesus as the Messiah. Some believed, but **some** were **hardened** against his message and **were disobeying** God's call, **speaking-evil of the Way before the multitude** in the synagogue, blaspheming its Founder Jesus as a deceiver and a false prophet. This Paul would not tolerate. He **withdrew** from the synagogue and **separated the disciples** of Jesus who had received his message, moving his meeting place to **the school of Tyrannus**. This separation happened fairly quickly, after **three months** of preaching in the synagogue.

The lecture hall of Tyrannus was available in the early afternoon, for most of the population in Ephesus took a siesta during this time. Accordingly, Paul would have plied his trade as a tentmaker in the morning hours and then, when most of the city was resting, would have continued to work at preaching and teaching when Tyrannus's hall was vacant. Paul's work continued for another **two years**, with the result that his message became known to **all dwelling in Asia** through word of mouth. This would have included the town of Colosse, to which Paul would later write a letter, and the other cities mentioned in Revelation 1:11. Paul's time in Ephesus was spent not only teaching in the house of Tyrannus, but also teaching the Christian families in their homes, declaring to them the whole of the divine plan, and praying for them with tears (Acts 20:19–20, 27).

> ৵ ৵ ৵ ৵ ৵
> 11 And God was doing not ordinary *works* of power through the hands of Paul,

VI. Paul's Further Journeys   Acts 19:11–17

> 12 so that even neckerchiefs or aprons were carried away from his skin to the sick, and the diseases left them and the evil spirits went out.
> 13 But also some of the Jewish exorcists who were going around set their hand to name over those who had the evil spirits the Name of the Lord Jesus, saying, "I adjure you by the Jesus whom Paul heralds."
> 14 And the seven sons of a certain Sceva, a Jewish chief-priest, were doing this.
> 15 And the evil spirit answered *and* said to them, "Jesus I know and Paul I know about—but you are who?"
> 16 And the man in whom was the evil spirit leaped upon them and mastered all of them and overpowered them, so that they fled out from that house naked and wounded.
> 17 And this became known to all dwelling in Ephesus, both Jews and Greeks, and fear fell upon them all, and the Name of the Lord Jesus was being magnified.

As an example of the Gospel's success, Luke mentions three things. The first is the role of Paul himself. Not only was he preaching daily, but God was also performing miracles **through the hands of Paul**. (The reference to **hands** probably reflects Paul's practice of laying his hands upon the sick and afflicted to heal them.) So strong was the power of God through His apostle that **God was doing not ordinary *works* of power** through him, but extraordinary ones—as if miracles were usually expected when Paul preached, but not ones like these! So great was his reputation as a healer **that even neckerchiefs or aprons were carried away from his skin** to the sick for their effectual healing and deliverance.

These neckerchiefs and aprons were the normal clothing Paul wore as he worked in his trade as a tentmaker, the **neckerchief** being the sweatband he wore around his head and the **apron** the garment he wore to wipe away his sweat. Because these had touched his **skin**, they were thought to be carriers of his miracle-working power—as indeed they were. They were, in fact, the first relics recorded in church history and were effectual for healing because of faith. We can imagine those who heard Paul's preaching asking for (or taking without asking?) such garments to place on those deemed too sick to be brought to Paul through the crowded city.

The second thing Luke relates (with his typical dry sense of humor) is the example of **some Jewish exorcists**. The ancient world was thronged with such peddlers of pretended power. They used incantations, borrowing them from whatever religious source they could find, offering to help the desperate for a fee. There were **seven** of them, **sons of a certain Sceva**, whom Luke describes as a **Jewish chief-priest** (that is, a member of one of the aristocratic high-priestly families of Jerusalem). They apparently had a family business, trading upon their Jewish heritage, perhaps telling the locals that Sceva's status as a chief-priest gave him special access to God's power. Seeing Paul's success, they **set their hand to name over those who had evil spirits the Name of the Lord Jesus, saying, "I adjure you by the Jesus whom Paul heralds."**

It was not a shrewd move. **The evil spirit** within the afflicted man **answered *and* said to them, "Jesus I know and Paul I know about—but you are who?"** That is, the demon acknowledged the power of Jesus (compare Mark 3:11) and knew Paul by reputation as the one who wielded Christ's authority as His true disciple (Mark 6:7)—but these men were who? (The pronoun *who* comes at the head of the clause in the Greek.) The demon knew that these men were no true disciples of Jesus, and thus had no authority to cast it out.

The man in whom was the evil spirit, controlled by the enraged demon, **leaped upon** the unfortunate exorcists and **mastered all of them and overpowered them**, tearing off their clothes and beating them up. The demon must have given the possessed man unusual strength (compare Mark 5:4), for the one man beat up seven. Their humiliating defeat as **they fled out from that house naked and wounded** (Gr. *traumatizo*, compare the English "traumatized"—as undoubtedly they were) only served to show all the more clearly the power of Paul. Obviously it was not the simple name of Jesus that was powerful in itself, but that Name uttered in faith by those who believed Paul's message. When news of the exorcists' debacle **became known to all dwelling in Ephesus, the Name of the Lord Jesus** was **magnified** by all who heard it and recognized as a name of salvation and power for those who were Christians.

> ৵ ৵ ৵ ৵ ৵
>
> 18 Many also of those who had believed were coming, confessing and announcing their practices.
> 19 And considerable *numbers* of those who practiced magic *arts* brought together their books and were burning them up before all; and they counted up the price of them and found *it* fifty thousand *pieces* of silver.
> 20 Thus the Word of the Lord was growing mightily and becoming strong.

Luke relates a third element in Paul's stay in Ephesus, one that began as people heard of the disastrous experiment of the sons of Sceva. Paul was presenting his Gospel as an alternative to the rival forms of spiritual power available in that day. Ephesus in particular was famous for **magic *arts***, and the city teemed with occult practices. Indeed, magic incantations and spells were referred to as "Ephesian letters." To **considerable *numbers*** of people, it was apparent that Paul's message was the true one, and they **were coming, confessing and announcing their practices** and spells, divulging their meaning to render them powerless.

As evidence of their repentance of such things, they **brought together their books** containing the spells and **were burning them before all**, to show publicly that they had truly destroyed such demonic things and had truly begun a new life. When the value of such scrolls was **counted up**, it amounted to **fifty thousand *pieces***

of silver. Assuming that the *piece* **of silver** was a drachma (a day's wage for the working man), this was quite a haul. Luke mentions the amount as an indication of Paul's amazing success. In this way (that is, through Paul's message finding public vindication), **the Word of the Lord was growing mightily and becoming strong** in Asia.

❧ EXCURSUS
On Writing the First Epistle to the Corinthians

About this time, Paul received news of trouble in Corinth and made a short and painful visit there, lasting perhaps only a few days, to attempt to remedy their troubles (compare 2 Cor. 2:1). The visit was not a success, for the problems of factionalism, disorder, and immorality continued. Hearing reports of continuing problems there, Paul fired off a brief letter, urging them to shun worldliness and not to associate with immoral people (see 1 Cor. 5:9).

This letter evidently did not solve the problem, for a reply came from the household of Chloe, outlining more problems and asking questions (1 Cor. 1:11). In response, Paul wrote his First Epistle to the Corinthians with many tears, sending it to Corinth by the hand of Titus and another brother (2 Cor. 12:18).

༄ ༄ ༄ ༄ ༄

21 Now after these *things* were fulfilled, Paul resolved in the Spirit, having gone through Macedonia and Achaia, to go to Jerusalem, saying, "After I have been there, it is necessary for me also to see Rome."

22 And having sent into Macedonia two of those serving him, Timothy and Erastus, he himself stayed in Asia for a time.

VI. Paul's Further Journeys   Acts 19:23–41

As Paul's time in Ephesus was drawing to its close, he **resolved in the Spirit to go to Jerusalem**. Since Paul was going to Jerusalem to deliver to the poor disciples there a collection he was gathering from the Gentile churches for them, he wanted to **go through Macedonia and Achaia** on his way to Jerusalem, so that he could collect money from these churches also. This resolve to visit Jerusalem was part of Paul's larger project and intention to **see Rome** and to use Rome as the jumping-off point for a trip to Spain (Rom. 15:23–28). Paul had finished his work in the eastern parts and had now set his sights on the western parts of the Roman world.

St. Luke says Paul's resolution was **in the Spirit** to show this was no personal whim on Paul's part, but was in accord with the will of God, probably being confirmed by prophecies given in the Ephesian church (compare the prophecies in 16:6, 7; 20:23; 21:4). That is why Paul does not say, "I intend to see Rome," but **"It is necessary for me to see Rome,"** for this visit to Rome is the will of God, confirmed by the words of the Christian prophets. (The circumstances of Paul's actual visit to Rome were of course somewhat different than Paul thought they would be.) Luke mentions such guidance to show that all that befell Paul subsequently in Jerusalem was the providential will of God.

As a preparation for Paul's trip to Macedonia and Achaia, he **sent** there **two of those serving him**, his assistants **Timothy and Erastus**. Timothy (last heard of in Corinth; 18:5) had come to join Paul in Ephesus, and he was sent **into Macedonia** and Achaia to arrange for the collection in advance of Paul's arrival.

The **Erastus** who was sent with him is probably different from the Erastus who was the city steward or treasurer at Corinth (mentioned in Rom. 16:23 and 2 Tim. 4:20). The name was common enough. Though it is possible the two Erastuses were the same, one would expect the city treasurer of Corinth to be too occupied with his work to undertake a mission to Macedonia.

ঌ ঌ ঌ ঌ ঌ
23 And during that time there occurred no small commotion about the Way.

24 For a certain *man*, Demetrius by name, a silversmith who made silver sanctuaries of Artemis, was giving no little profit to the craftsmen;

25 these he assembled with the workmen occupied with such things and said, "Men, you understand that our prosperity is from this profit.

26 "And you observe and hear that not only in Ephesus, but in almost all of Asia, this Paul has persuaded and changed a considerable crowd, saying that gods made with hands are no gods.

27 "And not only is there danger that this business of ours come into disrepute, but also that the temple of the great goddess Artemis be considered as nothing, and she is about to be brought down from her greatness, whom the whole of Asia and the world worships."

28 And when they heard this and were filled with wrath, they were crying out, saying, "Great *is* Artemis of the Ephesians!"

29 And the city was filled with the confusion, and they rushed with the same-impulse into the theater, having seized Gaius and Aristarchus, Paul's co-travelers from Macedonia.

30 And when Paul intended to enter into the people's *assembly*, the disciples would not let him.

31 And also some of the Asiarchs, being friends of his, sent to him and were urging him not to give himself to the theater.

32 Therefore some were crying out one thing and some another, for the assembly was in

confusion, and the majority did not know why they had assembled.

33 And some of the crowd concluded it was Alexander, since the Jews had put him forward; and having motioned with his hand, Alexander was wanting to defend himself before the assembly.

34 But when they recognized that he was a Jew, one voice came from them all as they cried out for about two hours, "Great *is* Artemis of the Ephesians!"

35 And after calming the crowd, the *town* scribe says, "Ephesians, who indeed is there among men who does not know the Ephesian city *as* being temple-guardian of the great Artemis, and of that which is Zeus-fallen?

36 "Since therefore these things are undeniable, it is necessary for you to be calm and do nothing reckless.

37 "For you have brought these men *here* who are neither temple-robbers nor blasphemers of our god.

38 "So therefore, if Demetrius and the craftsmen with him have a matter against any man, the assizes are in session and there are proconsuls; let them bring charges against one another.

39 "But if you seek after anything beyond this, it will be settled in the lawful assembly.

40 "For indeed we are in danger of being charged with a riot about today, since there is no cause *for it*; and about *this* we will not be able to render an account for this mob."

41 And after saying these *things*, he dismissed the assembly.

After this Luke relates an event in which there was **no small commotion about the Way**, but a major public demonstration. (We note in passing Luke's gift for understatement.) His purpose in relating this is to show how baseless were the accusations routinely leveled against the Christians, for the Ephesians almost started a riot without even knowing what for. Their opposition to Paul was not (as some said) because Paul was truly seditious, but only because their economic prosperity was threatened. The Ephesian commotion thus reveals how politically harmless the Christians really were.

It all began with a **certain *man*, Demetrius by name, a silversmith who made silver sanctuaries of Artemis**. Ephesus was the cult center of Artemis worship and the home of the goddess's huge temple. The Ephesian Artemis seems to have been a mother goddess, and an image of her many-breasted figure survives to this day. Her festival (the Artemisia) took place in the spring, and it is possible that the imminence of the festival provoked Demetrius's outburst. The devotees of Artemis would offer little images of the goddess, made either of terracotta or silver, and it was these images (miniature **sanctuaries** or silver shrines, representing the goddess in a niche) that Demetrius made and sold in connection with the festival. The success of **this Paul** (we can almost see Demetrius sneering when he says Paul's name) meant that fewer people were buying Demetrius's wares, for Paul was **persuading almost all of Asia** that **gods made with hands were no gods**. Christians were bad for the idol business!

Demetrius seems to have been a person of some civic importance (perhaps the head of the silver craftsmen), and he mobilized the other **workmen** who were **occupied with such things** (perhaps the workers in terracotta figurines also). He gave them a rousing speech, appealing not only to their economic fears (for if their **business** of making idols **came into disrepute**, they might find themselves impoverished), but also appealing to their civic pride and their religious zeal. **The temple of the great goddess Artemis** was the pride of the city, being 165 feet by 345 feet, adorned with splendid colors and gold leaf, and containing an altar 20 feet square. If Paul were allowed to continue his work, this wonderful temple would **be considered as nothing** and left neglected. There was the

VI. Paul's Further Journeys   Acts 19:23–41

real and present danger that the goddess whom the **whole of Asia and indeed the world worshipped** was **about to be brought down from her greatness** and dethroned from her rightful position. How could they let this happen? Ephesus, world-renowned as the keeper of her temple, would be universally blamed.

Demetrius played the crowd well, and **when they heard this**, they were **filled with wrath** at Paul and began **crying out, saying, "Great *is* Artemis of the Ephesians!"**

In the packed city, a mob quickly gathered, joining in the cry, and soon **the city was filled with confusion**. The mob **rushed into the theater**, the open-air amphitheater which could seat almost 25,000 people and which served for town meetings, to deal with the civic crisis of Paul's influence. On the way they **seized Gaius and Aristarchus, Paul's co-travelers from Macedonia** (being unable to seize Paul as they would have liked). By the time they arrived at the theater, Paul had caught wind of the events, and he intended to enter into the people's assembly to defend himself (and to rescue his friends). **Some of the Asiarchs, being friends of his, sent** word **to him, urging him not to give himself to the theater**. Such an act would be noble, but suicidal, for he risked being torn to pieces.

The **Asiarchs** were elected leaders of the province of Asia, charged with maintaining the emperor cult there. Luke stresses their friendly support of Paul to show that the Roman government had nothing to fear from Paul and the Christians.

Meanwhile, **some** of the crowd **were crying out one thing and some another, for the assembly was in confusion, and the majority did not know why they had assembled**. This was scarcely surprising, since this was not an official assembly (Gr. *ekklesia*) or people's assembly (Gr. *demos*), both words used for regularly convened town meetings. Rather it was simply a mob.

At some point, **the Jews put forward Alexander**, probably for the purpose of explaining that Paul was not one of theirs, and of distancing the Jewish community there from the hated Christians. They had worked hard to gain respectability in Ephesus and were not about to let it be lost because of Paul. Though Alexander **motioned with his hand** in hope of gaining a hearing, it was all for naught, for **when they recognized that he was a Jew,** they concluded that Alexander too was somehow behind the anti-idol rhetoric (the Jews being famous for the rejection of idols). **One voice came from them all as they cried out for about two hours, "Great *is* Artemis of the Ephesians!"** Mention of the long two-hour duration of the chant underscores how out-of-control the mob had become.

St. Luke calls attention to the Alexander incident to emphasize how easily it was for a Gentile audience to confuse Judaism with the Christian movement, and how little the Roman world really understood the Christians. The example of Alexander thus serves as a cautionary tale against jumping to conclusions about the Way.

After two hours of mob chanting, **the *town* scribe** stood up. His presence was enough to **calm** the crowd and gain him a hearing, for he was a person of importance, being the chief administrative officer of the city and the liaison between the city and Rome. He realized the mob was out of control and needed to be reined in. He begins by assuring them their beloved Artemis and the city's prestige are in no danger from the Christians. (Church history would later prove this assurance was too quickly given.) For **who was there among men who did not know** and respect **the Ephesian city *as* temple-guardian of the great Artemis,** and of her image **which is Zeus-fallen?** This **Zeus-fallen** image (Gr. *diopetes*) doubtless refers to a meteorite, whose shape suggested to them the many-breasted Artemis, that fell from the sky—from Zeus (Gr. *Dio*). Ephesus was in no danger of having her goddess dethroned, **since these things** were **undeniable.**

Moreover, they had **brought** into their midst by violence two **men who were neither temple-robbers nor blasphemers of their god.** That is, the public behavior of Gaius and Aristarchus was irreproachable, as they had done nothing that could be proven publicly sacrilegious to the Ephesian religion. (Missionaries may note this, for courtesy towards all religions was part of the apostolic approach.) **If therefore Demetrius and the craftsmen with him had a matter against any man,** they should avail themselves of the legal recourses available to them—the **assizes** and the **proconsuls,** who could try cases of personal wrong. Let them prosecute these

VI. Paul's Further Journeys   Acts 20:1–2

men there, if they thought they had a case, and not lynch them like this. If the matter were graver and a matter of public mischief and wrongdoing, it should be **settled in the lawful assembly** (which courts met regularly each month)—not like this.

The town clerk then comes to this point. It was not Paul and his company who were the proven danger to Ephesus—it was the mob. Demetrius had spoken of danger (v. 27)—but the real danger here was that the citizens would be **charged with a riot about today, since there was no cause *for it*,** and if the Romans inquired why such a large group had gathered this way, they would **not be able to render an account**. Such unlawful gatherings as this threatened the city's status with Rome. **After** he said **these *things*,** the crowd was sobered, and **he dismissed the** (so-called) **assembly**.

Luke spends a great deal of time narrating this story (in which Paul does not really feature), for he wants his Roman readers to see how easily the Christians can be falsely accused by an ignorant mob. In this instance, the presence of the Christians did indeed produce civil unrest (compare 17:6), but the blame rested entirely with the mob, not with the Christians.

To Greece

> ꙮ ꙮ ꙮ ꙮ ꙮ
>
> **20** 1 And after the uproar had stopped, Paul sent for the disciples, and having exhorted them, he greeted them and departed to go into Macedonia.
> 2 And having gone through those parts and having exhorted them with a long word, he came into Greece.

Luke ends his account of Paul's time in Ephesus with **the uproar**, making it clear that Paul was not driven from Ephesus, but left it of his own accord, having first **sent for the disciples** of the city and **having exhorted them** to stay firm in the Faith. It was only after this that Paul **greeted them** one last time and **departed** the city **to go into Macedonia**, probably to Philippi.

In going to Macedonia (by way of Troas), Paul was motivated by his desire to find Titus and to get news from him of how the Corinthians had responded to his first letter to them. After Paul got this news from Titus, he went **through those parts** around Macedonia (probably as far as the border of Illyricum, the land on the east side of the Adriatic Sea; see Rom. 15:9) and at length **came into Greece**, to make his long-promised visit to see the Corinthians. (See the Excursus following.) These pastoral matters, however, were none of Luke's concern in writing his own account, and so this aspect of Paul's work Luke passes over in silence, content to simply give a summary of Paul's movements.

❦ EXCURSUS
On Writing the Second Epistle to the Corinthians and the Epistles to the Galatians and the Romans

After sending his first letter to the Corinthians, Paul waited in Ephesus hoping for them to repent and correct themselves. (That was also the reason for his change of itinerary regarding them: while he was with them, he told them he planned to visit them on his way to Macedonia and then see them again after leaving Macedonia; see 2 Cor. 1:15–16. By the time he wrote 1 Corinthians, he planned to delay his visit until after he had visited Macedonia; see 1 Cor. 16:5. Paul hoped this delay would give the Corinthians time to amend; see 2 Cor. 1:23—2:1.)

Titus had been sent to Corinth to deliver Paul's first letter to them, and Paul had arranged to meet with Titus in Troas afterwards to get news of how things were in Corinth. After Paul left Ephesus, he headed north to Troas, probably sailing along the coast, to find Titus. Paul found many opportunities to preach the Gospel there, but he did not find Titus (2 Cor. 2:12). As week succeeded week, Paul became more and more concerned to get news of his beloved Corinthians from Titus, so he left the fruitful work in Troas to head to Macedonia to find him (2 Cor. 2:13). At length he did find him in Philippi, with the good news that Corinth had followed Paul's directive to excommunicate a notorious offender (see 1 Cor. 5:1f; 2 Cor. 2:6f).

But there was alarming news too, for some were accusing Paul of vacillation (why else would he change his itinerary and not fulfill his word to visit them before going to Macedonia?) and of weakness (see 2 Cor. 1:17f; 10:1f). Also, a collection still needed to be taken among them for the poor in Jerusalem (see 2 Cor. 8—9). So it was that Paul wrote his Second Letter to the Corinthians from Philippi. Titus took this letter to the Corinthians as a preparation for Paul's approaching visit.

Afterwards, Paul finally visited Corinth in Greece. Once there, he heard of difficulties in Galatia. After his recent visit there (Acts 18:23), his Judaizing opponents had dogged his steps, slandering him and his Gospel and encouraging his Gentile converts to accept circumcision. Paul knew that to accept circumcision as a condition of salvation undercut the entire Gospel of the love of Christ, and so in great turmoil of heart he wrote his Letter to the Galatians, urging them not to accept circumcision but to stand fast in the faith they had first received.

While in Corinth, Paul also turned his thoughts to more distant work. He planned, now he had finished his work of collecting money in Macedonia and Achaia, to deliver the money to the poor of Jerusalem and then proceed even further afield than he had ever gone before. His plan was to deliver the collection to Jerusalem and then to visit Rome, using this a base from which to travel to the furthest limit of the west, to Spain (see Rom. 15:22–28). Knowing that he and his Gospel were enduring much slander from the Jews, he wrote his Letter to the Romans from Corinth at this time, to secure a welcome for himself in the Eternal City and a base of operations from which he might proceed further west. This epistle was carried to Rome by Phoebe, a rich patron of the Church dwelling in the nearby port of Cenchrea (Rom. 16:1), probably in the spring of AD 57.

> 3 And he stayed three months *there*, and when a council was formed against him by the Jews as he was about to sail for Syria, he was of a mind to return through Macedonia.
> 4 And there were accompanying him Sopater of Berea, *the son* of Pyrrhus; and Aristarchus and Secundus of the Thessalonians; and Gaius of Derbe, and Timothy; and Tychicus and Trophimus of Asia.
> 5 But these had gone on ahead and were waiting for us at Troas.
> 6 And we *ourselves* sailed from Philippi after the days of Unleavened *Bread*, and came to them in Troas within five days; and there we spent seven days.

Paul **stayed three months** in Corinth, spending the winter there, since sea travel was difficult at this time. After this he intended **to sail for Syria** and thence to Jerusalem, probably aboard a ship that regularly took pilgrims there. A plot and **council was formed against him by the Jews**, who had learned of his intent to return to Jerusalem, and who were probably planning to assassinate him once he was aboard ship. Accordingly, Paul changed his plans and was **of a mind to return** to Jerusalem **through Macedonia** (doubtless Philippi), heading north and sailing from the Philippian port of Neapolis.

Luke lists his traveling companions: **Sopater of Berea,** *the son*

VI. Paul's Further Journeys Acts 20:7–12

of Pyrrhus (Pyrrhus being mentioned possibly to differentiate him from another Sopater in the Berean church); **Aristarchus and Secundus of the Thessalonians; Gaius of Derbe; Timothy** and **Tychicus** and **Trophimus of Asia**. These men were those from the various churches sent to accompany Paul as he brought the money collected from their churches. They accompanied him as a testimony that Paul would indeed take the collection to Jerusalem as promised. This group preceded Paul (and Luke; compare the **we** of v. 6; evidently Luke had remained in Philippi until this time) and **were waiting for** them **at Troas**. The reason for the advance delegation to Troas is not stated; perhaps more collecting there remained to be done, while Paul felt he had to remain in Philippi to deal with pastoral issues there. Paul and his companions **sailed from Philippi after the days of Unleavened** *Bread*, at Passover time, and came to **Troas within five days**. The seas were evidently contrary; earlier the journey from Troas to the Philippian port had been made in two days (16:11).

It is interesting that Luke does not mention the collection Paul was making among the churches of the area, which was the reason for the large group of people accompanying him from the various churches. Possibly he omits this detail lest he open Paul to the accusation that he was preaching the Gospel for monetary gain. This collection, though important to Paul, formed no part of Luke's apologetic purpose. His task was to reveal the divine spread of the Gospel, not to give a complete history of Paul's ministry.

It is also interesting that Titus is not mentioned among the traveling companions, since we know from 2 Corinthians 8:6, 16f that Titus was one of those taking care of the offering. It is possible that he is included in the "we" of verse 6, and that Luke does not mention him since he is Luke's brother.

Return to Jerusalem

> ॐ ॐ ॐ ॐ ॐ
>
> 7 And on the first *day* of the week, when we were assembled to break bread, Paul was discussing

> with them, about to depart the next day, and he was extending his word until midnight.
> 8 And there were many lamps in the upper-room where we were assembled.
> 9 A certain young man, Eutychus by name, was sitting upon the window *sill*, overwhelmed by a deep sleep as Paul was discussing for a long *time*. Overwhelmed by the sleep, he fell downwards from the third *floor*, and was taken up dead.
> 10 Paul, having gone down, fell upon him, and after *throwing his arms* around *him*, he said, "Do not be in an uproar, for his life is in him."
> 11 And having gone up, and having broken the bread and tasted *it*, and having conversed with them a long while, until daybreak, he thus departed.
> 12 And they led away the child alive, and were not moderately encouraged.

In narrating Paul's return to Jerusalem, St. Luke begins by narrating a miracle. This is narrated because it proves that God was still with Paul, and that Paul's arrest did not occur because God had abandoned him for his alleged impiety.

The miracle began on **the first *day* of the week** (probably Sunday evening, for that is how Luke's Gentile audience would have understood him. This accords with the practice of St. John, who was also writing for a Gentile audience. Despite the Jewish reckoning of days being from sundown to sundown, in John 20:19 he still refers to our Sunday evening as the evening "on that day, the first day of the week.") They had **assembled** in the evening **to break bread** in the regular fellowship meal that culminated with the Eucharist. Since Paul was **about to depart the next day**, he was **discussing with them** and teaching them at great length, **extending his word until midnight**. Luke relates that **there were many lamps in the**

VI. Paul's Further Journeys   Acts 20:13–16

upper-room. **A certain young man** (he is described in v. 12 as a **child**, and was perhaps eleven years old), **Eutychus by name** (literally "good fortune," or "lucky") **was sitting upon the window** *sill*. He was up past his bedtime, the room was hot and crowded (probably the window sill was the only place he could find to sit), and the lamps were using up the oxygen. His fight to stay awake was unsuccessful; eventually he was overwhelmed by sleep and nodded off completely. He then **fell downwards from the third** *floor* **and was taken up dead**. (Luke, as a physician, would be a good judge of his condition.)

The assembled company was thrown into terrified confusion (the word rendered **be in an uproar** is the Greek *thorubeo*, used in Matt. 9:23 to describe the confusion of an entire household wailing in mourning). Paul, however, did not immediately accept this as God's will. **Having gone down**, he **fell upon** the boy, and after throwing his arms around him in prayerful embrace (as Elijah did when he raised a child from death; 1 Kin. 17:21), declared **his life is in him**. This was not a diagnosis, but a miracle, for Luke plainly says that the child was **taken up dead**.

It was after this they all returned joyfully to the upper-room to **break the bread** in the eucharistic fellowship meal and to listen to Paul as he concluded his teaching. It was **thus he departed**—that is, after having raised a child to life, as a sign that the message and assemblies of the Christians were life-giving. No wonder the Christians of Troas were **not moderately encouraged**. They abounded in encouragement and were exuberant, having seen evidence of the truth of Paul's word through his miraculous work.

ॐ ॐ ॐ ॐ ॐ

13 But we *ourselves*, going ahead to the boat, sailed for Assos, intending from there to take Paul along; for thus he had directed, intending himself *to go* by land.
14 And when he met us in Assos, we took him along and came to Mitylene.

> 15 And sailing away from there, we arrived the following *day* opposite Chios; and the next *day* we crossed over to Samos; and the *day* following we came to Miletus.
> 16 For Paul had decided to sail past Ephesus that he might not have to spend time in Asia; for he was hurrying to be in Jerusalem, if possible, on the day of Pentecost.

After this, most of the group **sailed for Assos**, rounding Cape Lectum. Because of the prevailing winds, this would take longer than the twenty-mile journey by land. They were **intending** to go all together and **to take Paul along** with them, but Paul **had directed** that they go ahead without him, for he was **intending himself *to go by land***. The reason for Paul's delay is not clear; perhaps he wanted to stay to make sure Eutyches was indeed all right. Paul **met** the boat **in Assos** and joined his companions there. Together they came to **Mitylene**, and then to **Chios**, and to **Samos** and at length to **Miletus**. Luke delights to mention in detail Paul's travels (compare the details of the sea journey in chs. 27–28). It is the authentic touch of the eyewitness.

Paul had decided to take a larger seagoing vessel at Miletus, one that would take him to Palestine. He was in Miletus because he had already **decided to sail past Ephesus** (Ephesus was between Chios and Samos). Though perhaps tempted to call in at Ephesus, **he was hurrying to be in Jerusalem, if possible, on the day of Pentecost**, and he knew that if he visited his beloved Ephesians, he would never make it in time. He wanted to deliver his collection before the great feast.

Why the hurry to be in Jerusalem for Pentecost? Certainty is impossible, but perhaps St. Paul did not want to miss the opportunity of meeting the many pilgrims from foreign lands who would be in the Holy City for the feast (compare their presence there in 2:5f) and sharing the Gospel with them. The presence of so many foreign Jews in Jerusalem was an opportunity not to be missed.

VI. Paul's Further Journeys — Acts 20:17–21

> 17 And from Miletus he sent to Ephesus and called to him the elders of the church.
> 18 And when they had come to him, he said to them, "You *yourselves* know, from the first day that I set foot in Asia, how I was with you the whole time,
> 19 "serving *as slave to* the Lord with all lowliness and with tears and with testings which came upon me through the counsels of the Jews;
> 20 "how I did not shrink back from announcing to you anything that was profitable, and teaching you publicly and from house to house,
> 21 "testifying to both Jews and Greeks of repentance to God and faith in our Lord Jesus Christ.

Ephesus was thirty miles away, and Paul could not spend time in Asia visiting the churches there, for his ship would perhaps spend only a week in Miletus before sailing on. Nonetheless, he did want to see **the elders of the church** in Ephesus to encourage them in their work, and all the more so since he did not expect to see them again. The utterances of the Christian prophets in every place visited spoke of imprisonment and suffering in Jerusalem, and Paul perhaps expected that one of the many plots of the Jews would finally be successful, and he would be assassinated there. Therefore **from Miletus he sent to Ephesus**, asking that the clergy there come to visit him one last time before his ship sailed. They arrived perhaps three days later.

Paul begins his farewell address by reminding them of his own example while he had been with them. They knew well that **from the very first day that** he **set foot in Asia**, and consistently **the whole time** he was among them, he was **serving *as slave to* the Lord** with

all lowliness, not shunning any hardship or lowly task, nor exalting himself over others as if he were better than they. (The verb rendered *serve as slave* is the Greek *douleuo*, cognate with *doulos*, slave.) Rather, Paul worked side by side with the flock, exhorting them **with tears** and humbly enduring whatever **testings** and opposition **came upon** him **through the counsels** and plots **of the Jews** of Ephesus. Moreover, he did **not shrink back from announcing to** the faithful **anything that was profitable**, as he continued teaching **publicly** in the synagogue and lecture hall of Tyrannus, and from private **house to house** among the Christians. He refused to water down his teaching, despite the opposition it provoked. He taught all who would hear, **both Jews and Greeks**, of the Gospel of **repentance to God and faith in our Lord Jesus Christ**. In all his time among them, he poured himself out tirelessly for the Gospel.

In rehearsing his past, Paul is not commending himself in a spirit of self-praise. Rather, he is offering himself as an example to those who must now care for the flock he has gathered and saying they must do as he has done. He must leave his flock now (as he thought) forever, and he is concerned to leave them in the care of those who will love them as he loves them.

Paul's words are not meant only for the Ephesian elders, but for clergy throughout the ages. No presbyter must think he is too dignified for lowly and secular work. None must hold himself aloof from his flock. Rather, the true shepherd must so identify himself with his people that their stumblings become his, and he will anguish over their weaknesses, even to tears. And his concern will not be for his own people alone, but for the whole community, both Jews and Greeks, both believers and unbelievers. Only by so doing can the Church's shepherds be true to the pastoral legacy handed down by the great apostle.

ॐ ॐ ॐ ॐ ॐ

22 "And now, behold! having been bound in the Spirit, I *myself* am going to Jerusalem, not knowing what will meet me in it,

23 "except that the Holy Spirit in every city

VI. Paul's Further Journeys   Acts 20:22–27

> testifies to me, saying that bonds and tribulations are waiting for me.
> 24 "But I on no account make *my* life as precious to myself, that I may finish my course; and the service which I received from the Lord Jesus, to testify to the Good News of the grace of God.
> 25 "And now behold! I *myself* know that all of you, among whom I went about heralding the Kingdom, will no longer see my face.
> 26 "Therefore I witness to you in this day that I am clean of the blood of all.
> 27 "For I did not shrink back from announcing to you all the intention of God.

This legacy was all the more important, because he shares the surprising news (indicated by the word **behold!**) that he would be with them no longer. **Having been bound in the Spirit**, constrained by the direction given by the Spirit of God through the prophecies of the Christian prophets, he was **going to Jerusalem** to deliver the promised collection to the poor there. And he did **not know what would meet** him in the city exactly, **except that the Holy Spirit, in every city** he had been in, **testified** to him that **bonds and tribulations were waiting** for him. The prophets foretold that he must go to Jerusalem and meet his fate of suffering. Given the Jewish plots to assassinate him (as recently as his departure from Corinth; 20:3), he did not expect to survive. But that did not mean he would refuse to go, for **on no account** did he count his **life as precious**, to be preserved at all costs. Rather, his only consuming desire was to **finish** his **course**, running to the end the race set for him, and complete **the service** (Gr. *diakonia*) he **received from the Lord Jesus**. On the road to Damascus, Christ had called him to serve Him by **testifying** to all men about **the Good News of the grace of God**, and he would serve his Lord to the end.

He had testified to that Good News in Ephesus, as he **went about heralding the Kingdom**. He **did not shrink back from**

announcing all the intention of God. He had proclaimed all the fullness of the Gospel, the entire will of God for the salvation of humanity. The responsibility to preserve this tradition was now theirs. He had done his part. He now **witnessed** to them before God that he was **clean of the blood of** them **all**. As a watchman like Ezekiel, his part was to declare all that God told him to declare—what they would do with this was now up to them (see Ezek. 33:6). If they failed to be saved, it was no fault of his.

> ❧ ❧ ❧ ❧ ❧
>
> 28 "But pay attention to yourselves and to all the flock, among which the Holy Spirit has set you *as* bishops, to shepherd the Church of God which He acquired with the blood of His own *Son*.
> 29 "I *myself* know that after my departure burdensome wolves will enter in among you, not sparing the flock;
> 30 "and from among your own selves men will arise, speaking perverse *things*, to draw the disciples after them.
> 31 "Therefore keep alert, remembering that night and day for three years I did not cease to admonish each one with tears.

Having left them this apostolic tradition, he urged them to **pay attention to** themselves **and to all the flock**. Caring for this flock was a sacred trust. **The Holy Spirit** Himself had called them and empowered them for this task, **setting** them *as* **bishops**, those who must oversee the care of their brethren. (This phrase points to the Holy Spirit given through the laying on of hands in ordination, and possibly to prophetic utterance that accompanied it; compare 1 Tim. 4:14.) The task of the elders was to **shepherd the Church of God** committed to their care. This was an awesome task, for God had **acquired** this Church **with the blood**

VI. Paul's Further Journeys   Acts 20:32–35

of His own *Son*, and so the Church was inestimably precious to Him. Let the shepherds tremble and not fail in their care of God's own!

(We note in passing that it is grammatically possible to translate the last phrase of v. 28 as "the Church of God which He purchased in His own blood," so that Luke here calls Jesus "God." However, though Jesus Christ is indeed "true God from true God," all other New Testament usage reserves the title "God" for the Father, if the title is used alone. The use of the title "God" to describe Jesus, though theologically correct, is anachronistic in the New Testament. Paul is saying that God the Father has purchased His Church in the blood of His own one, His own Son.)

The pastoral vigilance on the part of the Ephesian clergy was necessary, for after Paul had gone, **burdensome** and fierce **wolves would enter in among** them, **not sparing the flock**. Heretical and false teachers had been held at bay to some degree by the presence and work of St. Paul, but in the years after his death, the wolves would menace the sheep. Indeed, **from among** their **own selves**, from the ranks of the Ephesian clergy, **men would arise, speaking perverse *things*** contrary to the holy tradition, **to draw the disciples after them** into schism.

The clergy must **therefore keep alert** and resist such men. They should not be blindsided by these future developments, or imagine that the teachings that would soon spread were a natural development of the true Gospel. They could **remember that night and day for three years** (reckoned in the Jewish manner, taking a part of a year for a whole), Paul did **not cease to admonish each one** of them **with tears**, urging all to hold fast to the traditions. Paul had expected such threats to come. They must be prepared. History relates that Paul's predictions were true. By the second century, Asia was a hotbed of heresy.

ॐ ॐ ॐ ॐ ॐ

32 "And now I commit you to God and to the Word of His grace, which is able to build up

> and to give the inheritance among all who are sanctified.
> 33 "I have desired no one's silver or gold or apparel.
> 34 "You yourselves know that these hands served my needs and those with me.
> 35 "In everything I showed you that by toiling thus it is necessary to help the weak and to remember the words of the Lord Jesus, that He Himself said, 'It is more blessed to give than to receive.'"

At the end, Paul could only **commit** them to the **God** who loved them **and to the Word of His grace**, the Gospel tradition he had preached among them. If they would hold to those apostolic traditions, God would keep them safe, for that Word was **able to build up and give** them **the inheritance** of eternal life **among all who were sanctified**, called from the world to be God's people. They did not need whatever additions the future heretical teachers might offer. Let them cling to the fullness of the Gospel and resist heretical innovations! Only so could they be finally saved.

Once again, Paul commends himself to them, making his own integrity a pledge of the truth of his message. He **desired no one's silver or gold or apparel**; he did not preach his message, or water it down, for the sake of gain. Rather, they themselves could recall that his own **hands** (here Paul doubtless held them up for them to see) **served** his **needs** and even the needs of **those with** him. They could trust his integrity.

In everything, in every situation, therefore, he **showed** them they must not be moved by avarice. Rather, **by toiling** as he did they must **help the weak**, caring for the sick who were unable to work. In this way they would fulfill **the words of the Lord Jesus** (not recorded in the canonical Gospels, but preserved in early oral tradition) that it was **more blessed to give than to receive**. God's blessing would be with them if they reached out selflessly to help the poor—as he had given them an example.

❦ EXCURSUS
On the Pastoral Office

In St. Paul's farewell address, we note that the elders or presbyters (Gr. *presbuteros*; v. 17) are also called bishops (*episcopos*; v. 28), so that the two terms are used more or less interchangeably. It was not until the end of the first century that a terminological shift arose. In the Letters of St. Ignatius of Antioch (who died about 107), the term "elder" or "presbyter" is used to describe the many pastoral leaders of the local church, all of whom are set under one single local leader, and the term "bishop" is now reserved for this local leader. That is, in the practice of Ignatius of Antioch, the term "bishop" no longer describes the many presbyters of the local church, but the head of the community alone.

I suggest this is not so much a radical change of church structure as it is simply a change in terminology. For even in the middle of the first century there was a single local leader who acted as the overseer of the community and the head of his fellow presbyters. This single leader at that time had no distinct title; he was simply called by his name. In first-century Jerusalem, the local leader was James; in the later first-century Rome, it was Clement (author of an epistle to the Corinthians).

As long as the apostles were alive, this single leader did not have as crucial a role as he was later to have, for all the pastors of the local churches (including the single leader) looked to the apostles as their ultimate heads. It was only after the death of the apostles and the growth of heresy and schism that it became urgent for the embattled Christian communities to coalesce, each around a single leader. The preservation of local unity became increasingly important, and the faithful had to know whom to look to in order to preserve this unity. It was these late-first-century developments that brought the local leader into greater prominence

> and necessitated giving him a specific title not shared by his fellow elders. From this time forth, he alone would be called "bishop," and his pastoral colleagues would be called "presbyters" (or in modern English, "priests").

ತ್ರಿ ತ್ರಿ ತ್ರಿ ತ್ರಿ ತ್ರಿ

36 And having said these things, he fell to his knees and prayed with them all.
37 And there was considerable weeping among all, and having fallen upon Paul's neck, they were *fervently* kissing him,
38 being especially pained over the word which he had said, that they were about to observe his face no longer. And they were sending him forth to the boat.

After his farewell, Paul **fell to his knees and prayed with them all**. The usual posture for prayer was standing; kneeling in prayer was only done during times of great emotion. His heart had been knit to these men, and it was with difficulty that he parted from them. On their part, **there was considerable weeping** among them too, and **having fallen upon Paul's neck, they were *fervently* kissing him** farewell. They embraced him as if they could not bear to be finally parted. What **pained** them the most was **the word which he had said that they were about to observe his face no longer**.

The word rendered *fervently kiss* is the Greek *kataphileo*, a more intensive form of the verb *phileo*, "to kiss." The word is used in Luke 15:20 (along with the phrase "to fall upon the neck" of another) to describe the overwhelming emotion the father had for his returning prodigal son. The love that united the apostle and his clergy converts was a mighty love indeed—and a testimony (Luke means his Roman reader to understand) to the apostle's integrity. For how else could a man inspire such loyalty, except by being above reproach? Obviously there was nothing in the slanders circulating about Paul.

After this final farewell, **they were sending him forth to the**

VI. Paul's Further Journeys   Acts 21:1–6

boat, escorting him back on board and (doubtless) providing him with food for the journey as well.

> ## 21
> 1 And it happened that having been withdrawn from them, we sailed, we ran a straight course to Cos, and the next *day* to Rhodes, and from there to Patara;
> 2 and having found a boat crossing over to Phoenicia, we embarked *and* sailed.
> 3 And having come in sight of Cyprus, leaving it on the left, we were sailing to Syria and came to Tyre; for there the boat was to unload the cargo.
> 4 And after searching out the disciples, we remained on there seven days; and they were telling Paul through the Spirit not to go up to Jerusalem.
> 5 And when it happened that our days there were ended, we departed and were going, while all, with wives and children, sent us forth until we were out of the city. And after falling to *their* knees on the beach and praying, we greeted one another.
> 6 Then we went up into the boat, and they returned to *their* own *homes*.

Paul and his companions, **having been withdrawn from them**, sailed on. The word rendered *withdrawn* is the passive of the Greek *apospao*, the same verb used in 20:30; the image is of Paul and his friends reluctantly being torn away from the embraces of their friends. They sailed to **Cos**, one of the islands in the Aegean forty miles south of Miletus, and **the next *day* to Rhodes**, the city on the northeast tip of the island of the same name. From there they sailed to **Patara**, a port city and capital of Lycia, a province south of

Asia Minor. Here they changed ships, and **embarked *and* sailed** to **Phoenicia,** the coastal strip of the province of Syria. Passing south of **Cyprus,** they eventually came to **Tyre**. Luke gives a characteristically complete itinerary, testimony of his eyewitness truthfulness. The open-sea journey from Patara to Tyre would have taken about five days.

In Tyre, **after searching out the disciples** there, they **remained on there seven days**. Since Luke uses the verb *search out* (Gr. *aneurisko*), it is possible Paul did not know the whereabouts of these believers and had to discover who and where the Christians were. (Perhaps things had changed since Paul's previous visit to Phoenicia, related in 15:3.) As in other Christian communities (20:23), the prophets of Tyre **through the Spirit** predicted that imprisonment and suffering awaited Paul in Jerusalem, and on the basis of these prophecies, the people were urging Paul **not to go up to Jerusalem**. Paul however, was still determined to fulfill his work, even though martyrdom might be his lot.

When the time came for his departure, **all** the community, including the **wives and children, sent** them **forth until** they **were out of the city**, escorting him back to the ship, unwilling to leave him to his fate. The presence of entire families testifies to the love they had for Paul, for even the children were reluctant to see him go. They **fell to *their* knees on the beach** in heartfelt prayer for him and were **praying** at length. Then they **greeted** one another, saying farewell for what they assumed would be the last time. It was only when Paul and his companions **went up into the boat** and were out of sight that **they returned to *their* own homes**. Their love for Paul is all the more impressive if they had only known him for the seven days he was with them. As with Paul's departure from the Ephesian elders, Luke relates this story of love for Paul to show how blameless was Paul's ministry among the Christians.

ॐ ॐ ॐ ॐ ॐ

7 And when we *ourselves* had completed the voyage from Tyre, we arrived in Ptolemais;

VI. Paul's Further Journeys — Acts 21:7–16

and after greeting the brothers, we remained one day with them.

8 And on the next *day*, having gone out, we came to Caesarea; and having entered the house of Philip the evangelist, who was one of the Seven, we remained with him.

9 Now this *man* had four virgin daughters who were prophesying.

10 And as we were remaining on there for many days, a certain prophet came down from Judea, Agabus by name.

11 And coming to us, he took Paul's belt and bound his own feet and hands, and said, "Thus says the Holy Spirit: 'The man who owns this belt—thus will the Jews in Jerusalem bind and deliver *him* into the hands of the Gentiles.'"

12 And when we heard these *things*, we *ourselves* as well as the locals were urging him not to go up to Jerusalem.

13 Then Paul answered, "What are you doing, weeping and pounding my heart? For I *myself* am ready not only to be bound, but even to die at Jerusalem for the Name of the Lord Jesus."

14 And since he would not be persuaded, we fell silent, saying, "The will of the Lord be done!"

15 And after these days we got ready *and* went up to Jerusalem.

16 And some of the disciples from Caesarea also came with us, bringing us to one with whom we were to lodge, Mnason, a certain Cypriot, an early disciple.

Ptolemais was about twenty-five miles to the south along the coast. They **greeted the brothers** in that city, but **remained** only

one day there (possibly because they were hastening to friends in Caesarea). The **next day** they came to the main Palestinian port city of **Caesarea**, another twenty-seven miles south. Though the journey from Ptolemais to Caesarea may have been by ship, it is probable they proceeded on foot, for the sea voyage was said to have Phoenicia as its destination (v. 2).

At Caesarea, they **entered the house of Philip**, who was **one of the Seven** (see 6:5), and **remained with him**. Philip is styled **the evangelist** because of his evangelistic work in Samaria, Azotus, and up the Palestinian coast to Caesarea, where he finally settled (8:12f, 26f, 40). (This is not to say that Philip was not then still continuing his evangelistic work, using Caesarea as a base.) By this time, he **had four virgin daughters who were prophesying**. Though we are not told the substance of their prophesying, given Luke's emphasis on prophecies of suffering accompanying Paul throughout his journey to Jerusalem (20:23; 21:4), it is difficult to resist the conclusion that these women had the same message.

This certainly was the message of **a certain prophet, Agabus by name**, who **came down from Judea**. (Technically, Caesarea was a part of Judea, but because it was such a Gentile city, it was separate from Judea in the popular mind.) He arrived after Paul and his companions had stayed **many days** with his host, and in his prophecy he used a dramatic action, as did the prophets of old (see 1 Kin. 11:29f; Jer. 13:1f; 19:1f). Coming up, he **took Paul's belt and bound his own feet and hands, and said, "Thus says the Holy Spirit, 'The man who owns this belt—thus will the Jews in Jerusalem bind and deliver *him* into the hands of the Gentiles.'"** The phrase **Thus says the Holy Spirit** (Gr. *tade legei to pneuma to agion*) echoes the prophetic formula, "Thus says the Lord" (Gr. *tade legei kurios*; Jer. 13:1 LXX); Agabus was speaking with the same authority as the prophets of old.

When all present **heard these *things***, they began **urging** Paul **not to go up to Jerusalem**—both **the locals** of Caesarea, as well as his traveling companions who had heard such things before. The dramatic binding of Agabus with Paul's belt, now that Jerusalem was so close at hand, was too much for them, and they could not bear

VI. Paul's Further Journeys   Acts 21:7–16

it that Paul was walking into what they thought was certain death.

Paul himself was grieved and besought them to stop **weeping and pounding** his **heart** by their entreaties. For it was no use—he was **ready not only to be bound** as Agabus had been, **but even to die at Jerusalem for the Name of the Lord Jesus**. Possibly they continued to press him and argue their point. But since it was all too evident Paul **would not be persuaded**, they **fell silent**, remarking only, **"The will of the Lord be done."** One gets the impression this was a reluctant acceptance of the divine will, and perhaps they were not entirely convinced this *was* the will of God. But Paul was not to be deterred, even when their entreaties broke his heart. Luke's mention of Paul's iron resolve highlights his point that Paul's arrest in Jerusalem was a voluntary one—it did not happen as a surprise to Paul, as if the judgment of God had caught up with him (as his foes alleged).

After their stay in Caesarea was over, they **got ready** (saddling pack animals) *and* **went up to Jerusalem**, the city where Paul would meet his fate. **Some of the disciples from Caesarea** accompanied Paul and his companions on the sixty-four-mile journey, escorting them to **Mnason, a certain Cypriot**, one who was **an early disciple**, converted from the early days. They lodged with him. Luke's mention of Mnason by name is characteristic of his concern to highlight Christian hospitality.

⚹ VII ⚹

PAUL IN JERUSALEM
(21:17—26:32)

§VII.1. Arrival

St. Luke next relates the events of Paul's arrival, arrest, and detention in Jerusalem. We know he places a great importance on this since he narrates it in such detail. Luke takes 112 verses (21:17—24:23) to narrate the events of the first twelve days in Jerusalem, while (for example) the two years subsequent are narrated in a mere four verses (24:24–27). For Luke, the precise events surrounding Paul's arrest are crucial. He wants his Roman audience to know the truth of the matter: that Paul's arrest was unjust and entirely unwarranted. Paul's foes were making the most of his long detention, saying it proved he was a dangerous criminal. Luke wants his readers to know this is not so.

⚹ ⚹ ⚹ ⚹ ⚹

17 And when we had come to Jerusalem, the brothers welcomed us gladly.
18 And on the following *day* Paul went in with us to James, and all the elders arrived.
19 And after he had greeted them, he was explaining one by one what God had done among the Gentiles through his service.
20 And having heard, they were glorifying God; and they said to him, "You observe, brother, how many myriads there are among the Jews of those who have believed, and they are all zealots of the Law;

21 "and they have been instructed about you, that you are teaching apostasy from Moses to all the Jews *who are* among the Gentiles, telling them not to circumcise their children, nor to walk in the customs.
22 "What therefore is *to be done*? They will doubtless hear that you have come.
23 "Therefore do this that we tell you. There are with us four men who have a vow;
24 "take them and purify yourself along with them, and pay *their costs* that they may shave *their* heads; and all will know that there is nothing *to the things* which they have been instructed about you, but that you yourself also walk-straight, keeping the Law.
25 "But about the Gentiles who have believed: we *ourselves* wrote, having judged that they should keep from things sacrificed to idols and from blood and from *things* strangled and from fornication."
26 Then Paul took the men the next day, and having purified himself, entered into the Temple with them, giving notice of the completion of the days of purification when the offering would be made for each of them.

At length Paul and his companions **came to Jerusalem**, and **the brothers** there (such as Mnason and other locals) **welcomed** them **gladly**, a sign that Paul did have supporters among the Jerusalem Christians despite his controversial status. After resting for the night, **Paul went in** with his companions to see **James**, perhaps at James's home. James was the leader of the church there, the other apostles having left by then.

Paul's presence in the city represented something of a crisis: he was *persona non grata* to most of the non-Christian Jews there, and even many of the Christian Jews had heard disquieting things about

VII. Paul in Jerusalem — Acts 21:17–26

him. He had come to deliver the collection of money he had taken among the Gentile churches for the Jerusalem poor. The money itself no doubt was appreciated, but the source was suspect. (That was why Paul asked his churches to pray that the gift would be accepted; see Rom. 15:30–31.) Wasn't this the one who was telling the Jews in the Diaspora not to be circumcised and turning them all into Gentiles? Perhaps the Jerusalem Christians should have nothing to do with this pagan gift. This crisis was the reason not just some, but **all the elders** of the church **arrived** there for the historic meeting.

After Paul **had greeted them** with the customary kiss of peace, he began **explaining one by one what God had done among the Gentiles through his** humble **service** (Gr. *diakonia*). His emphasis was not on what he had done, but rather on what God had done, as Paul was suggesting that all he had accomplished in converting the Gentiles was the work and will of God. When they heard of all the miracles and the many conversions, **they were glorifying God**. For Luke, this praise from the Jerusalem leadership was a clear sign God was indeed acting through Paul's ministry, for an outpouring of praise was always the hallmark of God's activity on earth (see Luke 2:13, 20; 7:16; 18:43; Acts 3:9; 8:8; 8:39; 16:34). Thus, to his great relief, Paul found the Christian leadership in the mother church supported him and his ministry.

But though James and the other elders supported Paul, the crisis remained. Acknowledging Paul as a beloved **brother**, they explained to him there were **myriads among the Jews** who had **believed** in Jesus, and how they were **all zealots of the Law**. The term *myriads*—literally "ten thousands"—is used hyperbolically, for there were at most 55,000 Jews in Jerusalem in total. The numbers of Jewish Christians were, however, very great, and they were **all zealots of the Law**. That is, they were fervently devoted to their ancestral way and indignant at those who scorned it. This was all the more so since at this time (around AD 57), Rome was moving against Israel in events that would soon culminate in the destruction of their Temple and extinction of their national life (Rome would invade in 66). The more the threat from Rome grew, the greater was their instinctive love for their national customs. They were in no mood to be philosophical about anyone who counseled apostasy from the Law.

Although Paul did *not* in fact **teach apostasy from Moses** to the Jews of the Diaspora, nor tell them **not to circumcise their children,** nor say they should not **walk in the customs** they had received (such as the Sabbath, the festivals, and the food laws), Paul did teach that such things no longer had ultimate significance (see Gal. 6:15). And he did say that his Gentile converts should not accept such things as if they were essential to salvation (see Gal. 5:2). Such teaching could easily be twisted by Paul's adversaries and his words taken out of context to make him sound as if he were indeed a renegade and opponent of Judaism. Something had to be done to show the Jerusalem Christians (to whom Paul proffered his gift of money from his Gentile churches) that he was still a good Jew, for all the city would soon **hear that** he **had come** and would be watching him suspiciously.

The leadership of the church suggested this plan: they had **four men** who **had a** Nazirite **vow** that was nearing completion. That is, these men were in a state of consecration, expressed by letting their hair grow. Once the time of their vowed consecration was completed, they were to **shave *their* heads** and offer their hair as part of the required sacrifices. These sacrifices were not cheap, but consisted of a male and female lamb, a ram, plus cereal and drink offerings—all of this times four. It was considered an act of piety to pay the expenses of such men (Herod Agrippa had done it once), and Paul was invited to pay these expenses now. He could do this when he **purified** himself by offering sacrifices (Jews would often purify themselves of ritual defilement when they returned to Israel after a long time in unclean Gentile countries), and so offer all the sacrifices at the same time. Since this was a public act (involving **giving** public **notice** of the time remaining for the vows' fulfillment), it would show all Jerusalem that the rumors about Paul were false and that he **also walked-straight** in the ancestral ways, **keeping the Law.**

The elders added that this keeping of the Law only applied to Jews like Paul. **About the Gentiles who had believed**, Paul's beloved converts, they would of course abide by what they themselves **wrote** at the Jerusalem Council (see Acts 15). The elders assured Paul that their suggestion did not imply any retraction of their previous policy. Paul agreed with this conciliatory course of action (since it involved no contradiction of his own principles; see 1 Cor. 9:20), and **took the men the next day** to begin the seven-day process of purification.

❧ EXCURSUS
On St. Paul's Judaism

It is apparent from 18:18 (which speaks of him keeping a Nazirite vow) that St. Paul was not opposed to Jews keeping the Jewish Law. His purifying himself from ritual defilement and paying for the expenses of four Nazirites cannot therefore be considered simply a political ploy. Paul was not presenting himself as other than he truly was. He really did keep the Jewish Law and "walk in the customs" of his ancestral Judaism.

Some have seen this as a problem. For how, they ask, can a Christian who believes in receiving God's forgiveness through Christ's sacrifice on the Cross continue to offer sacrifices according to the Law? The problem is more apparent than real, for it usually comes from modern Gentile Christians who know the Law only through book-learning. For St. Paul, however, the Law was a part of being Jewish, and as such it was "hard-wired" into his very being. He was, as he himself says, "a Jew by nature" (Gal. 2:15).

Even after believing that Jesus was the Messiah and that the Law was simply the historical means God used to bring His people to Christ (Rom. 10:4; Gal. 3:24), Paul continued to be a Jew. Believing in Christ did not mean that now he would eat pork (or anything else forbidden by the Law), or work on the Sabbath, or cease to say the prescribed Jewish prayers over food, or refuse to circumcise children. He would continue to relate to God and the world in a Jewish way, and not become a Gentile (as he was falsely accused).

The discovery that Jesus was the Christ did mean,

however, that these Jewish realities were not the final ones. Christ's Resurrection was now the final reality, transcending and (ultimately) superseding all other realities, just as the age to come transcended and will finally supersede this age. But that does not mean the Jewish realities *cease to be real*. The Jewish ways remain real conduits to divine life, authentic ways of relating to God. They are just not the ultimate ones. And now that the ultimate reality of Christ has come, these other realities and rites become merely relative in their significance, a part of the historical and cultural approach to God by which Israel was led to Christ.

To take several examples: The Sabbath was a divine reality in Israel, in that the pious Jew rested on the Sabbath to enjoy communion with God in thanksgiving for creation. The Jew could not dispense with this and still be obedient to God, for under the Mosaic covenant, the Sabbath still had ultimate significance. As part of the Law, it represented the ultimate in obedience to God, the high-water mark of God's provision for mankind.

But when Christ came, though a Christian Jew would still rest and read the Law in the synagogue on the Sabbath, the first day of the week came to have the ultimate significance. For on the first day of the week, he would meet with other Christians to celebrate the Lord's Supper, sacramentally uniting with Christ and participating in the powers of the age to come. The high-water mark of God's dispensation was now the Lord's Day, not the Sabbath. The Sabbath was the shadow; the reality was Christ (Col. 2:16–17). The Sabbath came to possess a relative and cultural significance, not an ultimate or eschatological one. It could be dispensed with, without apostasy from God, in a way that it never could before Christ. What now mattered was a new creation (Gal. 6:15).

It is the same with the sacrifices in the Temple. In the Law, the sacrifices were not just means of receiving God's forgiveness. Mere book-learning focuses only on this aspect of the sacrifices, but in St. Paul's life, they were so much more. They were also ways in which a Jew expressed his gratitude to God, giving away his possession (in this case, an animal) for God's sake. The offering was a time to pray in the holy place, to meet and pray with other Jews, to affirm one's fundamental identity as part of the chosen people, and to give oneself to God.

It continued to be all this even after Christ came. True, the aspect of "getting God's forgiveness" had become relativized. The writer to the Hebrews says that even under the Law, the sacrifices were more promise than fulfillment, more a request for cleansing than the actual cleansing itself (Heb. 10:1–4). The fulfillment, the actual cleansing, came through the Cross of Christ. But the sacrifices, even considered as prophecies of that cleansing, still had real value for the Christian Jew, in that they still accomplished all the other purposes related above. St. Paul therefore, as a loyal Jew, partook of the realities of the Temple. They were not the final or eschatological realities, for they pointed to Christ, who is Himself the final reality. But they were realities nonetheless and were gratefully received by the apostle to the Gentiles.

§VII.2. Arrest

27 And when the seven days were about to be finished, the Jews from Asia, having beheld him in the Temple, were stirring up all the crowd, and they laid hands upon him,
28 crying out, "Men of Israel, help! This one is the man who teaches everyone everywhere against the people, and the Law, and this place; and besides he has even brought Greeks into

> the Temple and has defiled this holy place!"
> 29 For they had before seen Trophimus the Ephesian in the city with him, and they supposed that Paul had brought him into the Temple.
> 30 And the whole city was moved, and the people ran together, and taking hold of Paul, they dragged him outside the Temple; and immediately the doors were shut.

All went as planned until the **seven days were about to be finished**. Paul's rites of purification required sacrifices to be offered on the third day and again on the seventh day. It was as he was entering the Temple on the seventh day to perform the last of the sacrifices that he was seen by **the Jews from Asia** (that is, from Ephesus). They were in Jerusalem for the Feast of Pentecost, and they carried with them a furious grudge. They had watched his success in Ephesus all during his time there with mounting envy and regarded him as utterly misled in supporting the Christian movement. And here before them was the great renegade himself!

They **had before seen Trophimus the Ephesian**, Paul's Gentile friend, **in the city with him**, where he had come to help present the offering to the Jerusalem church (20:4). Seeing Paul in the inner courts of the Temple (where Gentiles were forbidden to enter on pain of death), they gratuitously **supposed** that Paul had **brought** his friend with him through the Court of the Gentiles **into** these inner **Temple** courts, thereby defiling the Temple. Though Trophimus was nowhere to be seen (in fact Paul had not brought him into those Temple courts), they assumed he was somewhere in the crowd, so eager were they to believe the worst.

There they **laid hands upon** Paul, **crying out, "Men of Israel, help!"** All the crowd turned to see what was the emergency. Those who scuffled with Paul and held him fast began shouting, **stirring up all the crowd** with their false accusations that Paul had blasphemously **brought Greeks into the Temple** (note the plural: the number of Gentiles seems to have grown in their minds from Trophimus to include others as well). That would indeed have

VII. Paul in Jerusalem Acts 21:31–36

been a calamity, and the news spread like wild fire throughout **the whole city**. The people **ran together** to the Temple to avenge the outrage, and Paul soon found himself in the midst of a murderous mob, everyone trying to get at him and beat him. **They dragged him outside the Temple** into the outer Court of the Gentiles, and **immediately the doors** connecting the Court of the Gentiles to the Jewish Court of the Women **were shut** to prevent further profanation from any more Gentiles entering.

> 31 And while they were seeking to kill him, a report came up to the commander of the cohort that the whole of Jerusalem was in confusion.
> 32 Immediately they took along soldiers and centurions, *and* ran down to them; and when they saw the commander and the soldiers, they stopped striking Paul.
> 33 Then the commander drew near and took hold of him, and ordered him to be bound with two chains; and he was inquiring who he was and what he had done.
> 34 But among the crowd some were calling out one thing; others another. Not being able to know anything for certain because of the uproar, he ordered him to be brought into the barracks.
> 35 And when he was upon the steps, it so happened that he was borne by the soldiers because of the violence of the crowd;
> 36 for the multitude of the people were following, crying out, "Away with him!"

As things stood, Paul's end was at hand, for the crowd was about to stone him as they once had stoned Stephen, or even to tear Paul to pieces on the spot. But Roman soldiers were watching from the walls of the Tower of Antonia, located in the northwest corner of the Temple, with steps having access to the Court of the Gentiles (where Paul had been dragged). The fortress was garrisoned with Roman soldiers, who were especially vigilant for signs of riot during the Jewish festivals, when the city was swollen with patriotic pilgrims from around the world. One of them saw the riot and ran to bring the **report to the commander of the cohort**, Claudius Lysias (23:26).

The commander **immediately took along soldiers and centurions** and ran down to them to break up the riot. This show of Roman force was sizable: Luke mentions centurions in the plural (i.e. at least two), and each centurion was in charge of a force of a hundred men. Therefore at least two hundred soldiers ran down the steps of the Antonia Fortress into the Court of the Gentiles, into the midst of the teeming mob. Not surprisingly, **when they saw the commander and the soldiers, they stopped striking Paul**.

The commander of course assumed that Paul had committed some crime that had inflamed the popular wrath. He **ordered** Paul **bound with two chains** (possibly each hand to one soldier) and began **inquiring** of the crowd **who** Paul **was and what he had done**. The commander had heard of a Jewish Egyptian terrorist who had caused trouble and thought that perhaps this was he (21:38).

This was not the time or place for such an investigation, for **some were calling out one thing**, and **others another**, and the commander was **not able to know anything for certain because of the uproar**. There was nothing for it but to take the prisoner **into the barracks** of the Antonia fortress, so they could examine him in a place where they could hear themselves think. The crowd was reluctant to lose their victim and continued to cry out, **"Away with him!"** as if they would tear Paul to pieces then and there. It was difficult for Paul to walk with the soldiers up **the steps** into the interior tower, since he was encumbered by his chains. To avoid **the violence of the crowd**, therefore, Paul **was borne by the soldiers**, carried above the throng. Luke mentions these details to stress how mindless and murderous was the rage of the mob (and thus that Paul was the hapless victim, not the guilty criminal as some would allege).

VII. Paul in Jerusalem — Acts 21:37–39

§VII.3. Paul's Address to the Jerusalem Jews

> ॐ ॐ ॐ ॐ ॐ
>
> 37 And as he was about to be brought into the barracks, Paul says to the commander, "If I may be permitted to say something to you?" And he said, "Do you know Greek?
>
> 38 "Then you are not the Egyptian who before these days upset *the peace* and led out into the wilderness the four thousand men of the Sicarii?"
>
> 39 But Paul said, "I *myself* am a Jew of Tarsus of Cilicia, a citizen of no unimportant city; and I beseech you, allow me to speak to the people."

As Paul was nearing the top step and **was about to be brought into the barracks** for further interrogation, he made a request of the commander in Greek. The Greek (translated as, **"If I may be permitted to say something to you?"**) is very polished and polite—not what the commander was expecting from an Egyptian rabble-rouser—and he is caught off guard, as Paul intended. He asked Paul if he were **not the Egyptian** who in AD 54 **upset *the peace*** by starting a rebellion and **led out into the wilderness the four thousand men of the Sicarii**.

The **Sicarii** (from the Latin *sicarius*) were assassins who concealed on their persons small daggers (Latin *sica*) and used them to knife pro-Roman sympathizers in a crowd, then escape. The Egyptian referred to was a rebel who earlier duped some four thousand of these assassins, leading them into the wilderness of Judea and then coming to attack Jerusalem, promising that the walls of the city would collapse at his command by the power of God. They did not. Rather, the Romans moved in, capturing and killing a number of them, while the Egyptian false prophet himself escaped. The Roman commander thought Paul was perhaps this Egyptian and that the local populace was venting their fury on him for having previously duped them.

Paul, with some indignation at the social slur (even the Jews of Alexandria hated to be taken for Egyptians), assured his captor he was no Egyptian but **a Jew of Tarsus of Cilicia,** and furthermore, he was **a citizen of** that not **unimportant city**—he was no mere ruffian. Such citizenship required large land holdings, and Paul was asserting his dignity as one of the cultured class in his bid to get permission to **speak to the people**. Something there was in Paul's noble bearing that made the commander give in to the prisoner's extraordinary request. Doubtless he was hoping from the speech (which he probably expected would have been given in Greek, which he could understand) to discover what Paul's alleged crime was.

> 40 And when he had given permission, Paul, standing upon the steps, motioned to the people with his hand; and when there was a great silence, he spoke in the Hebrew language, saying,
>
> **22** 1 "Brothers and fathers, hear now my defense to you."
>
> 2 And when they heard that he was speaking to them in the Hebrew language, they became even more quiet. And he says,

---

Receiving permission to address the crowd, Paul **motioned to the people with his hand** to show that he wanted to speak (for the crowd was still shouting), and **when there was a great silence, he spoke in the Hebrew language**. Though all present would have understood Greek (the international language of the day), Paul spoke in Aramaic, the national language of the Jews. This was a forceful appeal to their patriotism, calculated to show that he too was a loyal Jew. He also addressed them very humbly and respectfully, calling them **brothers and fathers**. The combination of national language and respectful address worked, and **they became even more quiet**.

VII. Paul in Jerusalem — Acts 22:3–16

Not only could Paul be heard over the previous din, but all talking ceased as they gave him their undivided attention.

> ꙮ ꙮ ꙮ ꙮ ꙮ
>
> 3 "I *myself* am a Jewish man, born in Tarsus of Cilicia, but nurtured in this city, at the feet of Gamaliel, having been disciplined according to the strictness of the Law of our fathers, being zealous for God, just as you all are today.
>
> 4 "And I persecuted this Way to the death, binding and delivering up both men and women into prison,
>
> 5 "as even the chief-priest and all the *council of elders* testifies to me. From them I also welcomed epistles to the brothers in Damascus, and was going there to bring even those who were there to Jerusalem as prisoners to be punished.
>
> 6 "And it happened that as I was going, *drawing* near to Damascus about midday, suddenly from heaven a bright light flashed around me,
>
> 7 "and I fell to the ground and heard a voice saying to me, 'Saul, Saul, why are you persecuting Me?'
>
> 8 "And I *myself* answered, 'Who are You, lord?' And He said to me, 'I *Myself* am Jesus the Nazarene, whom you *yourself* are persecuting.'
>
> 9 "And those who were with me indeed beheld the light, but did not hear the voice speaking to me.
>
> 10 "And I said, 'What shall I do, Lord?' And the Lord said to me, 'Arise and go into Damascus; and there it will be told to you about all that has been appointed for you to do.'
>
> 11 "But since I was not able to see because of

Acts 22:3–16

> the glory of that light, I was led by the hand by those who were with me, and came into **Damascus.**
> 12 "And a certain Ananias, a man who was reverent according to the Law, witnessed to by all the Jews who dwelt *there*,
> 13 "came to me, and coming up, said to me, 'Brother Saul, see again!' And at that hour I *myself* looked up at him.
> 14 "And he said, 'The God of our fathers has preordained you to know His will, and to see the Righteous One, and to hear an utterance from His mouth.
> 15 "'For you will be a witness to Him for all men of what you have seen and heard.
> 16 "'And now why do you delay? Arise, and be baptized, and wash away your sins, calling upon His Name.'

Paul did not attempt to explain that he had not actually brought any Greeks into the Temple, for that was not the root cause of their hostility. Their hostility had its roots in their belief that Paul was a renegade Jew, one who was disloyal to the Law, the Temple, and all their holy ancestral ways. Why else would he be spending so much time among the Gentiles and telling them they did not have to be circumcised?

Paul therefore began by showing that he was a good Jew and by explaining why he was spending time among the Gentiles. That is, he rehearses for them the story of his conversion and his commissioning by the risen Christ.

He begins by giving his impeccable Jewish credentials: he was born **a Jewish man** (and was not a Gentile convert himself), **born in** foreign **Tarsus of Cilicia, but nurtured** and raised in the city of Jerusalem itself, educated **at the feet** of no less a rabbi than **Gamaliel** himself, a famous and respected teacher. As such, he was **disciplined** and trained **according to the strictness of the Law of our fathers**

VII. Paul in Jerusalem   Acts 22:3–16

(he was in fact a Pharisee; Phil. 3:5). He was **zealous for God**—just as they all were that day.

Moreover, he **persecuted this Way** (the Christian movement) **to the death**, even **binding and delivering up men** and even **women into prison**. Not content with arresting Christians in Jerusalem, he received and **welcomed epistles to the** Jewish **brothers in Damascus** from the **chief-priest and *council of* elders**, the Sanhedrin of Jerusalem, to the effect that the Damascus Jews should surrender to him any Jerusalem Christians who had fled the city and taken refuge there. This was quite a pedigree and showed amazing zeal. Paul's audience (who themselves opposed the Christian movement) would be impressed, for he was like them—only more so.

Paul then narrates the supernatural events of his conversion. For St. Luke, this is the unanswerable centerpiece of his presentation of the Gospel, and he tells the story three times in his narrative (9:1f; 22:1f; 26:1f). Paul tells his Jewish audience he was *drawing* **near to Damascus** when **suddenly from heaven a bright light flashed around** him, and he **fell to the ground**. This happened **about midday**, when the sun was bright in the sky; it was no middle-of-the-night dream or nocturnal fantasy. The light was bright enough even to outshine the midday sun.

Paul **heard a voice** addressing him in his native Hebrew (calling him **Saul**, rather than Paul, the name used among the Gentiles), and asking him **why** he was **persecuting** Him. Upon asking who the heavenly speaker was, he was told that He was **Jesus the Nazarene**, whom Paul was even then **persecuting**. Stunned and shaken, he asked, **"What shall I do, Lord?"** The question presupposes Paul's horror over his past actions and a burning desire to make amends. But how could he make such amends? What extraordinary act of penitence could he offer?

The Lord, however, was not thinking of Paul's past guilt, but his glorious future. For now, all He said was that Paul should **arise and go into Damascus** as he had originally planned (Paul had perhaps thought He would return him to Jerusalem). **There** he would **be told about all** that had been **appointed** for him **to do**. The mention of something **appointed** (Gr. *tasso*) suggests that the Lord indeed had

269

a specific task for Paul to do, a special mission and destiny long set aside for him (compare Gal. 1:15).

This vision was no mental delusion going on inside Paul's head, for **those who were with** him **indeed beheld the light**, though they **did not hear the voice speaking** to Paul. (That is, they did not hear words they could comprehend, but simply noise; see comments on 9:7.) They only heard Paul's half of the conversation. Because of **the glory of that light**, Paul was blinded, his outward condition now matching his previous inward one. Humbled and chastened, he had to be **led by the hand** of **those who were with** him and in that state **came into Damascus**.

Once there, **a certain Ananias** arrived to meet him. Paul presents Ananias's Jewish credentials as well, describing him as being **reverent according to the Law**, a truly pious and observant Jew, one **witnessed to** and well spoken of **by all the Jews who dwelt** in Damascus. Ananias acknowledged **Saul** as a **brother** (that is, a fellow Jew; Paul was presenting Ananias as a good Jew, so the term "brother" in this context does not mean "Christian"). He restores Paul's sight, saying, **"See again!"** (Gr. *anablepo*), and Paul does indeed **look up** to see him (the word rendered *look up* is the same Greek word, *anablepo*).

Ananias then delivers his message: **the God of** their **fathers** (note the classic Jewish term, reflecting Ananias's piety) had **preordained** Paul **to know** the secrets of **His will**, to know the truth regarding Jesus, hand-picking Paul to be His messenger even before he knew it. The word rendered *preordained* is the Greek *procheirizomai*; compare its use in 3:20. God had preordained that he should even **see the Righteous One** (an early title of the Messiah; see 7:52) and **hear an utterance from His mouth**. This vision on the Damascus road meant that Paul had been chosen to **be a witness** to Jesus **for all men** (even the Gentiles), telling them **what** he **had seen and heard** from Christ. This being so, there was no need to delay: Paul should **arise and be baptized** (doubtless at the hands of Ananias) and **wash away** his **sins, calling upon** Jesus' **Name**.

From this we see again the true significance of baptism: as the candidate invoked the Name of Jesus, confessing Him to be Lord

VII. Paul in Jerusalem — Acts 22:17–21

and Christ, the baptismal bath that followed washed away all the sins of his past, closing the door to the present dark age and opening the door to the bright age to come, bestowing a new birth. This was how one became a Christian, and Paul was obviously ready to take this step.

> ॐ ॐ ॐ ॐ ॐ
>
> 17 "And it happened that when I returned to Jerusalem and was praying in the Temple that an ecstasy came upon me,
> 18 "and I saw Him saying to me, 'Hurry, and quickly get out of Jerusalem, because they will not welcome your witness about Me.'
> 19 "But I *myself* said, 'Lord, they themselves understand that I was *the one who* was imprisoning and beating throughout the synagogues those believing in You.
> 20 'And when the blood of Your witness Stephen was being poured out, I was *the one who* was also standing by and consenting and guarding the garments of those destroying him.'
> 21 "And He said to me, "Go! For I *Myself* will send you out far away to the Gentiles.""

Up until now, Paul was holding his audience. He had presented both himself and Ananias as good observant Jews, narrating the story of his conversion in conventional Jewish terms. Paul omits the story of how his about-face astounded and confounded the Jews of Damascus (see 9:20–22), and of the plot on his life and his escape from there (9:23–25). He turns immediately to the story of what happened when he **returned to Jerusalem** (narrated in 9:26f).

Paul mentions that it was while he **was praying in the Temple** (like a good pious Jew—and thus one unlikely to defile that Temple by bringing Greeks into it) that **an ecstasy** or trance **came upon** him. In this vision, Paul saw Jesus telling him to **hurry, and quickly get out of Jerusalem**, because the local populace would **not welcome** his **witness** about Him. That is, the debates Paul was having with the Hellenistic Jews who put Stephen to death were about to reach a crisis, so that they would try to kill him too (see 9:29).

Paul tells his audience that even so, he was reluctant to leave the Holy City where he was nurtured and educated. He strove to persuade his Lord to let him stay—for surely (he reasoned) the local Jews **themselves understood** that he was the one **imprisoning and beating** the Christians in **synagogues** throughout the city, and that he was the one who was also **standing by and consenting** to the death of Stephen, and was even **guarding the garments of those destroying him**. Surely people who knew this could be persuaded the reasons for his change of heart must be convincing! The Lord, however, was adamant: Paul must **go**. Indeed, Christ Himself was now **sending** him **out far away**—even **to the** distant **Gentiles**.

---

22 And they were hearing him up to this word, and they raised their voices and said, "Away from the earth with such a one, for it was not proper for him to live!"

23 And as they were yelling and throwing off *their* garments and casting dust into the air,

24 the commander ordered him to be brought into the barracks, stating that he should be examined with scourges that he might find out the reason why they were thus calling out to him.

25 And when they stretched him out with straps, Paul said to the centurion who was standing by, "If a man *is* a Roman and uncondemned, is it permitted for you to scourge him?"

26 And having heard *this*, the centurion came to the commander and declared, saying, "What are you about to do? For this man is a Roman."

27 And the commander came and said to him,

VII. Paul in Jerusalem   Acts 22:22–30

> "Tell me, are you *yourself* a Roman?" And he said, "Yes."
>
> 28 And the commander answered, "I *myself* acquired this citizenship with a large sum." And Paul said, "But I *myself* was indeed born *a citizen*."
>
> 29 Immediately therefore those who were about to examine him withdrew from him, and the commander also was afraid when he found out that he was a Roman, and because he had him bound.
>
> 30 But on the next day, intending to know for certain why he had been accused by the Jews, he loosed him and ordered the chief-priests and all the council to be assembled, and having brought Paul down, he stood him before them.

Paul was probably intending to explain to his audience that his task was to proclaim to the Gentiles nothing other than what the Law and the Prophets had said would happen (see 26:22–23), and that there was nothing to the accusations that he counseled Jews to rebel against their ancestral Jewish ways.

He did not, however, get the chance to explain. As soon as the mob heard him mention going to the Gentiles, they jumped to the conclusion that Paul was about to justify the bringing of Gentiles into the sacred confines of the Temple, and their collective screams of outrage drowned out Paul's words, bringing his appeal to an end. They began **yelling, "Away from the earth with such a one, for it was not proper for him to live!"** The words translated **it was not proper** are in the past tense; the thought is that they had been about to kill him and the commander was wrong to save him. In their frantic rage, they began **throwing off *their* garments** to wave them angrily as so many banners of their fury, and **casting dust into the air** at Paul (there being no stones at hand to hurl). The whole scene was one of chaotic riot.

The commander saw it was no use to prolong the scene,

especially since the mere presence of the Jew from Tarsus was enraging the crowd. He could not understand the Hebrew Paul was speaking to the crowd, and was therefore at a loss to know what Paul had done to make them so angry. His only course of action was to have Paul **brought into the barracks** where he could **be examined with scourges** to **find out the reason why** the crowd below **were thus calling out to him** with such rage. The use of torture as an accompaniment to official investigation of slaves was routine in the empire at that time.

The use of scourges, however routine for slaves and non-Romans, was a fearful thing. The scourge was a whip embedded with sharp bits of bone and metal, and it laid open the back of the one being scourged. Men had died under the scourge. When they had stretched Paul out with straps as the preparation for scourging, Paul coolly asked the question, **"If a man *is* a Roman and uncondemned, is it permitted for you to scourge him?"** There is some irony in the obviously rhetorical question. It was as if Paul were inquiring, "Has the Roman law changed? I suppose it's legal now to scourge uncondemned Roman citizens."

It was not, and the question was calculated to stun the centurion and bring the proceedings to a screeching halt. It was in fact a serious crime to even bind an uncondemned Roman, much less to scourge him. Paul's question had the intended effect: The centurion in charge of the examination went to his commander and said, **"What are you about to do? For this man is a Roman."**

The commander, however, was not convinced. He came to Paul (presumably still bound in the leather straps and stretched out for his scourging) and asked, **"Tell me, are you *yourself* a Roman?"** The **you** is emphatic in the Greek, as if the commander thought such a thing unlikely. Paul doubtless presented quite the disheveled spectacle, and the commander was asking, "How could *you* be a Roman? *I* had to pay **a large sum** for my citizenship." The commander thought it unlikely Paul would have the necessary funds to buy his citizenship as he had done. But if he *were* a citizen, it was important to discover more precisely his social status, for if it were lower than his own, his offense in having him bound would be lighter.

Paul's answer was stunning. Paul replied that, on the contrary, *he* had actually been **born** *a citizen*. (The pronouns throughout the dialogue are emphatic in the Greek.) The effect of this answer was that the soldiers **withdrew from him**, treating him with a new respect, if not fear. The commander had cause to be **afraid**, for having a citizen **bound** without preliminary trial was a serious offense, especially since Paul's citizenship was older than his own. He was still, however, no closer to finding out why this mysterious man had so enflamed the locals, and so he **ordered the chief-priests and all the council to be assembled** and to have Paul **brought down before them** for examination. Then perhaps he could find out what this was all about.

Once again we may linger a bit on the question of why Paul only now revealed the fact of his Roman citizenship, for if he had declared it earlier, he would have avoided such rough treatment. But to have asserted it earlier would have meant to assert it publicly, not only to the Romans arresting him, but to his Jewish audience watching him, and Paul at all costs wanted not to alienate his Jewish audience. In his speech he took care to stress how Jewish he was, and he could hardly undercut this by claiming a Roman citizenship which they did not possess. So it was that he insinuated to his inquisitor that he was a Roman, but did this privately, far from the ears of his Jewish compatriots.

§VII.4. Paul's Address to the Sanhedrin

23 1 And Paul, staring at the council, said, "Brothers, I *myself* have conducted myself *as citizen* in all good conscience before God to this day."
2 And the chief-priest Ananias commanded those standing beside him to strike his mouth.
3 Then Paul said to him, "God is about to strike you, you whitewashed wall! And do you *yourself* sit judging me according to the Law, and

violating the Law you order me to be struck?"
4 But those who stood beside *him* said, "Do you abuse God's chief-priest?"
5 And Paul said, "I did not know, brothers, that he was chief-priest, for it is written, 'You shall not speak evil of a ruler of your people.'"
6 But knowing that one part were Sadducees and the other Pharisees, Paul was crying out in the council, "Brothers, I *myself* am a Pharisee, a son of Pharisees; I *myself* am being judged about the hope and resurrection of the dead!"
7 And as he said this, there arose a riot between the Pharisees and Sadducees, and the multitude was split.
8 For the Sadducees say that *there is* not to be a resurrection, nor an angel, nor a spirit; but the Pharisees confess all these things.
9 And there arose a great clamor; and some of the scribes of the parts of the Pharisees stood up and were quarreling *fiercely*, saying, "We find nothing wicked in this man; what if a spirit has spoken to him, or an angel?"
10 And as a great riot was happening, the commander was afraid Paul would be torn *to pieces* by them and ordered the soldiers to go down and snatch him from their midst, and bring him into the barracks.
11 But on the following night, the Lord stood by him and said, "Have courage; for as you have testified to the things about Me in Jerusalem, thus it is necessary for you to witness in Rome also."

St. Luke presents Paul as not cowering guiltily before his accusers, but as **staring at the council** with all the boldness of a good

VII. Paul in Jerusalem   Acts 23:1–11

conscience. He took the lead in a friendly spirit, referring to the Sanhedrin elders as his Jewish **brothers**, and began by declaring that he had **conducted** himself *as citizen* **in all good conscience before God**. The word rendered *conducted as citizen* is the Greek *politeuo*, cognate with *politeia*, "citizenship." Paul is saying he had conducted himself uprightly, discharging all public obligations as he should. No doubt Paul was about to continue by affirming that his recent conduct in the Temple reflected this, and that he had not in fact brought any Greeks into the forbidden precincts.

He did not, however, have the chance to continue. **The chief-priest Ananias commanded those standing beside** Paul **to strike his mouth**. It is not certain what in Paul's opening words so enraged Ananias. It seems that in his malevolent lust for power, he thought he had Paul cowed, and was furious to see him serene and bold. Such evil temper was consistent with the character of Ananias, who had a reputation for corruption, avarice, and cruelty.

Such an order to strike a defendant before he had been found guilty of anything was a flagrant breach of the Law, and Paul protested with righteous indignation. As he had spoken to a Jewish false prophet before (13:9–11), so he spoke to the corrupt Jewish elder now, saying, **"God is about to strike you, you whitewashed wall!"** For such hypocrisy as sitting to **judge according to the Law** while **violating the Law** invited the judgment of God, who declared in Exodus 21:23f that justice demanded an eye for an eye and a wound for a wound. Ananias had commanded that Paul be unjustly struck, and God would strike Ananias in turn. And Paul was not wrong. In less than ten years, Ananias would be assassinated by Zealots as war broke out with Rome.

Those in the Sanhedrin, however, were determined to condemn Paul now that they thought they had him at their mercy, and they refused to acknowledge that Paul had been unjustly struck. Instead, they defended Ananias, saying, **"Do you abuse God's chief-priest?"** Even in the face of such lawlessness, Paul continued to obey the Law, proving himself a better Jew than his accusers. He had not recognized Ananias as the chief-priest, and said that had he done so, he would not have spoken as he did, for the Law said, **"You shall**

not speak evil of a ruler of your people" (Ex. 22:28). St. Luke expects that his reader Theophilus, with the Romans' customary passion for justice, will side with Paul against his unjust accusers at this farcical proceeding.

It is not surprising that Paul did not recognize the one who gave the illegal order as the chief-priest. The Roman commander had summoned this meeting of the Sanhedrin hastily, and Ananias was probably not wearing his official robes. Also, Paul's visits to Jerusalem in the past years had been few and brief, and it is possible he did not know the chief-priest by sight.

What Paul *did* recognize, however, was that he would never receive a fair hearing from this gathering. Being as wise as a serpent, he decided to play off one side of his accusers against the other in order to survive to speak another day. He could see that **one part** of the council **were Sadducees and the other** part **Pharisees**—two groups who quarreled violently over many things, such as the role of **angel** and **spirit**, and (not least) the possibility of the future **resurrection**.

Paul was himself a Pharisee, from a long line of Pharisees, one who had sat at the feet of Gamaliel himself (22:3; Phil. 3:5). When finally allowed to speak, he began **crying out, "Brothers, I *myself* am a Pharisee, a son of Pharisees; I *myself* am being judged about the hope and resurrection of the dead!"** That is, he wrapped himself in the Pharisaical flag and presented himself as being persecuted by the Temple custodians (who were Sadducees) because of his adherence to a much-disputed Pharisaical doctrine. Paul's words were true (technically), but calculated to set off a firestorm among his accusers.

That storm broke out immediately. By **the resurrection of the dead**, Paul of course meant not just the possibility of future resurrection for all (affirmed by the Pharisees and hotly denied by the Sadducees), but also the resurrection of Jesus. By leaving out the Name of Jesus, he caused the two parties of his accusers to focus exclusively on the longstanding quarrel between them, giving vent to all the mutual sectarian hatreds they had been cherishing. **A riot** broke out, and **the multitude was split**, the Pharisees defending Paul and the Sadducees condemning him. In the Pharisees' eyes,

VII. Paul in Jerusalem — Acts 23:12–30

Paul may well have been misled about the Nazarene, but they were not going to abandon one of their own to those impious Sadducees. The trial was over.

As the yelling grew in intensity, the **commander was afraid that Paul would be torn *to pieces* by them**, and he **ordered the soldiers to snatch** Paul **from their midst** and **bring him** back into the safety of **the barracks**. It must have been frustrating for him, for he was no closer to finding out why these Jews hated Paul so much.

As for Paul, he also was dejected. He had come to Jerusalem full of hope that his gift for the poor there from the Gentiles would win support for his mission to the Gentiles. Instead, he had been arrested, beaten, and detained by the Gentiles, and every time he tried to explain his innocence to his own people, they refused to hear him.

Christ therefore **stood by** his apostle, appearing to him in a night vision and telling him to **have courage**. He must not think that all this was happening apart from the Lord's will. Paul had not failed, but had faithfully **testified to the things about** Him **in Jerusalem**. In the same way, it was **necessary** for him **to witness in Rome also**. Paul should not dwell on the past, but on the glorious work in the future. Christ would not abandon him, for he had yet more work to do. The word *necessary* (Gr. *dei*) shows that it was the providential plan of God to preserve Paul and see him safely to Rome.

ॐ ॐ ॐ ॐ ॐ

12 And when it was day, the Jews made a plot and put themselves under a curse, saying that they would neither eat nor drink until they had killed Paul.
13 And there were more than forty who made this conspiracy,
14 who came to the chief-priests and the elders, and said, "We have put ourselves under a curse to taste nothing until we have killed Paul.
15 "Now, therefore, you *yourselves* and the council explain to the commander so that he may bring him down to you, as though you were

about to decide more exactly the things about him; and we *ourselves* are prepared to destroy him before he *draws* near."
16 But the son of Paul's sister heard of their ambush, and he arrived and entered into the barracks and declared *this* to Paul.
17 And Paul called one of the centurions to him and said, "Bring this young man to the commander, for he has something to declare to him."
18 Having therefore taken him, he brought *him* to the commander and says, "Paul the prisoner called me to him and asked me to lead this young man to you, for he has something to say to you."
19 And the commander took him by the hand and having withdrawn, was inquiring of him privately, "What is it that you have to declare to me?"
20 And he said, "The Jews have agreed to ask you to bring Paul down tomorrow to the council, as though they were about to inquire somewhat more accurately about him.
21 "You therefore should not be persuaded by them, for more than forty of them are lying in wait for him, who have put themselves under a curse not to eat or drink until they destroy him; and now they are prepared and waiting for the promise from you."
22 Therefore the commander dismissed the young man, ordering him, "Tell no one that you have revealed these *things* to me."
23 And having called to *him* two of the centurions, he said, "Prepare two hundred soldiers, and seventy horsemen and two hundred

VII. Paul in Jerusalem   Acts 23:12–30

> spearmen by the third hour of the night to go to Caesarea."
>
> 24 *They were also to have* mounts stand by to put Paul on and bring *him* safely to Felix the governor.
>
> 25 And he wrote an epistle having this pattern:
>
> 26 "Claudius Lysias, to the most-excellent governor Felix, greetings.
>
> 27 "When this man was seized by the Jews and was about to be destroyed by them, I arrived with the soldiers and took *him* out, having learned that he was a Roman.
>
> 28 "And intending to find out the charge for which they were accusing him, I brought *him* down to their council.
>
> 29 "And I found him to be accused about debates of their Law, but under no accusation deserving death or bonds.
>
> 30 "And when a plot against the man was reported to me, I sent him to you immediately, also ordering his accusers to speak these things against him before you."

Paul's difficulties in Jerusalem, though, were not over. Hearing how Paul had been rescued by the Romans a second time, a group of **more than forty** fanatics met together secretly and **made a plot**. In their minds, Paul was a renegade Jew who had defiled the Temple and deserved to die for it. They despaired of him getting the punishment he deserved through legal means, and therefore decided assassination was the only option. They had to act fast, for soon he would be taken from Jerusalem, and they would lose their chance. They **put themselves under a curse that they would neither eat nor drink until they had killed Paul**—that is, that they would carry out their plot within the next twenty-four hours.

They came to those **chief-priests and the elders** of the Sanhedrin they thought would be sympathetic to their plot with the request that they gather the rest of the Sanhedrin Council (who were not in on the plot, such as the Pharisees) and **explain to the commander** they would like to examine Paul again to **decide more exactly the things about him**. The commander would surely agree to this, because he needed to know what the charges were against Paul, and a second meeting of the council (after the first had broken up so tumultuously) was not an unreasonable way to proceed. The assassins, for their part, were **prepared to destroy** Paul **before he drew** near, killing him as he was escorted from the Roman barracks to the council chamber. It was a courageous plot, for the assassins would certainly lose their lives in the bargain. Like all religious fanatics, they thought of themselves as martyrs, as offering service to God (John 16:2).

The large number involved in the conspiracy, however, meant that it was harder to keep their plans secret, and somehow **the son of Paul's sister heard of their ambush**. Paul had been raised in Jerusalem, and it is possible that some of his family still lived there. Possibly the boy overheard talk of the ambush, unnoticed by the plotters. The age of the boy is not given; the fact that he is called **young man** (Gr. *neaniskos*) and that the commander took him by the hand to lead him to one side (v. 26) indicates a young age of perhaps twelve or so. The boy left his home and **arrived and entered into the barracks and declared *this* to Paul** (who, as a Roman citizen, was given some liberty to receive visitors, if they were deemed harmless). Entering into the Roman fortress to inform on a group of assassins took some courage.

Luke narrates the boy's visit in dramatic detail, including such eyewitness touches as the commander gently taking the young Jewish boy by the hand to lead him away from the gruff centurion and the other soldiers so he could divulge his secret. The commander took the threat seriously and arranged for a heavily armed escort out of the city at 9:00 that evening (the **third hour of the night**). Since Paul was a Roman citizen, his case would in any case have to be dealt with by the procurator who resided in Caesarea, some sixty miles away, and the commander decided he should lose no time in transferring Paul to the procurator's jurisdiction. The commander

VII. Paul in Jerusalem   Acts 23:31–35

was taking no chances in protecting his Roman prisoner, for whose safety he was responsible: the escort of **two hundred soldiers, seventy horsemen, and two hundred spearmen** was almost half the forces he had at his disposal in Jerusalem.

Luke quotes the gist (the **pattern**; Gr. *tupos*) of the **epistle** the commander **Claudius Lysias** sent to **Felix the governor**, the procurator at Caesarea. In Luke's summary, we note his wry sense of humor, for the commander predictably recounted the events in such a way as to make himself look good. Indeed, the commander does twist the truth a bit: he did not **take** Paul **out** from the Jews who were about to **destroy** him **having learned that he was a Roman**. Rather, he only discovered Paul was a fellow Roman *after* he had rescued him. And regarding that discovery, the commander (prudently, as far as his own career is concerned) omits the fact that he had bound Paul when he was yet uncondemned, and was even about to scourge him.

More significantly for Luke's apologetic purpose, the commander is quoted as affirming that Paul was **under no accusation deserving death or bonds**. Whatever Luke's readership had heard about Paul as a dangerous rebel, the people in the know acknowledged him as completely innocent of sedition. In exonerating Paul, Luke means his readers to see that the Christian movement also should not be blamed for any treason.

§VII.5. Paul's Address to Felix at Caesarea

> 31 Therefore the soldiers, according to their direction, took Paul along *and* brought *him* down by night to Antipatris.
> 32 But the next day, allowing the horsemen to depart with him, they returned to the barracks.
> 33 And when these had entered into Caesarea and given over the epistle to the governor, they also presented Paul to him.

> 34 And when he had read it, he asked from what province he was, and when he learned that he was from Cilicia,
> 35 he said, "I will give you a hearing after your accusers arrive also," ordering him to be kept in Herod's Praetorium.

After these preparations, Paul was taken from Jerusalem to Caesarea, moving from a Jewish to a Roman court, being **brought down by night to Antipatris**. Antipatris was a military station some thirty-five miles from Jerusalem, about halfway to their final destination. Once they had reached Antipatris, the threat from Jewish assassins was no longer a factor, and **the next day**, the foot-soldiers of the Roman escort were permitted to **return** to their **barracks** in Jerusalem. Paul went on to Caesarea accompanied by the **horsemen** only.

When these horsemen had **entered into Caesarea and given over the epistle to the governor, they also presented Paul to him**. The governor first ascertained that he had legal jurisdiction over this case, and so **he asked from what province** Paul had come. **Cilicia** at this time belonged to the united jurisdiction of Syria-Cilicia, so that Paul indeed was his responsibility alone, and he need not consult with any other ruler. Having assured himself of this, he ordered that Paul be **given** a formal **hearing** and had him **kept in Herod's Praetorium**, which served as the official Roman residence. Paul would be safe there until the time for his trial.

St. Luke presents all these details as a good historian, and to contrast the efficiency of Roman justice with the choleric chaos which accompanied Paul's trial before the Sanhedrin (23:1–10).

> ಞ ಞ ಞ ಞ ಞ
>
> **24** 1 And after five days the chief-priest Ananias came down with certain elders, with a certain attorney Tertullus, and they made known to the governor *charges* against Paul.
> 2 And after he had been called, Tertullus began

VII. Paul in Jerusalem   Acts 24:1–9

> to accuse him, saying, "Since through you we have attained much peace, and since by your foresight reforms are coming to this nation,
>
> 3 "we welcome *this* in every way and everywhere, most-excellent Felix, with all thanksgiving.
>
> 4 "But, that I may not hinder you any further, I urge you to hear us briefly in your forbearance.
>
> 5 "For we have found this man a pestilence and one who stirs up riot among all the Jews throughout the world, and a ringleader of the faction of the Nazarenes,
>
> 6 "who even tried to profane the Temple, whom also we seized.
>
> 8 "And by investigating *him* yourself about all these things, you will be able to find out the things of which we *ourselves* accuse him."*
>
> 9 And the Jews also joined in the charge, claiming that these things were thus.
>
> *Some manuscripts add, "And we would have judged him according to our own Law, but Lysias the commander came and with much violence took him out of our hands, ordering his accusers to come before you." But such older manuscripts as Sinaiticus, Alexandrinus, and Vaticanus omit this verse, and it is unlikely that it is part of the Lukan original.

After five days Paul's accusers did arrive from Jerusalem. **The chief-priest Ananias came down with certain elders** from the Sanhedrin, and also with **a certain attorney**, named **Tertullus**. It seems he was a pagan lawyer hired by the Jews to deal with the Romans; in verse 9 Luke seems to differentiate Tertullus from the Jews. When Paul had been summoned, the trial finally commenced, and **Tertullus began to accuse him**. Luke does not relate his full speech, but only the flattering way it began, in order to show how flimsy was the actual case against Paul.

285

The details of the flowery introduction also appeal to Luke's ironic humor, for Tertullus's description of Felix was wildly off the mark (Luke wants his reader to see how absurd were Tertullus's accusations against Paul). Felix began life as a slave, and an ancient historian (Tacitus) said though he exercised the power of a king, he did so with a slave's mind. Despite Tertullus's assertion that through him Judea had **attained much peace**, his reign as governor was accompanied by increasing terrorism, including the rise of the Sicarii, or assassins. Tertullus praised his **foresight** and the **reforms** and improvements he brought to the nation, saying that the Jews **welcomed** these developments in **every way and everywhere, with all thanksgiving**. In actual fact, Felix's brutal rule was universally resented, for he had made life miserable for the Jews.

The actual accusations Tertullus brings against Paul (whom he denounces as a poison-spreading **pestilence**) begin with the assertion that he **stirs up riot among all the Jews throughout the world**—that is, that he is a disrupter of the public peace. And Paul was no minor character in this disruptive and dangerous **Nazarene** movement, but **a ringleader** of this **faction**. The charge was calculated to appeal to the Romans, for they regarded such disruptions as very serious indeed. And the charge was cleverly made, for there was indeed evidence that disturbances accompanied Paul's preaching. What was not said was that these disturbances were created by the Jews themselves.

The further charge about desecrating the Temple by bringing a Gentile into the sanctuary is also cleverly made. Tertullus does not say that Paul actually did this (for there was absolutely no evidence for it), but rather that he **tried to profane the Temple**. The suggestion is that he was about to do so, but was prevented—a harder thing to disprove (or prove). Tertullus describes the event in the Temple by saying the Jews **seized** Paul to prevent him from carrying out the profanation. This was quite a twist of the truth, for that was no orderly and legal arrest, but an illegal mob lynching—one that required Roman intervention. It is implied that Lysias's intervention was unnecessary and wrong.

Tertullus concludes his introduction by confidently asserting

VII. Paul in Jerusalem   Acts 24:10–21

that if Felix will only **investigate** Paul himself, he will quickly **find out** that all this is true. Just give the prisoner rope, and he will hang himself!

> ᪥ ᪥ ᪥ ᪥ ᪥
>
> 10 And when the governor gestured to him to speak, Paul answered, "Knowing that for many years you have been a judge to this nation, I cheerfully make my defense,
>
> 11 "since you are able to find out that it was not more than twelve days since I went up to Jerusalem to worship.
>
> 12 "And neither in the Temple, nor in the synagogues, nor in the city did they find me discussing with anyone, or putting pressure on a crowd,
>
> 13 "nor are they able to prove to you that about which they now accuse me.
>
> 14 "But this I confess to you, that according to the Way, which they call a faction, I thus worship the God of *our* fathers, believing everything *that is* in accord with the Law and that is written in the Prophets;
>
> 15 "having a hope in God, which these *men* anticipate themselves also, that there is about to be a resurrection of both the righteous and the unrighteous.
>
> 16 "For this *reason*, I myself also do my best to maintain always an unoffending conscience before God and before men.
>
> 17 "Now after many years I arrived to do almsgiving to my nation and to make offerings,
>
> 18 "in which *task* they found me in the Temple, having been purified, not with a crowd nor an uproar. But certain Jews from Asia—
>
> 19 "who ought to have been present before you,

> and to make accusation, if they should have anything against me.
> 20 "Or these *men* themselves—let them tell what unrighteous *deed* they found when I stood before the council,
> 21 "unless it is about this one utterance which I cried out while standing among them, 'About the resurrection of the dead I *myself* am being judged today before you!'"

St. Paul, after **the governor gestured to him** that he might speak, made his defense. (We note the touch of the eyewitness in recording the silent gesture of Felix.) Paul begins not with flattery (as Tertullus did), but simply acknowledges that Felix, since for **many years** he had **been a judge** and ruler of Judea, would be able to ascertain the facts for himself and to confirm the truth of Paul's assertions.

Paul says that it was **not more than twelve days since** he **went up to Jerusalem**—not enough time to arrange for a rebellion. (See Excursus following on the chronology of Paul's time in Jerusalem.) Moreover, he had gone up to Jerusalem **to worship** as a pilgrim, and thus was unlikely to try to profane the very place to which he had come for such a sacred purpose. Far from fomenting rebellion, **neither in the Temple, nor in the synagogues, nor** anywhere **in the city** did they find him **discussing** contentious points **with anyone** to stir up trouble, nor **putting pressure on a crowd** to incite them to riot, and his accusers had to acknowledge they were completely unable **to prove that about which they now accuse** him. Let them produce one witness who saw him fomenting rebellion!

On one point, however, he would agree with them and **confess**—that he *was* a ringleader of the faction of the Nazarenes (compare v. 5). But **the Way, which they call a faction**, was not just a Jewish sect, but was the true hope of Israel and the fulfillment of all their ancestral hopes. In this Way he did indeed **worship the God** of Israel, not in heretical innovation, but simply **believing everything *that is*** in accord with the Law, and that is written in the Prophets. He **anticipated** the same **hope in God** as his accusers, that there was **about to be a resurrection of both the righteous and the unrighteous**, and a final judgment. Far from being a heretic and an extremist, Paul was simply a loyal Jew like them. And because of this belief in the future judgment, he strove to **maintain always an unoffending conscience before God and men**. A man who feared the judgment was unlikely to impiously profane the Temple or be an evildoer, as they alleged.

Paul continues that he had **arrived** in Jerusalem **to do almsgiving to** his **nation** (a reference to delivering his collection for the Christian Jewish poor there) and **to make offerings** in the Temple for himself and the Nazirites. Indeed, he had **been purified** ceremonially for this very work, and it was while he was performing this task of offering sacrifices that they **found** him **in the Temple**. Obviously he was not trying to desecrate the Temple, for he was scrupulously offering sacrifices there. And his worship there was orderly and law-abiding, with no inciting of a **crowd** or creating of an **uproar**.

In narrating the circumstances of his arrest, Paul begins by saying it was all the fault of **certain Jews from Asia**, who misunderstood his intention and who themselves created the riot. But as he says this, he looks about and notices they are not present at the trial. This was serious, for it meant that his main accusers had defaulted and were not able to provide any supporting evidence for the prosecution. Paul therefore stops in mid-sentence and affirms that they **ought to be present to make** their **accusation**. In their absence, there was no one who could provide eyewitness evidence of any wrongdoing in the Temple.

Perhaps the witnesses for the prosecution who were there could tell of some other crime he had committed when he was tried before the Sanhedrin? **Let them tell what unrighteous *deed* they found when** he **stood before** that **council!** With superb irony, Paul says the only thing he can think of is this **one utterance** of his which he **cried out while standing among them, "About the resurrection of the dead I *myself* am being judged today before you!"**—which utterance obviously was no crime at all. It was apparent that the prosecution had no case whatsoever.

> ## ❧ EXCURSUS
> ### ON THE CHRONOLOGY OF PAUL'S TIME IN JERUSALEM
>
> Paul's statement that he had arrived in Jerusalem only twelve days before (24:11)—not sufficient time for him to organize any rebellion—has occasioned much debate. In particular, scholars are concerned about how these twelve days are to be reckoned. (We must be clear at the outset: Paul's point here is not to account for all his free time; it is to stress the shortness of his present time in Jerusalem, and thus the fact that much of that time was spent in Roman custody, where he was not free to organize a rebellion, is irrelevant.) I would offer the following chronology.
>
> **Day 1**: Paul arrives in Jerusalem (21:17).
>
> **Day 2**: He visits James and the elders (21:18). Paul agrees to pay the expenses for men under a vow, worshipping in the Temple with them (21:23f).
>
> **Day 3**: He purifies himself, joins the men under a vow, and worships in the Temple (21:26).
>
> **Day 4**: Paul worships in the Temple a second day, and while there, he is mobbed by his opponents and taken by the Romans (21:27). He attempts to speak to the crowd, and his words are drowned out (22:1f). He is interrogated by the Romans (22:24f). He spends the night in Roman custody (22:30).
>
> **Day 5**: Paul is examined before the Sanhedrin (23:1f). The meeting breaks up, and Paul spends another night in Roman custody (23:10). That night he has a vision of Christ (23:11).
>
> **Day 6**: A conspiracy is formed to assassinate Paul within twenty-four hours (23:12f). Paul's nephew discovers this and informs the Romans (23:16f). Paul is taken at 9:00 that night to Antipatris under heavily armed guard (23:23f).

VII. Paul in Jerusalem — Acts 24:22–27

> **Day 7**: Paul is taken from Antipatris to Caesarea (23:31–33). He meets governor Felix and is remanded to trial (23:35).
>
> **Days 8–12**: After these five days, Ananias and his delegation from Jerusalem arrive in Caesarea for Paul's trial before Felix (24:1).
>
> **Note:** This chronology assumes that the seven days of vowed sacrifices for which Paul was paying were almost completed when Paul joined the men. This is consistent with the actual wording of 21:26, which does not say that Paul purified the men offering the sacrifices but that he "took the men the next day and purifying himself" went into the Temple—that is, the men were already purified and were well on with their sacrifices. It was Paul who newly purified himself to join them—and to pay their expenses.

༄ ༄ ༄ ༄ ༄

22 But Felix, knowing more exactly about the Way, adjourned, saying, "When Lysias the commander comes down, I will decide your case."

23 And he directed the centurion for him to be kept and *yet* to have *some* relief, and not to prevent his own from attending him.

24 But after some days, Felix arrived with Drusilla, his own wife, *who* was a Jewess, and he sent for Paul, and heard him *speak* about faith in Christ Jesus.

25 And as he was discussing righteousness, self-control, and the coming judgment, Felix became afraid and said, "Go away for now, and when I find an *appointed* time, I will call for you."

26 At the same time also, he was hoping that

> money would be given him by Paul; therefore he also used to send for him very often and converse with him.
> 27 But when two years were fulfilled, Felix received a successor, Porcius Festus; and wanting to offer the Jews a favor, Felix left Paul bound.

After Paul's defense, Felix's course was clear, for Paul's testimony coincided with the report of the commander Lysias (who had already said Paul had done nothing that deserved death or imprisonment), and the prosecution had no real evidence to present to the contrary. Felix **knew more exactly** than other Romans **about the Way**, and that the Christian movement was not the seditious threat the Jews said it was. It was clear, therefore, that Felix should simply acquit Paul and release him. But for political reasons, he did not want to antagonize the Jews, and so he **adjourned** the case on the pretext that he wanted more information from **Lysias the commander**. Though he **directed** that Paul **be kept** in custody, he allowed him to **have *some* relief** from the rigors of strict imprisonment, so that none of **his own** friends (including his fellow-Christians?) were **prevented from attending him**.

After some days, Felix arrived with Drusilla, his own wife, *who* was a Jewess. Drusilla was his third wife. She had been wed to a Syrian king at the usual age of fourteen, but was unhappy. She was very beautiful, and Felix desired her for himself. She left her husband to be married to Felix at the age of sixteen. Being a Jewess, she was probably the one who informed Felix more exactly about the Way.

On hearing Felix had a famous leader of the movement imprisoned, she wanted to hear for herself about the movement's teachings, and so Felix **sent for Paul, and heard him *speak* about faith in Christ Jesus**. Doubtless Felix was interested too, for he sat in on these discussions.

Paul took the opportunity to preach the Gospel to the governor and his wife, **discussing** the Lord's precepts about the need for

VII. Paul in Jerusalem — Acts 25:1–5

righteousness and **self-control** in face of **the coming judgment**. To one as passion-driven and worldly as Felix, the relevance of Paul's message was all too obvious. **Felix became afraid** (Gr. *emphobos*, "terrified," a stronger word than *phobos*, usually rendered "afraid"), abruptly terminated the discussion, and sent Paul away.

It was not the only interview he had with the apostle. He also **used to send for him very often and converse with him**. This was perhaps because he knew in his heart that Paul's message was right. But it was also because **he was hoping that money would be given him by Paul** to effect a verdict and Paul's release. Other Roman governors were known for this practice and would only release prisoners when given a bribe.

After **two years were fulfilled, Felix received a successor**, as he was recalled to Rome to answer charges of mismanagement and was finally removed from office. The Jews of Palestine hated him (indeed, they helped bring about his downfall), and Felix **wanted to offer** them **a favor**, in hopes of placating the opposition. He therefore refused to hear Paul's case before he left and **left Paul bound** in prison. Luke mentions these details to show that Paul's long imprisonment was not the result of any real wrongdoing, but of administrative corruption and politics.

§VII.6. Paul Appeals to Caesar

25 1 Festus therefore, having set foot in the province, after three days went up to Jerusalem from Caesarea.
2 And the chief-priests and the leading men of the Jews made known *the charges* against Paul; and they were urging him,
3 asking a favor against Paul, that he might send him to Jerusalem, lying in wait to destroy him along the way.
4 Festus therefore answered that Paul was to

> be kept at Caesarea and that he himself was about to go *there* quickly.
> 5 "Therefore," he says, "let the powerful among you come down with *me*; if there is anything improper about the man, let them accuse him."

When Felix's successor, Porcius **Festus**, set foot in the province, he wasted no time in familiarizing himself with the local situation. **After** only **three days he went up to Jerusalem from** his capital of **Caesarea** to see the Jewish leadership of the Sanhedrin.

These leaders also lost no time in making their demands known, not least of which were the ***charges* against Paul**. The **chief-priests**, along with **the leading men** of the Sanhedrin, began **urging** Festus, **asking** as **a favor that he might send** Paul **to Jerusalem** to be tried under their jurisdiction. Doubtless they hoped the new governor would think it politically wise to begin his administration there by winning over the local leaders. What they had in mind secretly, of course, was the resumption of their previous plan to have men **lying in wait to destroy** Paul **along the way**.

Festus, though, saw no reason to turn over a Roman citizen to Jewish justice, and he **answered that Paul was to be kept at Caesarea**. Since Festus himself **was about to go *there* quickly**, he suggested that their **powerful** and influential men **come down with** him so that the matter could be dealt with there.

> ꙮ ꙮ ꙮ ꙮ ꙮ
>
> 6 And after he had spent among them not more *than* eight or ten days, he went down to Caesarea; and on the next day he sat upon the judgment-seat and ordered Paul to be brought.
> 7 And after he had arrived, the Jews who had come down from Jerusalem stood around him, bringing many and weighty charges against *him* which they were not able to prove,

VII. Paul in Jerusalem   Acts 25:6–12

> 8 while Paul defended *himself, saying*, "I have sinned neither against the Law of the Jews nor against the Temple nor against Caesar."
> 9 But Festus, wanting to offer the Jews a favor, answered Paul and said, "Do you want to go up to Jerusalem and there be judged by me about these *charges*?"
> 10 But Paul said, "I am standing before Caesar's judgment-seat, where it is necessary for me to be judged. I have wronged no one, as you *yourself* also recognize well.
> 11 "If therefore I do wrong, and have practiced anything worthy of death, I do not refuse to die; but if there is nothing in *those things* of which these *men* accuse me, no one is able to grant me to them. I appeal to Caesar."
> 12 Then when Festus had spoken with *his* council, he answered, "You have appealed to Caesar; to Caesar you shall go."

Festus was as good as his word. After **not more *than* eight or ten days** in Jerusalem, **he went down to Caesarea** for the trial of the controversial prisoner, which began promptly **the** very **next day**. (The promptness of the trial was an indication of its importance for Festus, for Paul was a Roman citizen.)

It was an impressive scene, and Luke relates it with dramatic flourish: the governor **seated upon** the high **judgment-seat, Paul brought** into the legal arena and surrounded by his foes who **stood around him** like a pack of baying dogs or roaring bulls (compare Ps. 22:12), **bringing many and weighty charges**—charges, Luke adds, they were not able to prove. Paul refuted their charges one by one, asserting he **had sinned neither against the Law of the Jews** (by counseling Jews to forsake their Law; compare 21:21), **nor against the Temple** (by profaning it by bringing Gentiles into it), **nor against Caesar** (by causing seditious tumult).

It was clear to Festus, as to Felix before him, that Paul was innocent. But he still **wanted to offer the Jews a favor**. (Luke expects his Roman audience to see how the justice due to Paul was constantly compromised by such considerations, for Felix also was more concerned to curry Jewish favor than to do the right thing; compare 24:27.) Though unwilling to relinquish jurisdiction to them, Festus asked Paul if he was willing **to go up to Jerusalem and there be judged** by him, evidently suggesting a Roman court on Jewish turf, where more Jewish witnesses might be found, or perhaps with some Jews on his advisory council.

Paul could see that strict Roman justice (his only hope of acquittal) was giving way before political expediency. He replied that he was already **standing before Caesar's judgment**-seat, receiving Roman justice, as was his right as a citizen. Defiantly, he declared that he had **wronged no one**, and that Festus himself **also recognized** this very **well**. His refusal to go to Jerusalem was not based on a desire to avoid justice by stretching out his trial for as long as he could, and if he had truly **practiced anything worthy of death**, he would **not refuse to die**. But as **there was nothing in *those things*** of which he was accused, he refused to be **granted to them** as a favor (the word rendered *grant* is the Gr. *charizomai*, cognate with *charis*, a favor; compare v. 9). He refused Festus's suggestion of reconvening at Jerusalem. Instead, he exercised his right as a Roman citizen, uttering the fateful words, "*Ad Caesarum provoco*"—**I appeal to Caesar**.

Every Roman citizen had the right of having his case heard before the emperor in Rome and of thus bypassing the local courts. While there was a hope of local justice from the governor, Paul pursued this. But it was apparent that the local scene would yield no justice. His only hope now lay with the higher and more distant court. **Festus** consulted with his **council** of legal advisors for a moment before bowing (one imagines gratefully) to the inevitable. Paul's appeal to Caesar certainly rescued Festus from the political dilemma of either condemning a citizen unjustly or enraging the local Jews. He had **appealed to Caesar** as was his right; **to Caesar** now he must **go**. The court was adjourned.

VII. Paul in Jerusalem   Acts 25:13–22

§VII.7. Paul's Address to Agrippa

13 Now when some days had passed, King Agrippa and Bernice arrived at Caesarea and greeted Festus.

14 And while they were spending many days there, Festus laid before *them* the things with respect to Paul before the king, saying, "A certain man was left a prisoner by Felix;

15 "about whom, when I was at Jerusalem, the chief-priests and the elders of the Jews made known *charges*, asking for a sentence against him.

16 "I answered them that it is not a custom of the Romans to grant any man before the accused meets his accusers face *to face, and* has a place to defend *himself* against the accusation.

17 "Therefore, after they had assembled here, I made no delay, but on the next *day* sat upon the judgment-seat and ordered the man to be brought.

18 "And when the accusers stood up, they were bringing no charge against him of such evils as I *myself* was suspecting;

19 "but they had against him some debates about their own religion, and about a certain dead *man*, Jesus, whom Paul claimed to live.

20 "And being perplexed about *the* investigation of these *things*, I asked whether he would like to go to Jerusalem and there be judged about these.

21 "But when Paul appealed to be kept *in custody* for the emperor's decision, I ordered him to be kept *in custody* until I send him to Caesar."

> **22** And Agrippa *said* to Festus, "I also would like to hear the man myself." "Tomorrow," he says, "you will hear him."

Festus, however, still had a problem, for when he sent Paul to Caesar for trial, he must also indicate the charges on which he was being tried, and this was by no means clear to him, for the case seemed to him to be simply a debate about Jewish theology. He had an opportunity to consult an expert on such matters when **King Agrippa and Bernice arrived at Caesarea** to pay their official respects to the new governor. King Agrippa would surely be able to get to the bottom of things.

This **Agrippa** was the son of Herod Agrippa (whose end was narrated in 12:20f). He presently ruled over the mainly Gentile territories of Philip and Lysanias (see Luke 3:1), though not over the Jewish populations of Judea, Samaria, and Galilee, as his father did. Nonetheless, he was an acknowledged expert in Jewish affairs, knowing their Scriptures well (see 26:27). He was accompanied by his sister **Bernice**. She had been previously married to her uncle at the age of thirteen, and moved in with her brother after her husband's death. It was rumored that her relationship to her brother Herod (one year older than she) was one of man and wife. She would later accompany Agrippa to Rome, where she became the mistress of Titus, the Emperor's son. During their official visit, Festus took the opportunity of mentioning the **prisoner left by Felix** and asking their help. Agrippa said he would indeed **like to hear the man**, and Festus promptly arranged for such a hearing.

Luke relates Festus's conversation with Agrippa and Bernice because it makes clear that in Festus's view, Paul was not guilty of any crimes against Rome. Rather, his imprisonment was simply over **some debates about** the Jewish **religion**. With a fine irony, Luke quotes Festus's puzzled comment about **a certain dead *man*, Jesus, whom Paul claimed to live**. Though Festus could not know it, this was indeed the heart of the matter before him. It was apparent from Festus's report of the situation to Agrippa that Paul was now only being **kept *in custody*** because he had appealed to **the emperor's**

decision, and not because he was dangerous (as his enemies alleged). These are important words for Luke, and he expects his Roman audience to get the message: Paul and the whole Christian movement are no danger to the Roman peace.

> 23 Therefore, on the next day, when Agrippa and Bernice had come with great pageantry and had entered into the auditorium, with the commanders and the prominent men of the city, and when Festus ordered, Paul was brought.
> 24 And Festus says, "King Agrippa, and all here present with us, you observe this *man* about whom all the multitude of the Jews appealed to me, both at Jerusalem and here, shouting that he ought not to live any longer.
> 25 "But I *myself* found him to have practiced nothing worthy of death, and since he himself appealed to the emperor, I judged to send him *to him*.
> 26 "Yet I do not have anything certain about him to write to *my* lord. Therefore I have brought him forward before you *all* and especially before you, King Agrippa, so that after the investigation has occurred, I may have something to write.
> 27 "For it seems to me irrational in sending a prisoner, not to signify also the charges against him."

When the time for the hearing arrived, **Agrippa and Bernice** came **with great pageantry into the auditorium, with the** five **commanders and the** many **prominent men of the city**. The word rendered *pageantry* is the Greek *phantasia* (compare our English "fantasy"); it indicates a showy parade with much pomp. Luke, who has revealed Paul as a man of miraculous power (see 13:9f; 14:3f; 16:18; 19:11–12), means for his readers to contrast this outward show of glory with the true glory of God manifested by Paul, and to see the glory of the world for the empty shadow it is.

History has proven Luke to be spectacularly right: Even the mighty Roman governor and the Jewish king have vanished into the mists of history, and would not be remembered at all were it not for their accidental association with the lowly prisoner who stood bound before them. The eyewitnesses present that day could not have guessed this. For them, the pageantry and long parade revealed the greatness of Rome and its representatives, while the controversial prisoner was doubtless doomed to be forgotten in a matter of months, as irrelevant as yesterday's news—so blind is the wisdom of this age.

In his opening remarks, Festus introduced the case of Paul, whom **the multitude of the Jews**—from **Jerusalem** in the south to **here** in Caesarea in the north—thought to be so evil that they loudly **shouted**, insisting he **ought not to live any longer**. For his part (the **I** is emphatic), Festus **found him to have practiced nothing worthy of death**. (Luke again emphasizes this for his Roman audience.) If he was to send the prisoner to his **lord** the emperor, he must send also the charges on which he was to be tried, and he hoped that **after the investigation** was concluded, he would **have something to write**, for to send him for trial without a list of charges was **irrational** (Gr. *alogos*)—and also (he no doubt thought) suicidal for a Roman's career.

---

26 1 And Agrippa said to Paul, "You are allowed to speak about yourself." Then Paul stretched out *his* hand and defended *himself*:

2 "About all the things of which I am accused by Jews, I consider myself blessed, King Agrippa, that I am about to defend *myself* before you today,

VII. Paul in Jerusalem — Acts 26:4–12

> 3 "especially because you are knowledgeable in all customs and debates among Jews; therefore I beseech you to hear me patiently.

After Festus turned over the inquiry to Agrippa, Agrippa gave Paul permission to speak. Striking the pose of an orator, Paul **stretched out *his* hand and defended *himself*.** This was not a legal defense (for this was not a trial), but a defense of his life and work—as well as an opportunity to preach the Gospel to those in power (as the Lord said; compare 9:15). Paul delivers his speech in elegant language, calculated to impress his Gentile hearers and add persuasiveness to his message.

As the inquiry was about the religious disagreement between Paul and his foes (which is why Agrippa, the expert in Jewish matters, was conducting it), Paul omits any assertion that he was innocent of sedition and Temple sacrilege. These things were not the issue here. Rather, the issue was solely Paul's "heretical" faith in Jesus and his participation in the Christian movement. Paul therefore concentrates his efforts on defending his faith in Jesus, telling the story of his conversion in such as a way as to focus on Christ's commission to him (for this proves that Jesus is alive; compare 25:19).

In the usual and required rhetorical introduction, Paul says he considers himself **blessed** that it is before **King Agrippa** he must **defend** himself, for the king (who knew **customs and debates**) was in a position to verify Paul's appeal to the Jewish Scriptures. He asked the king to **hear** him **patiently**, for a patient hearing (Luke wants his readers to know) would certainly vindicate the Christian Faith.

> 4 "Therefore, all Jews know my manner of life from *my* youth up, which from the beginning was *spent* among my nation and in Jerusalem;
> 5 "since they have previously known about me for a long time, if they are willing to witness, that I lived *as* a Pharisee according to the strictest faction of our religion.

> 6 "And now for the hope of the promise made by God to our fathers I am being judged,
> 7 "to which our twelve tribes hope to attain as they worship with earnestness night and day—about which hope I am being accused by Jews, O King!
> 8 "Why is it judged unbelievable among you *all* if God raises the dead?
> 9 "Therefore, I *myself* thought it was necessary to practice many things against the Name of Jesus the Nazarene,
> 10 "which also I did in Jerusalem: not only did I *myself* lock up many of the saints in prisons, having received authority from the chief-priests, but also when they were being destroyed I cast a vote against them.
> 11 "And as I punished them often throughout all the synagogues, I was *trying to* compel them to blaspheme, and raving against them, I was pursuing them even to outside cities.
> 12 "In this *pursuit* I was going to Damascus with authority and permission of the chief-priests.

Paul asserted he was no impious renegade from Judaism or lax worldling. On the contrary, **all Jews knew** his **manner of life from youth up**. He had not lived in decadence among the Gentiles, but **among** his **nation** in Palestine **and in Jerusalem** itself. And he had **lived** *as* **a Pharisee, according to the strictest faction** of Judaism—indisputable facts to which his accusers could **witness**, if they were **willing**. As a Jew, he had longed for the **hope of the promise made by God to** the **fathers**, the coming of the Messiah, the hope to which not only Paul, but all the **twelve tribes hoped to attain**. It was for this hope that they **worshipped with earnestness night and day**, praying at the time of the twice-daily Temple sacrifices and clinging to Judaism in the midst of a Gentile world. Incredibly, it was because of the fulfillment of this

VII. Paul in Jerusalem — Acts 26:13–18

very hope that Paul was now **being accused by** those very **Jews**!

The heart and proof of this hope was the resurrection of Christ, and before speaking about it, Paul turns to the mainly Gentile audience present to forestall an objection. Paul knew that Gentiles considered the entire concept of resurrection absurd (see 17:31–32), and so he challenged this prejudice, asking, **"Why is it judged unbelievable among you *all* if God raises the dead?"** To show that Christ was raised from the dead, Paul goes on to relate his own experience.

He was not always a member of the Christian movement. Indeed, though he was a pious Jew, he once thought **it was necessary** and required of him by God that he **practice many things against the Name of Jesus the Nazarene**. That is exactly what he did: **in Jerusalem** he would **lock up in prisons many** of the Christians (whom he labels **saints**, God's faithful people, not heretics, as some said). When they were **being destroyed**, he **cast a vote against them** (that is, he gave his hearty consent). The reference is to the stoning of Stephen, here taken as representative of the Christian sufferers generally. And not only this, but Paul **punished them often throughout all the synagogues**, insisting they be flogged in discipline for their heresy (see Mark 13:9). In his **raving** and fury, he even began **pursuing them even to outside cities**, hunting them down as far as Damascus.

꣠ ꣠ ꣠ ꣠ ꣠

13 "At midday, along the way, I saw, O King, a light from heaven, beyond the brightness of the sun, shining around me and those going with me.

14 "And when we had all fallen down to the earth, I heard a voice saying to me in the Hebrew language, 'Saul, Saul, why are you persecuting Me? It is hard for you to kick against the goads.'

15 "And I *myself* said, 'Who are you, lord?' And the Lord said, 'I *Myself* am Jesus whom you *yourself* are persecuting.

> 16 "'But arise and stand on your feet. For to this *purpose* I have appeared to you, to preappoint you an attendant and a witness, both of the *things* you have seen, and also of the *things* in which I will appear to you;
> 17 "'taking you out from the people and from the Gentiles, to whom I *Myself* am sending you,
> 18 "'to open their eyes, to turn them from darkness to light and from the authority of Satan to God, that they may receive forgiveness of sins and an inheritance among those who have been sanctified by faith in Me.'

It was while he was going to Damascus for this purpose that his life was suddenly turned upside-down. For he **saw a light from heaven, beyond the brightness of the sun, shining around** him. This was no midnight dream or delusion, Paul insists, but happened **at midday**. Furthermore, it affected not just him, but also **those going with** him, and they **all fell down to the earth**. These could verify his words! Paul then **heard a voice** speaking to him **in the Hebrew language** and saying, **"Saul, Saul, why are you persecuting Me? It is hard for you to kick against the goads"** (that is, to resist your destined fate; the **goads** stood for the divine decree calling Paul to his destiny, not any supposed pricks of conscience). Not surprisingly, Paul asked who the voice belonged to (**lord** is the usual term of respect for any exalted person). He was stunned to hear the reply, **"I *Myself* am Jesus whom you *yourself* are persecuting."** The pronouns are emphatic in the Greek: Jesus was alive, and Paul, the one who was so zealous for God, was persecuting Him.

In this address to Agrippa, Paul telescopes the information given him by Ananias (9:15–16; 22:14–15) and his later vision in the Temple (22:18–21) with the account of his conversion. Paul's purpose is not to outline a strict chronological account, but to show how the risen Christ had commissioned him to do the work he was doing. He therefore tells Agrippa that Christ said He **appeared** to him to make him His humble **attendant** and **witness, both**

of the heavenly vision he **had seen, and also of** the later visions **in which** He **would** yet **appear** to Him. The appearance on the road to Damascus was **to preappoint** Paul, preparing him for this holy work.

Christ would continue to be with him, **taking** him **out from the** Jewish **people and from the Gentiles**, rescuing him time and again from their snares (compare 14:5, 19; 16:19f; 21:31f; 23:16f). This protection was necessary, for Christ was **sending** him far away, to the Gentiles throughout the world, **to open their eyes, to turn them from** the **darkness** of paganism to the **light** of the Kingdom, and **from the authority** and power **of Satan to God, that they may receive forgiveness of sins and an inheritance among those** of His chosen people who had **been sanctified by faith** in Him, Jesus. It was not, as Paul's foes alleged, that he was working among the Gentiles to take Jews away from the Law. He was working to bring Gentiles into the Kingdom promised to Israel.

ॐ ॐ ॐ ॐ ॐ

19 "Afterwards, King Agrippa, I was not disobedient to the heavenly vision,

20 "but both to those in Damascus first, and also in Jerusalem, and *also* all the region of Judea, and to the Gentiles, I was declaring that they should repent and turn to God, practicing works worthy of repentance.

21 "Because of these *things* Jews seized me in the Temple and tried to lay *violent* hands on me.

22 "Therefore, having attained help from God, I stand to this day witnessing both to little and great, saying nothing but what both the Prophets and Moses said was about to happen;

23 "that the Christ was to suffer, that by His resurrection from the dead He should be the first to proclaim light both to the people and to the Gentiles."

Paul related to the King that he was **not disobedient to** that **heavenly vision**, but was engaged in doing what he was ordered, both **in Damascus** and **also in Jerusalem**, and then in all **the region of Judea** and even in the lands of **the Gentiles** far away. To these Gentiles he declared **that they should repent and turn to God, practicing works worthy of repentance**. What Jew could object to this?

Yet it was **because of these *things*** (his Gentile mission) that **Jews seized** him **in the Temple and tried to lay *violent* hands** on him, killing him then and there. But he had **attained help from God** (not just the Romans), and so was rescued to **stand** before them **to this day, witnessing both to little and great** (that is, to all, regardless of their wealth and position, for he was not doing this for money). He was **saying nothing but what both the Prophets and Moses said was about to happen—that the Christ was to suffer,** and **by His resurrection from the dead He should be the first to proclaim light to the** Jewish **people and to the Gentiles**. The Prophets said that Messiah would be a light to the nations (Is. 49:6; Acts 13:46–47), and through Paul, this prophecy was being fulfilled before their eyes.

❦ EXCURSUS
On the Resurrection of Christ

The theme of Christ's Resurrection runs through the entire Book of Acts and forms the central theme of Paul's addresses in Jerusalem. Even in his Gospel, Luke presents for his readers compelling evidence of Christ's Resurrection, narrating how He appeared to two men on the road to Emmaus, and to Simon Peter, and even how He proved He was no ghost or figment of imagination by eating a piece of broiled fish in the presence of the apostles (Luke 24:13–43). In his Acts, Luke summarizes this by saying Christ proved He was risen "by many proofs" (1:3).

Christ's Resurrection was the main theme of the

apostolic message (2:24f; 3:15f; 4:10; 5:30; 13:30f; 17:31), and Luke focuses on the conversion of St. Paul (narrating the conversion story three times, in 9:1f; 22:1f; 26:1f) because this more than anything else throws that Resurrection into high relief. For Luke, Paul's conversion was the undeniable proof that Jesus had indeed been raised from the dead.

For Luke as for Paul, the truth of the Christian movement stood or fell with the truth of Christ's Resurrection. That was the central issue Luke would bring before his readers. This concern underlies his report in 23:6 of Paul's outcry before the Sanhedrin, "I am being judged about the hope and resurrection of the dead!" as well as his report in 25:19 of Festus's hearing about "a certain dead man, Jesus, whom Paul claimed to live." Luke means his readers to detect in these two references the crux of the whole matter. Though St. Luke is concerned to show his Roman readers the Christians are not dangerously seditious, he also writes as an evangelist, to convince his readers of the truth of the Christian Faith.

༄ ༄ ༄ ༄ ༄

24 And while he was saying these *things* in his defense, Festus says in a great voice, "Paul, you are raving! *Your* many studies are turning you to *raving*-madness!"

25 But Paul says, "I am not raving, most-excellent Festus, but I declare words of truth and restraint.

26 "For the king knows about these *matters*, and I *speak* to him boldly, since I am persuaded that none of these things escapes him, for this has not been practiced in a corner.

27 "King Agrippa, do you believe the Prophets? I know that you believe!"

> 28 And Agrippa *said* to Paul, "In a little you are persuading me to act a Christian!"
> 29 And Paul *said*, "I could pray to God that whether in a little or long *time*, not only you, but also all who hear me today might become such as I *myself* am—except for these bonds."
> 30 And the king arose and the governor and Bernice, and those sitting with them.
> 31 And when they had withdrawn, they were speaking to one another, saying, "This man is practicing nothing worthy of death or bonds."
> 32 And Agrippa said to Festus, "This man could have been dismissed if he had not appealed to Caesar."

This was as far as Paul got in his address before Festus burst in with an interruption. He had listened as patiently as he could, becoming ever more incredulous at what he was hearing from his fellow citizen. When he could stand it no more, he **says in a great voice, "Paul, you are raving!** *Your* **many studies are turning you to** *raving***-madness!"** The word rendered *raving*-madness is the Greek *mania* (related to the verb *mainomai*, "to rave"; compare its use in 1 Cor. 14:23). A Gentile like Festus could not make sense of the idea of resurrection, much less the idea that an executed Jewish felon was now alive again and directing Paul. He knew Paul was well educated. The only thing that could account for him spouting such nonsense was that the greatness and burden of his **many studies** and reading had obsessed him and overthrown his mind.

Paul was not thrown off. He replied calmly, addressing his interrupter as **most-excellent Festus**, and asserting that he was **not raving** at all, but **declaring words of truth and restraint**. (The word rendered *declare* is the Gr. *apophtheggomai*, used for the utterances of prophets.) And for corroboration of the truth and reasonableness of his words, he appealed to **the king**, Agrippa. He **knew about these** *matters*. Paul could *speak* **to him boldly**, asking him to back

VII. Paul in Jerusalem — Acts 26:24–32

him up. Surely **none of these things escaped him**, for the Christian witness **had not been practiced in a corner**, but publicly. The facts about Jesus' death and the Church's claim that He had been raised were matters of open and public record. Turning to Agrippa himself, Paul asked earnestly, **"King Agrippa, do you believe the Prophets? I know that you believe!"** The king knew what the Prophets had said and could confirm for Paul how Christ fulfilled them completely.

Here was a delicate situation! The prisoner had somehow turned the tables on his judges and was putting the king on the spot. Paul was not now defending himself, but pressing home the claims of the Gospel, boldly trying to convert the Jewish king and the Roman governor. King Agrippa felt the heat of the spotlight very keenly. He could not deny he believed the Prophets. But he could scarcely say publicly like this that the chained prisoner was correct and be seen supporting his cause. He therefore evaded the whole question by making a wry joke, saying to Paul, **"In a little you are persuading me to act a Christian!"** That is, "I better not let you go on any longer, or you will make one of these crazy Christians out of me!" It was probably said with a self-conscious smile and a laugh, looking around at his fellows, inviting them to laugh as well.

Paul was equal to the situation. He responded by saying, **"I could pray to God that whether in a little or long *time*, not only you, but also all who hear me today** (here he doubtless held up his shackled wrists as he pointed to all those in the audience) **might become such as I *myself* am—except for these bonds."** It was the perfect reply, for it took Agrippa's words seriously and pressed them home, but it also followed Agrippa's quip with one of his own. "I could wish all of you were like me," he says, and then, looking at his upheld shackled wrists: "well, except for the fact of being in chains!" The joke doubtless drew appreciative laughter as was intended, showing that the Christians were no humorless fanatics, but had a sense of humor even in such circumstances. His earnestness and wit went a long way to commend the Christian Faith to his audience.

That was all Agrippa needed to hear. (Also, the inquiry had taken an alarmingly personal turn!) He arose, with **the governor and Bernice,** to leave, indicating the inquiry was over. Luke leaves his readers with their consensus about the prisoner: **"This man is practicing nothing worthy of death or bonds."** Indeed, in Agrippa's view, Paul **could have been dismissed** there and then **if he had not appealed to Caesar**. For Luke, this is the climax of all his narrative about Paul's arrest and imprisonment, for it shows clearly that the Christian movement is blameless of any wrongdoing.

❦ EXCURSUS
On the Church's Interaction with the Romans

St. Luke writes his two-volume Luke-Acts with an eye on his Roman audience, having dedicated both volumes to "the most excellent Theophilus"—and through him, to the Roman world at large. Theophilus casts his shadow, therefore, over all of Luke's narrative and is never far from his thought.

A large part of Luke's didactic purpose and his subtext is to show his Roman audience that the Christian movement has been unjustly slandered, especially by the Jews, and that the Christians are no threat to the Roman peace. He therefore spends much time narrating the various interactions of the Christian missionaries with the Roman authorities.

Thus early in his narrative we see a Roman centurion being converted (ch. 10). Moreover, Luke delights to show how the Roman governing authorities interacting with the Christians found them guilty of no offense. The authorities of the Roman colony of Philippi apologized to Paul and Silas for wrongfully imprisoning them (16:38f); the authorities of Thessalonica let Paul and his companions depart in peace, which they never would have done had they considered them an actual threat (17:9f); and the proconsul Gallio refused even to hear a case against Paul, but instead turned a blind eye to the beating of his adversaries (18:14f). Those in Ephesus who opposed the Christians were rebuked by the town clerk there (19:35f). The soldier Claudias Lysias rescued Paul and had him sent safely to Caesarea (ch. 22f). The governor Felix allowed Paul quite a bit of liberty while awaiting trial (24:23), and only kept him imprisoned because he wanted to do the Jews a favor (24:27). His successor Festus heard Paul's case and said he could have been released on the spot, had he not appealed to Rome (26:32).

Luke devotes a lot of space to detailing Paul's time spent in Roman custody (eight chapters out of twenty-eight), for Paul's innocence (and the harmlessness of the Christian movement) is a major theme and concern. Many doubtless had heard that Paul, a ringleader of the Christian sect, had constantly been in trouble with the authorities, and now had been arrested by the Romans while in Jerusalem and had spent no little time in prison. Luke gives a detailed treatment of those days to show that Paul was completely innocent of any wrongdoing, and that his incarceration was due solely to unjust Jewish malevolence and Roman corruption (compare 23:12; 24:26–27).

On his voyage to Rome, Paul enjoyed the confidence of the Roman centurion aboard ship (27:1–3, 42f). At Malta, the chief man of the island, Publius by name, received Paul hospitably, and Paul healed his father (27:7f). When Paul finally arrived at Rome, even though of course he was detained in prison while awaiting trial, the authorities allowed him to receive visitors and to spread his message openly and unhindered (28:30–31), which would not have been the case had his message been dangerous to Rome.

In all these details, Luke is making his case to Theophilus that Paul was favorably received by the Roman authorities, and that therefore the Christian movement was no threat to Rome, but that Christians should enjoy Rome's protection.

❧ VIII ❧

PAUL AND THE GOSPEL IN ROME
(27:1—28:31)

§VIII.1. Voyage to Rome and Shipwreck on Malta

27 1 And when it was judged that we sail for Italy, they were delivering up Paul and some other prisoners to a centurion, Julius by name, of the Augustan cohort.
2 And embarking in an Adramyttian ship, which was about to sail to places along *the coast* of Asia, we put out *to sea*—Aristarchus, a Macedonian of Thessalonica, being with us.
3 And on another *day* we put in at Sidon; and Julius treated Paul with benevolence, and allowed *him* to go to *his* friends and obtain care.
4 And from there we put out *to sea* and sailed under the lee of Cyprus because the winds were against *us*.
5 And when we had sailed through the open sea along *the coast* of Cilicia and Pamphylia, we came down to Myra in Lycia.
6 And there the centurion found an Alexandrian ship sailing for Italy, and he put us aboard it.
7 And when we had sailed slowly for considerable days, and with difficulty had arrived off

> Cnidus, since the wind did not let us go farther, we sailed under the lee of Crete, across from Salmone;
> 8 and with difficulty sailing past it we came to a certain place called Good Harbors, near which was the city of Lasea.
> 9 And when considerable time had passed and the voyage was already unsafe, since even the fast had already gone by, Paul was advising them,
> 10 and said to them, "Men, I observe that the voyage is about to be *attended* with hardship and much loss, not only of the load and the ship, but also of our lives."
> 11 But the centurion was more persuaded by the pilot and the ship-owner than by the things spoken by Paul.
> 12 And because the harbor was unsuitable for wintering, the majority made a decision to put out *to sea* from there, if somehow they might be able to reach Phoenix, a harbor of Crete, facing southwest and northwest, and winter *there*.
> 13 And when a south wind blew gently, thinking that they had attained their purpose, they raised *anchor* and were sailing past Crete, close *to the shore*.

Luke then narrates the voyage to Rome, doing this in great dramatic detail as a careful historian and to show the reliability of all his narratives. In addition, these details show the divine Providence that protected Paul and thereby marked him out as an innocent man of God. Luke also wishes to draw his Roman readers emotionally into the story, so that they cheer for the protagonist Paul as he endures his misfortunes and attains to his happy ending and safe arrival in Rome.

Luke tells the story in the first person ("we"), having rejoined Paul to accompany him to Rome, boarding the hired ship as a

VIII. Paul and the Gospel in Rome — Acts 27:1–13

paying passenger. The ship chosen for the first leg of this voyage was **an Adramyttian ship**, that is, a ship returning to its home port of Adramyttium, southeast of Troas, by way of **places along *the coast* of Asia**. Paul and **some other prisoners** were in the custody of **a centurion, Julius, of the Augustan** (or imperial) **cohort**. Julius chose this ship because no ships were departing from Caesarea for a direct voyage to Rome, and because in Myra he could find another ship to continue the journey, for grain ships regularly sailed from Myra to Rome. Also accompanying him was **Aristarchus of Thessalonica**, Paul's companion who accompanied him to Jerusalem, bringing the collection of money to the poor there (see 20:4). He is not mentioned again in the narrative. Perhaps he was heading home to Thessalonica and disembarked at Adramyttium, looking for another ship to take him home. He was, however, in Rome at some time during Paul's extended imprisonment there (see Philemon 24; Col. 4:10).

When for cargo purposes the ship **put in at Sidon** (about seventy sea miles to the north, a voyage taking less than twenty-four hours), **Julius treated Paul with benevolence, and allowed *him* to go to *his* friends and obtain care** (obviously accompanied by a Roman guard). His **friends**, the church in Sidon, would have heard news of Paul's arrest, trial, and transfer to Rome. Their **care** refers to giving him food and supplies for his journey—as well as prayer and words of encouragement. This **benevolence** from the centurion testifies to the esteem with which he regarded Paul—and (Luke wants his readers to see) how politically harmless the prisoner was.

From Sidon they **sailed under the lee of Cyprus**, under the shelter of the eastern part of the island, to avoid the prevailing winds then blowing from the west. They then went north **through the open sea along *the coast* of Cilicia and Pamphylia**, using the westerly current along the shore to move westward **to Myra** in the province of **Lycia**. The port of Myra was Andriace, three miles to the southwest, a main port for grain ships that sailed between Alexandria and Rome (for Myra was directly north of Alexandria). From there it would be easy to lease a grain ship going to Rome. Julius **found** such **an Alexandrian ship, sailing for Italy**, and continued his journey. From the size of its crew (v. 37), it seems to have been quite a large vessel, perhaps over a thousand tons in weight and over a hundred feet in length. Haste was necessary, for it was late in the sailing season, as sailing was too dangerous in the winter.

Owing to contrary winds, they **sailed slowly for considerable days**, and only **with difficulty arrived off Cnidus**. The voyage from Myra to Cnidus was only 130 nautical miles and should have been concluded in less time. It seems owing to the winds they were already somewhat off course, for Cnidus was northwest of Myra, on the coast of Asia Minor, and a direct route would have taken them south of Rhodes towards Crete. As they made for Crete, the northwest wind forced them to **sail under the lee of Crete**, on the south of the island, **across from** Cape **Salmone**, on the northeastern tip of the island. At length they **came to a certain place called Good Harbors** (usually rendered "Fair Havens"), twelve miles east of Cape Matala on the south coast.

Here a decision needed to be made, for **considerable time had passed and the voyage was already unsafe. Even the fast** (the Day of Atonement) **had already gone by**, so that it was late in the sailing season. Travel on the open sea was becoming dangerous, and they would have to winter somewhere. But where? Good Harbors (despite its name) **was unsuitable for wintering**, for it was too exposed and faced eastward, where it would get the full blast of the easterly winter winds. The sailors knew of another place, **Phoenix**, to the west, which was much better sheltered from the winds.

Paul, however, **was advising them** against going there, saying that if they attempted this, **the voyage** would be *attended* **with hardship and much loss, not only of the** cargo **load and the ship**, but the **lives** of the crew also would suffer injury. It is a testimony to Paul's credibility that he, as a prisoner, was included in the discussion at all. He spoke not only out of much experience (he had been shipwrecked three times and had spent a day and a night in the deep; 2 Cor. 11:25), but also as a prophetic man of God.

Not surprisingly, though, **the centurion was more persuaded by the pilot and the ship-owner than by the things spoken by Paul**. As the ship had been contracted for the imperial grain shipment, the centurion was the ranking officer, and the final call was his. He decided to follow the advice of the majority and make for Phoenix. **When a south wind blew gently,** they **thought they had attained their purpose** and began **sailing past Crete**, making for the more sheltered harbor. The journey was only thirty-six miles or so and should have taken but a few hours.

> 🙙 🙙 🙙 🙙 🙙
>
> 14 But after not much *time*, a typhonic wind rushed down against it, the one called the Northeaster;
> 15 and when the ship was caught and was not able to face the wind, we gave way and let ourselves be carried along.
> 16 And running under *the lee* of an islet called Cauda, we were with difficulty able to get the lifeboat under control.
> 17 And after they had taken *it* up, they used supporting *cables* in undergirding the ship, and being afraid that they might run aground on *the shallows of* Syrtis, they let down the equipment, and thus they were carried along.
> 18 The next *day* as we were being violently storm-tossed, they began to throw out *the cargo load*;
> 19 and on the third *day* they threw away the ship's equipment with their own hands.
> 20 And since neither sun nor stars appeared for many days, and no little stormy *weather* was pressing upon *us*, finally all hope of our being saved was being taken away.

They were never to make Phoenix. **After not much *time*, a typhonic wind rushed down**, one only too familiar to the sailors, the one they called **the Northeaster** (Gr. *Euraquilo*). It swept down from the high mountains of Crete, causing the clouds and sea to whirl as contrary air currents met. It hit the ship broadside, and the ship **gave way, carried along** by the hurricane force. Eventually the ship came **under *the lee* of an islet called Cauda**, about twenty-five miles southeast. The **lifeboat** or ship's dinghy was filling with water, threatening the ship, and so **with difficulty** they got it **under control** and **took *it* up** into the ship. (Luke uses the first person, saying, **we were able to get the lifeboat under control**, and it is likely he was involved in this arduous effort himself, helping the crew.)

Also, **they used supporting *cables* in undergirding the ship** (probably wrapping the cables under the ship several times to hold the hull together), lest the ship be torn apart by the storm. Further, **being afraid that they might run aground on *the shallows* of Syrtis** (some 400 miles south) if the storm persisted for days, **they let down the equipment** to slow their progress towards those shoals. What is meant by *equipment* is not clear. It is possible it refers to lowering the gear for the topsail and only setting the small storm sail, or perhaps to lowering a floating anchor into the sea to slow their progress. Having taken what measures they could, they **thus were carried along** before the storm.

The storm continued unabated **the next day**. The ship possibly had developed leaks, and it was deemed necessary to **throw out** some of the cargo load to lighten the ship. On the day after that, they still needed to lighten the ship, and so they **threw away the ship's equipment.** They did this **with their own hands** for they knew their survival depended on it. Once again, the nature of this **equipment** is not clear. It may well have been the long spar used to support the mainsail, which would have needed the help of all the crew to cast it overboard.

The storm continued for **many days**, so that **neither sun nor stars appeared**, and there was no way for them to know where they were. The ship was leaking badly, with **no little stormy *weather* pressing** upon them, and was in danger of sinking. Their only hope was to make for land, but they had no idea of which direction that was. No wonder that in their terror, hunger, seasickness, and misery, **all hope of being saved** was finally **taken away**, and they all despaired of life.

VIII. Paul and the Gospel in Rome

Acts 27:21–26

> 21 And when they had been long without eating, then Paul stood up in their midst and said, "Men, you ought to have obeyed me and not to have put out *to sea* from Crete, and spared yourselves this hardship and loss.
> 22 "And now I advise you to cheer up, for there shall be no loss of life from you, but *only* of the ship.
> 23 "For this night an angel of the God whose I am and whom I worship stood by me,
> 24 "saying, 'Do not be afraid, Paul; it is necessary for you to stand before Caesar; and behold! God has granted you *as gift* all those sailing with you.'
> 25 "Therefore, cheer up, men, for I believe God, that it will be thus, exactly as it was spoken to me.
> 26 "But it is necessary for us to run aground on a certain island."

All despaired, that is, but the Christians. After many days **without eating** (due to the need to conserve provisions), **Paul stood up in their midst** to encourage them. He began by reminding them that they **ought to have obeyed** him **and not to have put out *to sea* from Crete**. This was not motivated simply by the human desire to say, "I told you so!" Rather he wanted to win their assent for the advice he was about to give them. He thus reminded them that he knew what he was talking about, and they should follow his advice this time.

His advice was that they should **cheer up**, for he promised them there would be **no loss of life**, but loss *only* **of the ship**. This assurance was not based on wishful thinking, but on divine revelation, for **an angel of the God** to whom Paul belonged and whom he **worshipped stood by** him, assuring him that **it was necessary** for him to **stand before Caesa**r in Rome, for this was God's will. Paul, then, would surely survive. Moreover, **God had granted** him *as gift* (Gr. *charizomai*, cognate with *charis*, "grace") **all those sailing** with him, so that they would survive too. But first, Paul said, it was God's will that they **run aground on a certain island**. This last utterance must have seemed wildly improbable to the sailors, for they knew they had missed Sicily and had no idea where they were. The fulfillment of Paul's words about running aground would confirm his status as one guarded by God.

---

27 But when the fourteenth night had come, as we were being carried about in the Adriatic *Gulf,* toward the middle of the night, the sailors were supposing that they were approaching some land.

28 And they took soundings, and found *it to be* twenty fathoms; and having sailed a little *farther*, again they took soundings and found *it to be* fifteen fathoms.

29 And being afraid that we might run aground against the rough places, they threw out four anchors from the stern and were praying *for it* to become day.

30 And as the sailors were seeking to flee from the ship, and had let down the lifeboat into the sea, on the pretense of being about to lay out anchors from the bow,

31 Paul said to the centurion and to the soldiers, "Unless these *men* remain in the ship, you *yourselves* cannot be saved."

32 Then the soldiers cut away the ropes of the lifeboat and let it fall away.

33 And until the day was about to come, Paul was encouraging everyone to receive food, saying, "Today *is* the fourteenth day that you have

VIII. Paul and the Gospel in Rome   Acts 27:27–38

> been continually expecting *help* and going without eating, having taken nothing.
> 34 "Therefore I encourage you to receive food, for this is for your salvation, for not a hair from the head of any of you shall perish."
> 35 And having said these *things*, and having taken bread, he gave thanks to God before *them* all, and he broke *it* and began to eat.
> 36 And everyone was cheered up, and they *themselves* also took food.
> 37 And all the souls in the ship were two hundred and seventy-six.
> 38 And when they were satiated with food, they were lightening the ship by casting out the wheat into the sea.

So it turned out. After **the fourteenth night** of being adrift had come, they **were being carried about in the Adriatic *Gulf*.** (This **Adriatic** is not the Adriatic Sea as we know it, but the Ionian Sea between Italy and Greece, stretching between Malta and Crete.) **Toward the middle of the night** (when they could not see), the sailors **supposed they were approaching some land**, and so **took soundings**, being afraid they would dash against the rocks. This revealed they were at **twenty fathoms**, or 120 feet of water. About half a hour later, **again they took soundings and found** *it to be* **fifteen fathoms**, or 90 feet of water. (We see Luke's talent for vivid and dramatic storytelling, as he builds the suspense.) Since they were fast approaching shore, **they threw out four anchors from the stern** (using the stern so that the ship would keep pointing at the shore and not turn about), and began **praying *for it* to become day**, so that they could see where they were. The picture is a vivid one, and ironic: hundreds of frightened pagan men praying to their pagan gods for help, when true help lay only with the God of Paul, who trusted in His help with serene confidence.

There were yet more difficulties to be faced. After all their danger, **the sailors** seemingly did not believe Paul's word about his

God granting rescue to all on board for Paul's sake. They decided therefore to abandon the ship and its passengers to their doom and make for shore. They wanted **to flee from the ship** to safety and so had **let down the lifeboat into the sea**, to use it to abandon ship. (The **pretense** they used was that they were simply using the lifeboat to **lay out anchors from the bow**.) **Paul** could see what they were doing and **said to the centurion and to the soldiers** that unless the crew **remained in the ship** to man it, no one else could **be saved**. (The reader is expected to discern the subtext: being **saved** depended on believing the apostolic word of vv. 22–24 and trusting in Paul's God, remaining with Paul in the ship.) Paul had amassed much credibility with the centurion, so **the soldiers** therefore **cut away the ropes of the lifeboat and let it fall away** into the sea, thereby preventing the sailors' escape.

Once again, the crew needed a word of encouragement and unity, for the sailors had watched the soldiers deprive them of what they thought was their best hope for survival. In the darkness before the dawn, in the pouring rain (see 28:2), Paul again arose and began **encouraging everyone to receive food**. This, he assured them, was **for** their **salvation** and survival. That is, they would need the strength the food would give if they were to carry out the rescue attempt successfully in the morning. Let them eat and do their best when morning dawned. For, Paul promised, **not a hair from the head of any** would **perish**, but God would save them all, as He promised (v. 24).

After this, he encouraged them by example: **having taken bread, he gave thanks** (the normal Jewish blessing over food), **broke** the bread, **and began to eat**. Heartened by his example, they indeed **cheered up** and **also took food. When they were satiated** and had eaten all they could hold, they began **lightening the ship by casting out the** rest of the **wheat** cargo **into the sea**. Paul's example was powerfully effective, for all the crew of **two hundred and seventy-six** joined him in this predawn meal.

This meal was not, of course, the Eucharist, for it was shared with the unbelieving crew. Nonetheless, Luke uses eucharistic language to describe it, speaking of Paul taking the bread, blessing and breaking it, and of the meal being for their salvation (vv. 34–35). Indeed, the word "saved" is often used in the narrative (vv. 20, 31). It seems Luke wants his Christian readers to take this lesson from Paul's experience—that in the midst of persecution's storms, the eucharistic Church will be saved (Gr. *sozo*) and come safely through (Gr. *diasozo*, v. 44). As the Lord promised in such persecution as Paul was enduring, not a hair of their head would perish (Luke 21:18; compare Acts 27:34; the echo from the Gospel is deliberate).

> 39 And when day came, they were not recognizing the land; but they did consider a certain bay with a beach, and they intended to drive the ship onto it if they were able.
> 40 And casting off the anchors, they left them in the sea while at the same time they were unfastening the ropes of the rudders, and raising the foresail to the breeze, they were steering for the beach.
> 41 But striking a place where two seas met, they ran the vessel aground, and the prow stuck and remained immovable, but the stern was being destroyed by the force of the waves.
> 42 And the soldiers' intention was to kill the prisoners, lest any swimming out should flee away.
> 43 But the centurion, intending to bring Paul safely through, prevented them from *carrying out* the intention, and ordered that those able to swim should throw themselves *overboard* first and get out upon the land,
> 44 and the rest *should follow*, some upon planks, and others upon some *things* from the ship. And thus it happened that everyone was brought safely upon the land.

When day came, they were not recognizing where they were, for they were not at the main port of Malta, which was further to the west. However, **they did consider a certain bay with a beach** as being a suitable place to land. They **cast off the anchors** from the stern, **unfastened the ropes of the rudders** and let the rudders back into the water, and **raising the foresail to the breeze, were steering for the beach**. They soon **ran the vessel aground**, and **the prow** of the ship **stuck** on the sandbar and **remained immovable**, while the stormy waves continued to pound **the stern** of the ship and break it to pieces. There was now no alternative but to abandon ship.

The soldiers feared their prisoners would use this opportunity to escape, and the soldiers were responsible for them at the cost of their own lives. Their **intention** was therefore to **kill the prisoners** to prevent this escape. **The centurion**, however, had become a friend of sorts to Paul and was **intending to bring** him **safely through**. He therefore **prevented** this and **ordered that those able to swim should throw themselves** *overboard* **first and get out upon the land**. Those who could not swim should follow, floating upon **planks** from the ship that was breaking up, or upon anything else from the ship they could use.

Thus **everyone was brought safely upon the land**, even as Paul had foretold. They escaped sinking in the sea, being abandoned by the crew, shattering against the rocks, and being killed by the soldiers. Against all odds, they had survived, thanks to Paul and his God. The place where they landed in Malta came to be known as St. Paul's Bay.

§VIII.2. Malta

> **28** 1 And when they had been brought safely through, then we recognized that the island was called Malta.
> 2 And the barbarians showed us not ordinary benevolence, for because the rain had set in and because of the cold, they kindled a fire and received us all.

VIII. Paul and the Gospel in Rome   Acts 28:1–6

> 3 But when Paul had gathered together a certain multitude of sticks and laid *them* upon the fire, a viper came out because of the heat and fastened on his hand.
>
> 4 And when the barbarians saw the beast hanging from his hand, they were saying to one another, "Doubtless this man is a murderer, whom, though he has been brought safely through the sea, Justice has not allowed to live."
>
> 5 However, he shook off the beast into the fire and suffered no harm.
>
> 6 But they were expecting that he was about to swell up or suddenly fall down dead. But after they had expected *such* a long *time* and had observed nothing unusual happening to him, they changed *their minds* and were saying that he was a god.

After they **had been brought safely through** to shore, they **recognized that the island was called Malta**. This might simply mean that the sailors at last recognized where they were. But the name Malta means "refuge" in the Phoenician language of the native Maltese, and it is possible Luke means the sailors recognized how well-named the island was.

The inhabitants of the island spoke a Phoenician dialect and were considered **barbarians** by Greek-speakers, such as Luke. Luke acknowledges, however, that these natives **showed not ordinary benevolence**, but extraordinary kindness, for **they kindled a fire** so that the many strangers could warm themselves against **the rain** and **the cold**, and hospitably **received** them **all**.

Paul (like his Master before him, who humbly washed the feet of His disciples) did not disdain the lowliest of duties. To keep a fire going large enough to warm 276 men against the storm, much wood was continually needed, and Paul undertook to scavenge for it. He **had gathered together a certain multitude of sticks** and was bringing the huge bundle to the fire. A viper was lying among the sticks, in a stupor from the cold. When **the heat** from the fire warmed it, it **came out** and **fastened on his hand** as he added sticks to the blaze. The term *viper* here denotes simply a small poisonous snake, not the snake we know as a viper. Whatever the actual species of the snake, the natives were well familiar with it and knew its bite was extremely lethal. **When** they **saw the beast hanging from** Paul's **hand**, they began quietly **saying to one another, "Doubtless this man is a murderer, whom, though he has been brought safely through the sea, Justice has not allowed him to live."** The Greeks worshipped the goddess Justice (Gr. *dike*), and the natives here apparently had their local Phoenician equivalent. As far as they could see, the deity was meting out punishment to the guilty Paul through this serpent. How else could someone survive such a shipwreck against all odds, only to be killed by such a freak accident when safely on land?

Paul, however, served the One who promised immunity from such venom (see Mark 16:18), and **he shook off the beast into the fire**, trusting in his Lord. The natives watched him as he continued to feed the fire and warm himself, **expecting** every moment that he would **swell up or suddenly fall down dead**. When at length they **observed nothing unusual happening to him, they changed** *their minds* and began **saying** among themselves **that he was a god**. Luke reports this dramatic *volte-face* with his usual quiet humor, perhaps as a kind of dramatic comedy relief after the suspenseful story of the storms and the shipwreck. (The natives were barbarians after all, in religion as well as language.) The incident reveals that the God who saved Paul from death on the seas protected him from peril on land as well. The angel had said God willed that Paul reach Rome (27:24), and nothing would overturn that divine decree.

> ॐ ॐ ॐ ॐ ॐ
>
> 7   Now in the *lands* around that place were lands *belonging* to the first man of the island, Publius by name, who welcomed us and lodged us hospitably three days.

VIII. Paul and the Gospel in Rome — Acts 28:7–10

> 8 And it happened that the father of Publius was lying down, distressed with fever and dysentery; *and* Paul went in, and after he had prayed, he laid his hands on him and cured him.
> 9 And after this had happened, the rest of the people on the island also who had ailments were coming to him and being healed.
> 10 And they also honored us with many honors, and when we were putting out *to sea*, they supplied us with the things for *our* need.

The group had three months to spend there over the winter as they waited for safer seas to travel. **In the *lands* around** the place where they beached **were lands *belonging* to the first man of the island** (his official title), **Publius by name**. He was evidently a Roman whose estate was nearby. He **welcomed** Paul and the others (not all 276 of the crew, but at least the centurion, his fellow citizen Paul, and Paul's companion Luke), and **lodged** them **hospitably three days**, entertaining them by having them eat with him in his home.

During these meals, it was mentioned that **the father of Publius was lying down, distressed with** recurrent **fever and dysentery**. Paul offered to help and **went in** to the place where the sick man lay, and **after he had prayed, he laid his hands on him and cured him**. Not only was Publius grateful, but word spread to others on the island, and soon **the rest of the people** there **who had ailments were coming to** Paul **and being healed**. Thus, when it came time for them to leave, **they honored** them **with many honors** (probably including gifts) and **supplied** them with all they needed for the voyage.

Luke mentions these miraculous events to show even after his arrest, Paul continued in God's favor, coming to Rome as an innocent man. Also, it reveals that those who welcomed Paul and showed him benevolence (such as the Romans Julius and Publius, and the natives of Malta; see 27:3; 28:2) eventually enjoyed the blessing of God.

§VIII.3. Voyage to Rome

> ૐ ૐ ૐ ૐ ૐ
>
> 11 And at the end of three months we put out *to sea* in an Alexandrian *ship* which had wintered on the island, and which was marked by the Dioscuri.
> 12 And after we put in at Syracuse, we remained there three days.
> 13 And from there we went around and arrived in Rhegium, and after one day a south wind sprang up, and on the second *day* we came to Puteoli.
> 14 There we found brothers and were called by them to remain on with them for seven days, and thus we came to Rome.
> 15 And the brothers, having heard the things about us, came from there, as far as Appius Market and Three Taverns, to a meeting with us; and when Paul saw them, he gave thanks to God *and* took courage.

When the winter ended in February **at the end of three months**, they found another **Alexandrian** grain ship **which had wintered on the island**, probably in the main port of Valetta, and which was going to Rome. This ship **was marked by the Dioscuri**. All ships like these were distinguished by some figurehead carved on the ship, and this ship was named for the **Dioscuri** (literally, "sons of Zeus"), the Twin Brothers Castor and Pollux. These two gods were venerated as protectors of sailors, and sighting their constellation (Gemini) in a storm was considered by sailors a lucky omen. Luke mentions this detail here to show his Roman audience that this coincidence (divinely sent from the true God?) was indeed a sign that Paul was innocent and would now reach Rome safely.

The grain ship sailed from Malta and **put in at Syracuse**, ninety miles from Malta, on the eastern tip of Sicily. They **remained there**

VIII. Paul and the Gospel in Rome   Acts 28:16–24

three days, possibly waiting to do their appointed business. They next sailed on to **arrive in Rhegium**, opposite Sicily, on the tip of the boot of Italy, seventy miles away. After only a **second** *day* of sailing, having made good time, they **came to Puteoli**, the main port for the grain ships. Rome was now only 130 miles away by foot. In Puteoli, Paul and Luke **found brothers**, and this small Christian community **called** them **to remain on with them for seven days**. Evidently Paul's centurion guard had business there, and so Paul was able to accept the Church's offer of a week's hospitality.

It is **thus**, Luke says, that they **came to Rome**—that is, welcomed by the Christians there, who, despite the controversy swirling around Paul, still acknowledged him as God's chosen vessel. This could not be taken for granted, for Paul had spent many months in prison, unable to defend himself fully against the many foes who would slander him. Yet his integrity and divine mission were recognized by the Church at large, even in the environs of faraway Rome.

Luke confirms this by mentioning that it was not just the brothers in Puteoli who believed in Paul, but also those who came **from as far as Appius Market and Three Taverns**, towns 43 and 33 miles from Rome respectively. Christians from these towns along the Appian Way to Rome met Paul and escorted him to his destination, encouraging him as he traveled his five-day journey from Puteoli to the Roman capital. **When Paul saw** that the shame of his imprisonment had not turned them against him but that they still believed in him, **he gave thanks to God** *and* **took courage**. Their fidelity was another sign that God was still with him.

§VIII.4. Paul at Rome

> ༄ ༄ ༄ ༄ ༄
>
> 16 And when we entered into Rome, Paul was allowed to remain by himself with the soldier who was guarding him.
> 17 And it happened that after three days he called together those who were the leading *men* of the Jews, and when they had come together,

he was saying to them, "Brothers, though I *myself* had done nothing against our people or the customs of our fathers, I was delivered prisoner from Jerusalem into the hands of the Romans.

18 "And when they had examined me, they were intending to dismiss *me* because there were no grounds for death in me.

19 "But when the Jews contradicted, I was compelled to appeal to Caesar, not that I had anything to accuse my nation of.

20 "For this reason therefore, I called you to see and to speak with *you*, for I am wearing this chain for the sake of the hope of Israel."

21 And they said to him, "We *ourselves* have neither welcomed letters about you from Judea, nor have any of the brothers arrived and declared or spoken anything evil about you.

22 "But we request from you to hear what you think, for about this faction, it is known to us that everywhere it is contradicted."

23 And having appointed a day for him, many came to him at his guest room, and he was explaining to them, testifying about the Kingdom of God, and *trying* to persuade them about Jesus, from both the Law of Moses and the Prophets, from morning until evening.

24 And some were being persuaded by the things he said, but others were unbelieving.

At Rome, **Paul was allowed to remain by himself** in his own quarters (possibly one storey of the many tenements available for rent), along with, of course, **the soldier who was guarding him**. Since he was obviously no threat, he was permitted the maximum freedom while he awaited trial (for example in being guarded by

VIII. Paul and the Gospel in Rome — Acts 28:16–24

only one soldier, not the usual two), so that he could receive as many visitors as he liked.

Paul's concern was to connect with his Jewish friends in Rome, to try to win them over for the Gospel. Had he been free, he would have attended their synagogues on the Sabbath days. But since he was not free, **he called together those who were the leading *men* of the Jews** and asked them to come and visit him. He wasted no time in this, but contacted them **after** a mere **three days** in Rome.

In his first brief meeting with the leaders of the synagogues, he stressed that he **had done nothing** to offend his **people** (such as profaning their Temple), or against **the customs of** their **fathers** (such as saying that Jews should forsake the Law of Moses). Whatever his foes had said about him deserving death because he had profaned the Temple (see 21:22), when **the Romans examined** him, they **were intending to dismiss** him and set him free, because they realized that such charges were not true, and that **there were no grounds for death** in him. Paul was now in Rome only because **the Jews contradicted** and protested this, so that he was **compelled to appeal to Caesar**.

Thus, he was in Rome simply to further defend himself, **not** because he **had anything to accuse** his **nation of**. He was not there to lodge a counter-complaint against his Jewish brothers (as the Jews of Rome may have feared), simply to vindicate his innocence. He was a good Jew, and in fact was **wearing** a **chain** because of his faith in his ancestral hope—that chain, far from being a shameful sign of his guilt, was an adornment of the faith that both he and his hearers held dear. **The hope of Israel** was that Messiah would come, and Paul was being persecuted for believing in the fulfillment of what all good Jews hoped to see.

The leaders replied very diplomatically. They said that for their part, they **neither** received **letters about** him, denouncing him as someone to be avoided, **nor** had any Jewish **brothers arrived** or said that. They thus had no preformed judgments about him. But they politely **requested from** him **to hear** his own statement of the Christian case, for **about** that **faction**, they **knew that everywhere it was contradicted** and maligned. But they were willing (they said) to be convinced, and would accede to Paul's desire to speak with the Jewish community at large. They therefore **appointed a day for him** when not just the leaders but **many** from the Jewish community in Rome would **come to him at his guest room**, to hear him make his case.

Some have found it a bit surprising that no Jew came from Jerusalem to Rome to mobilize the Jews there against Paul, and more surprising that the Jews of Rome had so little contact with the Christians of Rome. It is possible the Jewish leaders of Rome were being more diplomatic than candid and were simply giving Paul the chance to make his case for himself. Perhaps the Jews of Jerusalem decided not to hound Paul as far as Rome, because they wanted to keep a low profile there. It was not long since Claudius expelled the Jews from Rome (compare 18:1), and they may have felt that mounting an attack on a Roman citizen in the capital itself might backfire. Perhaps letters were yet coming, but had not yet arrived.

When the scheduled meeting took place, Paul **was explaining to them, testifying about** how **the Kingdom of God** was fulfilled in **Jesus**. He argued this by showing how Jesus fulfilled the hopes in **the Law of Moses and the Prophets**, speaking **from morning until evening. Some were persuaded** and became Christians, **but others** (the majority perhaps, given the parting words of v. 25f?) **were unbelieving**, refusing to accept his message.

ॐ ॐ ॐ ॐ ॐ

25 And when they did not agree with one another, they were dismissed after Paul had spoken one word: "Well did the Holy Spirit speak through Isaiah the prophet to your fathers,

26 "saying, 'Go to this people and say, "Hearing, you will hear, but never have insight; and seeing you will see, and will never perceive;

27 "'"for the heart of this people has been made dull, and with their ears they are heavy of hearing, and their eyes are closed; lest they

VIII. Paul and the Gospel in Rome — Acts 28:25–28

> should see with their eyes, and hear with their ears, and have insight with the heart and turn back, and I should cure them."'
>
> 28 "Let it be known to you, therefore, that this salvation of God has been sent to the Gentiles; and they *themselves* will hear."*
>
> * Verse 29, which speaks of the Jews debating among themselves as they departed, is omitted by the best manuscripts.

As in other Jewish communities, the Gospel of Jesus divided the Jews, so that **they did not agree with one another**. Paul ended the meeting and **dismissed** them to their homes, but not before he had left them with **one word**, one final challenge. Let the majority who rejected the Gospel know that they were fulfilling Isaiah's prophecy of doom. Their refusal to believe shows how **well** and truly **the Holy Spirit spoke through Isaiah** (Is. 6:9–10).

For it was written that the people would keep on **hearing** God's announcement of salvation and **never have insight** into it. However long messengers like Paul spoke to them, they would **never perceive** the truth, for their **heart had been made dull** and calloused. **Their ears** were **heavy of hearing** and scarcely able to take anything in, **their eyes** completely **closed**, unable to see the truth when it stood before them. They thus were unable to **turn back** to God so that He could **cure them**. As long as they refused to humble themselves and open themselves up to new things, there was no hope.

But their refusal to accept **this salvation of God** would not frustrate His purposes. Salvation had **been sent to the Gentiles** also, and **they** would **hear** and believe. Surely Israel would not want to miss out on a blessing that even the Gentiles would accept (see Rom. 11:13–14)?

In leaving his hearers with his prophecy of doom, Paul did not mean simply to have the last word and to denounce them. Nor was he giving up on reaching Israel. His intention was to leave this scriptural prophecy of doom in their minds as they left so that they might think about it in the days to come and repent. Luke ends his presentation of Paul's message with this word as a challenge to Israel to save themselves from the doom decreed for the hard of heart (compare 13:40–41).

> ᪥ ᪥ ᪥ ᪥ ᪥
>
> 30 And he remained on two whole years in his own rented *quarters* and was welcoming all those coming in to him, heralding the Kingdom of God and teaching the things about the Lord Jesus Christ with all boldness, unhindered.

St. Luke concludes his long narrative of the Church's progress with a last look at St. Paul, the apostle to the Gentiles. **He remained on two whole years** in those **rented *quarters* and was welcoming all those coming in to him, heralding** to them about **the Kingdom of God and teaching the things about** how **the Lord Jesus Christ** fulfilled this. He spoke **with all boldness**, completely **unhindered** by his Roman jailers.

This itself (Luke wants his Roman readership to see) proved that the Christian message was not seditious, for Paul would never have been allowed to preach for so long in the Roman capital itself, under the very nose of those guarding him, if his message were truly treasonous. His message was therefore not seditious. Romans like Theophilus (1:1) could rest assured that the Christians had been unfairly accused. God was plainly guiding the Christian movement, bringing it from Jerusalem to faraway Rome, offering salvation to all men everywhere. Thoughtful men like Theophilus should consider the Church's claims.

❧ A POSTSCRIPT ❧

Luke's Narrative and Paul's Subsequent Fate
It is commonly believed that Paul was released after this first Roman imprisonment, as he himself expected (see Phil. 1:19, 25–26), and as the Fathers and early church historians record. He was later imprisoned a second time, and this time he was martyred (see 2 Tim. 4:6).

The question arises, if Paul was released after this first imprisonment, why did not St. Luke record it? It would seem Luke would have known of Paul's release by the time Acts was completed and ready to be published, for Paul was tried and released shortly after the two years of which Luke speaks were completed. This being the case, why was his release not reported in Acts?

In the absence of a definitive word from St. Luke himself, we can never be sure. I would, however, offer the following.

Some have suggested that, if Paul was indeed not condemned and was later released, Luke might be expected to narrate this, since (it is argued) this development would have furthered his purpose of vindicating Paul (and the Church) of any charge of sedition. But to focus on the fate of Paul would have been counterproductive for Luke's political apologetic, for to report that Paul was released after his *first* trial would have left Luke open to the obvious retort that Paul was *not* released after his *second* trial. Far better not to focus on the legal verdicts of men at all, for God's truth is not subject to the wisdom of human courts.

For Luke, the fate of St. Paul was not the point, and the Christian movement did not stand or fall with him. Certainly, Luke focuses on Paul for the latter half of his book because Paul's conversion points so clearly to Christ's Resurrection, and because Paul's obvious innocence throughout his ministry points to the political harmlessness of the Christian Faith. But for all that, Luke was still writing about the Acts of *the Apostles*, not the Acts of *Paul*, and Paul is scarcely present in the first part of Luke's narrative.

Thus, to end his work by focusing on Paul's fate would give the erroneous impression that the story was about Paul. It was not. It was about Jesus, and Luke's two-volume work of Luke-Acts was the story of what Jesus began to do and teach during His ministry, and of what Jesus continued to do through His Church (compare Acts 1:1). Luke ends his story with Paul's open and unhindered preaching while in Roman chains to show his Gospel was clearly not seditious. But the fate of Paul himself was ultimately irrelevant. By leaving the final fate of Paul in Rome unreported, Luke allows the reader to see that what matters is the fate of the Christian movement as a whole and the truth of its claims.

"Acts 29": The Ongoing History of the Orthodox Church

St. Luke's narrative ends with chapter 28, but the story of Christ's work through His Church does not end there. After Paul's arrest, as we have suggested, he was later released and continued his ministry, which included writing his so-called Pastoral Epistles to Timothy and Titus. And Peter, whose ministry is in part narrated by St. Luke, also continued his work until he won a martyr's crown in Rome under Nero in the same persecution that swept away Paul, as well as many others in Rome and its immediate environs. The other apostles also continued their work (tradition locates Thomas in India), as did many other Christian workers, known and unknown.

Even after the end of the first century and the writing of all the other books of the New Testament, the Church continued its mission. We justly refer to the first century as "the apostolic age" because that time was characterized by the work of the apostles who laid the foundations on which those who came later were to build, but a solid dividing line cannot be drawn between the life of the Church in the apostolic age and the ages that came after. Reference to "the apostolic age" is a handy term of convenience, but it should not blind us to the fact that many people "straddled" the apostolic age and the decades succeeding it—men such as Ignatius, bishop of Antioch, who died about AD 107, and who therefore labored as bishop in the closing decades of the first century.

Historical division of time into different ages is handy, but real

A Postscript — "Acts 29"

history is never that tidy. One decade flows seamlessly into the next, and people living in these times are rarely aware that they belong to a particular age. History is a continuity, with changes usually happening slowly. In other words, Acts 28 was succeeded in history without a break by the unwritten "Acts 29," and then by "Acts 30." The story of the Church is an ongoing one.

Certain things of course characterized the apostolic age more than subsequent ages, since each generation knows its own challenges and has its own characteristics. In particular, miracles seem to have abounded more in the first century through the hands of the apostles than they did later. Paul himself refers to these miracles as "the signs of an apostle" (2 Cor. 12:12), which could only function as "signs of an apostle" if the apostles did more of them than others. But that did not mean miracles abruptly ceased as soon as the last apostle expired. Miracles continued to be found in some measure, and other things that occurred in the apostolic age also continued to abound in the history of the Church in succeeding ages—including our own.

Thus, for example, the Church continued to hold councils or synods as the way of resolving controversial issues, as it did in the days related in Acts 15. Most of these later councils were local; some drew from all over the world and concerned issues of worldwide importance (and thus were styled "ecumenical councils," since they were accepted throughout the *ecumene* or world).

Further, the Church continued to exercise spiritual gifts of healing, as local presbyters anointed the faithful with oil, laid hands on them, and healed them (compare James 5:14f) in what would later be called "the sacrament of unction." The Church continued to cast out demons, which became an essential part of the baptismal rite as the Church received converts from the pagan world, which worshipped the demons. People continued to exercise prophetic gifts; healings continued to be wrought, especially through the prayers of the martyrs. In short, the Holy Spirit who was active in the first century did not desert the Church after that century gave way to the next. The apostolic Faith was handed down from father to son, from grandparent to grandchild, from pastor to flock, without a break.

It is necessary, therefore, to read the Acts of the Apostles not in isolation from the later history of the Church, but as a part of its ongoing narrative. This is what is ultimately meant by "apostolic Tradition"—the teaching, life, and experiences of the first-century apostolic Church continue to flow through history in a continuous stream, and we can receive that teaching, life, and experience even today.

The Church of the Acts of the Apostles did not vanish after the first century. It continued its pilgrimage through history, wending its way through time year after year and century after century, starting in Jerusalem and spreading out to the ends of the earth (Acts 1:8). It can be found and encountered even today, in Orthodoxy. The latest chapter of its sacred and sanctifying history can be experienced now, and by anyone. Simply walk into your nearest Orthodox church and let the stream that sprang up on the Day of Pentecost sweep you along in its saving flow.

⁕ APPENDIX ⁕

A CHRONOLOGY OF ACTS

The following chronology is offered as a possible outline for the events in Acts. Its dating is based on certain secular chronological anchors, events that are known from secular history. These would include the date of the beginning of the building of Herod's Temple in 20–19 BC (and therefore, adding the 46 years of Temple construction brings one to the beginning of Christ's ministry in AD 27; compare John 2:20); the date of the famine in about AD 44 (compare 11:27f); the date of Herod's death in the same year (compare 12:20f); the date of Claudius's order for Jews to leave Rome (compare 18:2), which occurred sometime in AD 49; the date of Gallio's term of office in Corinth (compare 18:12f), which was from the summer of 51; the late date of the Day of Atonement in the year of Paul's voyage to Rome (compare 27:9), which occurred only in the year 59.

The chronology is also based on certain factors internal to the New Testament. Some of these include the three years (Judaically reckoned) between Paul's conversion and his visit to Peter in Jerusalem (Gal. 1:18); the 14 years (Judaically reckoned) between that and his next visit to Jerusalem (Gal. 2:1); the length of time Paul spent in Corinth (Acts 18:11); and the time he spent in prison in Caesarea (24:27).

AD 27 – Christ begins His ministry
29 – Christ's Death, Resurrection, Ascension; the Pentecostal outpouring of the Spirit (2:1)
34 (approx.) – Martyrdom of Stephen (ch. 7)
35 – Conversion of St. Paul (ch. 9)

A Chronology of Acts

37 – Paul's first visit to Peter at Jerusalem (Gal. 1:18)
42 or 43 – Herod begins persecution of Jerusalem church (12:1f)
43 – Agabus prophesies the coming famine; collection of relief funds begins (11:27f)
44 – Famine begins in Palestine; Herod dies in summer (12:20f)
45 – Famine relief arrives
46 – Paul at Antioch (13:1f)
47 – **First Missionary Journey**: to Cyprus, Pisidian Antioch, Iconium, Lystra, Derbe (13:4—14:20)
48 – then back through those cities to Antioch (14:21–28)
49 – Council of Jerusalem (ch. 15; Gal. 2:1f)
49 – Claudius expels Jews from Rome (18:2)
50 – Aquila and Prisca leave Rome
50 – **Second Missionary Journey**: Paul to Cilicia, Lycaonia, Galatia, Troas, Philippi, Thessalonica, Berea, Athens (15:36—17:34)
50 – Paul arrives in Corinth (in fall? 18:1–2)
51 – in Corinth (18:11); trial before Gallio (18:12–17)
51 – writes 1 and 2 Thessalonians from Corinth
52 – Paul leaves Corinth in spring; reaches Jerusalem by summer; thence to Antioch (18:18–22)
53 – **Third Missionary Journey**, through Galatia, Phrygia (18:23)
54 – to Ephesus (by spring?), spends two years in Ephesus (19:1–10)
56 – writes 1 Corinthians from Ephesus (in spring); leaves Ephesus for Macedonia (in summer; 20:1); writes 2 Corinthians from Macedonia (in fall); travels to Corinth in Greece (20:2); in Corinth (in winter); writes Galatians
57 – in Corinth (in spring); writes Romans; leaves Corinth for Philippi and Miletus (20:3–15); arrives in Jerusalem (ch. 21)
57 – Paul arrested in Jerusalem; kept in Caesarea prison for two years by Felix (24:27)
59 – Festus succeeds Felix; Paul sent to Rome
59 – shipwrecked on Malta in the fall (ch. 27); winters on Malta
60 – sails for Rome in spring; arrives in Rome (ch. 28)
61 – writes Philippians, Ephesians, Colossians, Philemon from prison in Rome
62 – Roman trial and release (28:30)

About the Author

Archpriest Lawrence Farley currently pastors St. Herman of Alaska Orthodox Church (OCA) in Langley, B.C., Canada. He received his B.A. from Trinity College, Toronto, and his M.Div. from Wycliffe College, Toronto. A former Anglican priest, he converted to Orthodoxy in 1985 and studied for two years at St. Tikhon's Orthodox Seminary in Pennsylvania. In addition to the books in the Orthodox Bible Study Companion series, he has also published *The Christian Old Testament: Looking at the Hebrew Scriptures through Christian Eyes; A Song in the Furnace: The Message of the Book of Daniel; Unquenchable Fire: The Traditional Christian Teaching about Hell; A Daily Calendar of Saints: A Synaxarion for Today's North American Church; Let Us Attend: A Journey Through the Orthodox Divine Liturgy; One Flesh: Salvation through Marriage in the Orthodox Church; The Empty Throne: Reflections on the History and Future of the Orthodox Episcopacy;* and *Following Egeria: A Visit to the Holy Land through Time and Space.*

ANCIENT FAITH RADIO

Visit www.ancientfaithradio.com to listen to Fr. Lawrence Farley's regular podcast, "No Other Foundation: Reflections on Orthodox Theology and Biblical Studies."

A Complete List of the Books in the Orthodox Bible Study Companion Series

The Gospel of Matthew
Torah for the Church
- Paperback, 400 pages, ISBN 978-0-9822770-7-2

The Gospel of Mark
The Suffering Servant
- Paperback, 280 pages, ISBN 978-1-888212-54-9

The Gospel of Luke
Good News for the Poor
- Paperback, 432 pages, ISBN 978-1-936270-12-5

The Gospel of John
Beholding the Glory
- Paperback, 376 pages, ISBN 978-1-888212-55-6

The Acts of the Apostles
Spreading the Word
- Paperback, 352 pages, ISBN 978-1-936270-62-0

The Epistle to the Romans
A Gospel for All
- Paperback, 208 pages, ISBN 978-1-888212-51-8

First and Second Corinthians
Straight from the Heart
- Paperback, 319 pages, ISBN 978-1-888212-53-2

Words of Fire
The Early Epistles of St. Paul to the Thessalonians and the Galatians
- Paperback, 172 pages, ISBN 978-1-936270-02-6

The Prison Epistles
Philippians – Ephesians – Colossians – Philemon
- Paperback, 224 pages, ISBN 978-1-888212-52-5

Shepherding the Flock
The Pastoral Epistles of St. Paul the Apostle to Timothy and Titus
- Paperback, 144 pages, ISBN 978-1-888212-56-3

The Epistle to the Hebrews
High Priest in Heaven
• Paperback, 184 pages, ISBN 978-1-936270-74-3

Universal Truth
The Catholic Epistles of James, Peter, Jude, and John
• Paperback, 232 pages, ISBN 978-1-888212-60-0

The Apocalypse of St. John
A Revelation of Love and Power
• Paperback, 240 pages, ISBN 978-1-936270-40-8

Other Books by the Author

The Christian Old Testament
Looking at the Hebrew Scriptures through Christian Eyes
Many Christians see the Old Testament as "the other Testament": a source of exciting stories to tell the kids, but not very relevant to the Christian life. *The Christian Old Testament* reveals the Hebrew Scriptures as the essential context of Christianity, as well as a many-layered revelation of Christ Himself. Follow along as Fr. Lawrence Farley explores the Christian significance of every book of the Old Testament.
• Paperback, 200 pages, ISBN 978-1-936270-53-8

A Song in the Furnace
The Message of the Book of Daniel
The Book of Daniel should be read with the eyes of a child. It's a book of wonders and extremes—mad kings, baffling dreams with gifted interpreters, breathtaking deliverances, astounding prophecies—with even what may be the world's first detective stories added in for good measure. To argue over the book's historicity, as scholars have done for centuries, is to miss the point. In *A Song in the Furnace*, Fr. Lawrence Farley reveals all the wonders of this unique book to the receptive eye.
• Paperback, 248 pages, ISBN 978-1-944967-31-4

A Daily Calendar of Saints
A Synaxarion for Today's North American Church
Popular biblical commentator and church historian Fr. Lawrence Farley turns his hand to hagiography in this collection of lives of saints, one or more for each day of the calendar year. His accessible prose and contemporary approach make these ancient lives easy for modern Christians to relate to and understand.
• Paperback, 304 pages, ISBN 978-1-944967-41-3

Unquenchable Fire
The Traditional Christian Teaching about Hell
The doctrine of hell as a place of eternal punishment has never been easy for Christians to accept. The temptation to retreat from and reject the Church's traditional teaching about hell is particularly strong in our current culture, which has demonstrably lost its sense of sin. Fr. Lawrence Farley examines the Orthodox Church's teaching on this difficult subject through the lens of Scripture and patristic writings, making the case that the existence of hell does not negate that of a loving and forgiving God.
• Paperback, 240 pages, ISBN 978-1-944967-18-5

Let Us Attend
A Journey Through the Orthodox Divine Liturgy
Fr. Lawrence Farley provides a guide to understanding the Divine Liturgy, and a vibrant reminder of the centrality of the Eucharist in living the Christian life, guiding believers in a devotional and historical walk through the Orthodox Liturgy. Examining the Liturgy section by section, he provides both historical explanations of how the Liturgy evolved and devotional insights aimed at helping us pray the Liturgy in the way the Fathers intended.
• Paperback, 104 pages, ISBN 978-1-888212-87-7

One Flesh
Salvation through Marriage in the Orthodox Church
Is the Church too negative about sex? Beginning with this provocative question, Fr. Lawrence Farley explores the history of the Church's attitude toward sex and marriage, from the Old Testament through the Church Fathers. He persuasively makes the case both for traditional morality and for a positive acceptance of marriage as a viable path to theosis.
• Paperback, 160 pages, ISBN 978-1-936270-66-8

The Empty Throne
Reflections on the History and Future of the Orthodox Episcopacy
In contemporary North America, the bishop's throne in the local parish stands empty for most of the year. The bishop is an honored occasional guest rather than a true pastor of the local flock. But it was not always so, nor need it be so forever. Fr. Lawrence Farley explores how the Orthodox episcopacy developed over the centuries and suggests what can be done in modern times to bring the bishop back into closer contact with his flock.
• Paperback, 152 pages, ISBN 978-1-936270-61-3

Following Egeria
A Visit to the Holy Land through Time and Space
In the fourth century, a nun named Egeria traveled through the Holy Land and wrote an account of her experiences. In the twenty-first century, Fr. Lawrence

Farley followed partially in her footsteps and wrote his own account of how he experienced the holy sites as they are today. Whether you're planning your own pilgrimage or want to read about places you may never go, his account will inform and inspire you.
• Paperback, 160 pages, ISBN 978-1-936270-21-7

Three Akathists:
Akathist to Jesus, Light to Those in Darkness
• Staple-bound, 32 pages, ISBN 978-1-944967-33-8

Akathist to the Most Holy Theotokos, Daughter of Zion
• Staple-bound, 32 pages, ISBN 978-1-944967-34-4

Akathist to Matushka Olga Michael
• Staple-bound, 32 pages, ISBN 978-1-944967-38-3

For complete ordering information, visit our website: store.ancientfaith.com.

Other Books of Interest

The Orthodox Study Bible: Old and New Testaments
Featuring a Septuagint text of the Old Testament developed by outstanding Orthodox scholars, this Bible also includes the complete Orthodox canon of the Old Testament, including the Deuterocanon; insightful commentary drawn from the Christian writers of the first ten centuries; helpful notes relating Scripture to seasons of Christian feasting and fasting; a lectionary to guide your Bible reading through the Church year; supplemental Bible study articles on a variety of subjects; a subject index to the study notes to help facilitate Bible study; and more.
• Available in various editions. Visit store.ancientfaith.com for more details.

The Whole Counsel of God
An Introduction to Your Bible
by Stephen De Young
In *The Whole Counsel of God*, popular writer and podcaster Fr. Stephen De Young gives an overview of what the Bible is and what is its place in the life of an Orthodox Christian, correcting many Protestant misconceptions along the way. Issues covered include inspiration, inerrancy, the formation of the biblical canon, the various texts and their provenance, the place of Scripture within Orthodox Tradition, and how an Orthodox Christian should read, study, and interpret the Bible.
• Paperback, 128 pages, ISBN: 978-1-955890-19-9

The Names of Jesus
Discovering the Person of Jesus Christ through Scripture
by Fr. Thomas Hoko
In this book based on his popular podcast series of the same name, the late Fr. Thomas Hopko shares meditations on over 50 different names and titles used for Jesus in the Bible. Learn what each name uniquely has to tell us about the character of the Son of God, His role in our salvation, and the relationship we can choose to cultivate with Him.
• Paperback, 400 pages, ISBN 978-1-936-70-41-5

The Rest of the Bible
A Guide to the Old Testament of the Early Church
by Theron Mathis
A beautiful widow risks her life to defend her people while men cower in fear. A young man takes a journey with an archangel and faces down a demon in order to marry a woman seven times widowed. A reprobate king repents and miraculously turns back toward God. A Jewish exile plays a game of riddles in a Persian king's court. Wisdom is detailed and exalted. Christ is revealed.

These and many other stories make up the collection of writings explored

in this book—authentic books of the Bible you've probably never read. Dubbed "Apocrypha" and cut from the Bible by the Reformers, these books of the Greek Old Testament were a vital part of the Church's life in the early centuries, and are still read and treasured by Orthodox Christians today. *The Rest of the Bible* provides a brief and intriguing introduction to each of these valuable texts, which St. Athanasius termed "the Readables."
• Paperback, 128 pages, ISBN 978-1-936270-15-6

Christ in the Psalms
by Patrick Henry Reardon
A highly inspirational book of meditations on the Psalms by one of the most insightful and challenging Orthodox writers of our day. Avoiding both syrupy sentimentality and arid scholasticism, *Christ in the Psalms* takes the reader on a thought-provoking and enlightening pilgrimage through this beloved "Prayer Book" of the Church. Which psalms were quoted most frequently in the New Testament, and how were they interpreted? How has the Church historically understood and utilized the various psalms in her liturgical life? How can we perceive the image of Christ shining through the psalms? Lively and highly devotional, thought-provoking yet warm and practical, *Christ in the Psalms* sheds a world of insight upon each psalm, and offers practical advice for how to make the Psalter a part of our daily lives.
• Paperback, 328 pages, ISBN 978-1-888212-21-7

Christ in His Saints
by Patrick Henry Reardon
In this sequel to *Christ in the Psalms,* Patrick Henry Reardon once again applies his keen intellect to a topic he loves most dearly. Here he examines the lives of almost one hundred and fifty saints and heroes from the Scriptures—everyone from Abigail to Zephaniah, Adam to St. John the Theologian. This well-researched work is a veritable cornucopia of Bible personalities: Old Testament saints, New Testament saints, "Repentant saints," "Zealous saints," "Saints under pressure" . . . they're all here, and their stories are both fascinating and uplifting. But *Christ in His Saints* is far more than just a biblical who's who. These men and women represent that ancient family into which, by baptism, all believers have been incorporated. Together they compose that great "cloud of witnesses" cheering us on and inspiring us through word and deed.
• Paperback, 320 pages, ISBN 978-1-888212-68-6

For complete ordering information, visit our website: store.ancientfaith.com.

We hope you have enjoyed and benefited from this book. Your financial support makes it possible to continue our nonprofit ministry both in print and online. Because the proceeds from our book sales only partially cover the costs of operating **Ancient Faith Publishing** and **Ancient Faith Radio**, we greatly appreciate the generosity of our readers and listeners. Donations are tax deductible and can be made at **www.ancientfaith.com**.

To view our other publications,
please visit our website: **store.ancientfaith.com**

ANCIENT FAITH RADIO

Bringing you Orthodox Christian music, readings, prayers, teaching, and podcasts 24 hours a day since 2004 at
www.ancientfaith.com